Bound for Africa

Bound for Africa

COLD WAR FIGHT ALONG THE ZAMBEZI

By Douglass H. Hubbard Jr.

Naval Institute Press
Annapolis, Maryland

Naval Institute Press
291 Wood Road
Annapolis, MD 21402

LIBRARY OF CONGRESS CATALOGING-IN-PUBLICATION DATA
Hubbard, Douglass H., 1945–
Bound for Africa : Cold War fight along the Zambezi / Douglass H. Hubbard, Jr.
p. cm.
Includes bibliographical references and index.
ISBN 978-1-59114-394-9 (alk. paper)
1. Zimbabwe—History—Chimurenga War, 1966–1980. 2. Zimbabwe—Foreign relations—1965–1980. 3. Africa, Southern—History—1899–1975. 4. Africa, Southern—History—1975– 5. Africa, Southern—Description and travel. 6. Hubbard, Douglass H., 1945—-Travel. I.Title.
DT2988.H83 2008
967.9—dc22

2008015588

Printed in the United States of America on acid-free paper

14 13 12 11 10 09 08 9 8 7 6 5 4 3 2
First printing

This book is dedicated to the people of Africa,
whose perseverance, spirit, and determination have
inspired me for more than three decades.

In memory of Guy Houghton
Leader, mentor, and friend

CONTENTS

ILLUSTRATIONS

PREFACE AND ACKNOWLEDGMENTS

THIS IS A STORY that I never expected to be telling. It is a very personal tale about a young American's journey that ultimately took him to the battlefield of Cold War southern Africa after three years of service in Vietnam. My hope is that this work will provide readers with an intimate snapshot of some of the factors and events that cumulatively formed the counterinsurgency war in Rhodesia and its neighboring countries—now more than thirty years past.

I must first thank Naval Institute Press director Mr. Richard Russell for his vision and encouragement, for it was he who said he thought mine was a story worth telling—and who ultimately encouraged me to actually write it. I also wish to thank my copy editor, Gary Kessler, for his excellent work and insightful suggestions.

Though this is my story, a number of former colleagues enthusiastically assisted with their recollections and memorabilia. Winston Hart, one of Rhodesia's most effective Special Branch operatives and who effectively became intelligence officer to the Selous Scouts, made historic photographs available and recalled important events in the war. Lieutenant Colonel Ron Reid-Daly, legendary commander of the Selous Scouts, gave useful advice about events of the day. Peter Cooper, former Grenadier Guardsman and later regimental sergeant major and training officer at the School of Infantry, Gwelo, Rhodesia, provided photographs from the school and identified personalities long vanished from my memory. Guy Houghton supplied valuable information about British South Africa Police (BSAP) Support Unit organization and its expansion.

Ormonde Power and Eric Kennelly helped confirm three-decades-old recollections of events we shared. Brian and Jo Cullingworth, ever dear friends, supported both my efforts to write the manuscript and to identify important personalities in the story.

Particular thanks go to former detective section officer of the BSAP Special Branch, Nick Russell, who shared images and reference material from the era. Geoff Hill, noted author of *The Battle for Zimbabwe* and *What Happens after Mugabe,* gave of his time to answer important questions about contemporary issues in the country that was once Rhodesia—and those relating to the languages and customs of the region.

Judith Anderson, who featured prominently in the story, encouraged me through some difficult pages in the book's early days and provided her insightful mind to questions of clarity and context. It was she who gave the manuscript its final examination.

My parents, Doug and Fran Hubbard, gave of their five decades of experience as authors as well as constant support and encouragement. Without them, this book would not exist.

This work encapsulates a period in which the Cold War developed in many forms and reached its zenith. The antagonists and their allies and sympathizers formed distinct factions in the world. For a young American, educated and trained to counter potential enemies of his country and tempered by three years of service in the Vietnam War, the machinations of the former Soviet Union and Communist China formed a distinct threat to peace in the world, wherever they occurred. Today, where the face of terrorism and its causes seem more ambiguous, my observations from those days may seem simplistic. I thus request that readers consider this work in the context of the period in which the described events occurred.

I would also ask my reader's indulgence about matters that are entirely my recollections and those of a few peers. Thirty years after the fact, we have done the best we could with fading memories—but in the end, any errors of fact are my responsibility alone.

INTRODUCTION

By John P. Cann, PhD

DOUGLASS HUBBARD arrived in Johannesburg, South Africa, in January 1974, during what would prove a pivotal juncture in a conflict that would come to be known as the Rhodesian Front War of 1972–79. In his twenty-nine years, the young American had seen more than his share of the world and experienced the horrors of combat and the consequences of failed international strategy and policy on the most fundamental human level.

Trained as a special agent of the U.S. Naval Investigative Service, Hubbard had served for three years in Southeast Asia during the Vietnam War, working in the field with Marines and sailors. By 1972 he had grown tired and disillusioned and left government service to establish a business in Australia. Hubbard's predictable and subsequent disenchantment with the easy life in "The Lucky Country," as Australia was then known, led him to the jungles of nearby Papua New Guinea, where he spent time recovering World War II relics.

All the while, he wrestled with wistful memories of an earlier adventure to Africa while on leave from the war and the notion of becoming a district policeman in the back blocks of Rhodesia. Hubbard in 1974 accepted an appointment with the British South Africa Police (BSAP), the original police force of Cecil Rhodes' British South Africa Company. Before long, Hubbard found himself embroiled in the violent political upheavals of an Africa in historic transformation.

The BSAP enjoyed a long and venerable history, formed in 1889 as a paramilitary, mounted infantry protecting the column of pioneer settlers who moved into present-day Zimbabwe in 1890. As the Rhodesian Front

War unfolded, Hubbard's unit was a key force in the counterinsurgency campaign against the black insurgents—trained and supported by the Soviet Union and its Eastern Bloc allies, as well as Communist China—and his account provides a fascinating snapshot of the country as its people became embroiled in war amid successive efforts to find a political solution that would embrace the nation's majority black citizenry while protecting the rights of minority whites.

Eight years before Hubbard's arrival, Rhodesia had become the only territory in history other than the United States to separate successfully from Great Britain without the Empire's consent. As an impoverished British government began divesting itself of colonial aspirations in the wake of World War II, Southern Rhodesia appeared to be the first colony in line for independence; it was already self-governing and possessed the right of self-defense. It was, in fact, in the same political condition as had been New Zealand before its grant of dominion status, so Rhodesia seemed destined to move along a similar trajectory.

Unfortunately, the British government chose to advance Rhodesia's neighbors, Malawi and Zambia, to independence, based on universal suffrage, which meant majority rule and in reality single-party dictatorships. This left Britain with the awkward problem of Rhodesia.

Rhodesia had long-established democratic institutions based on the British pattern but under conditions that centered control of a country with six million black citizens among a white minority of 250,000. While the constitution installed in 1961 was administratively efficient, its political structure was difficult to reconcile with African nationalist movements. Nevertheless, Southern Rhodesia had been a loyal British colony, and sympathies ran high in the United Kingdom for the aspirations of the Rhodesian settlers. In 1964 Rhodesian whites overwhelmingly elected Ian Smith of the Rhodesian Front Party as premier. When the Rhodesian government reached an impasse with Great Britain over conditions for continued autonomy, Smith on 11 November 1965, with the wide backing of the white settler population, declared Rhodesia independent.

The Unilateral Declaration of Independence was immediately condemned as illegal and an "act of treason" by the British government, the Commonwealth, and the United Nations (UN). The newly independent Rhodesia was not recognized by any country—not even apartheid nation South Africa—and Britain and the UN imposed economic sanctions.

Over the next decade, there were a series of negotiations between Britain and Rhodesia, in which Britain insisted on majority rule with various plans that would eventually lead to a black government. Smith and his Rhodesia Front government, distrustful of British intentions, procrastinated and ultimately decided to find their own internal political solution separate of British politicians. Many of Rhodesia's whites had been driven from newly independent nations to the north, memories of the Congo massacres were still fresh, and there was not a single example of a functioning democracy in black Africa to provide them with reassurance that Rhodesia could expect to be different if control was prematurely turned over to the majority under a formula evolved by foreign politicians who would not have to live with the results.

The political vacuum between the white minority's position and the majority black population's desire for a government elected by universal suffrage allowed the emergence of Robert Mugabe, a Marxist intellectual and leader of the Chinese-backed Zimbabwean African National Union (ZANU), and Joshua Nkomo of the Soviet-backed Zimbabwe African People's Union (ZAPU), both of whom aspired to overthrow the white regime.

In the early years of what might be called the Zambezi Valley Campaign (1966–71), Rhodesia succeeded in its counterinsurgency operations because of an effective, well-disciplined national military organization that exploited its enemy's debilitating strategic and tactical mistakes. In the field, for example, insurgents moved across the Zambezi in columns and wore green uniforms with a standardized boot that simplified tracking. On the strategic level, ZAPU in August 1967 formed an alliance with the African National Congress (ANC), the South African insurgency, and together with its military wing, launched a campaign into northern Rhodesia. Recognizing the benefits of using Rhodesia as a buffer, South Africa dispatched two thousand paramilitary police to help defeat the ANC in Rhodesia, a contingent that remained until 1975.

The insurgents had attacked Rhodesia at its strongest point from their sanctuary in Zambia and had unwittingly cooperated in their own destruction through multiple mistakes. In a series of some twenty-seven operations between 3 April 1966 and 29 August 1971, Rhodesian security forces killed more than three hundred insurgents and captured nearly five hundred against a loss of fourteen dead and twenty-seven wounded.[1]

In December 1972, ZANU launched a new offensive from an unexpected quarter. The Rhodesian insurgents found a break from their monolithic tactical approach by way of the remote but neighboring Portuguese district of Tete in Mozambique. The Mozambican insurgent movement, the

Mozambique Liberation Front (Frente de Libertação de Moçambique, or FRELIMO), had begun its assault on the Portuguese colony in 1964 through its northern border with Tanzania, poorly executing a program of infiltration, subversion, and raids. With FRELIMO's campaign failing, Chinese advisers suggested a flanking approach through the remote wasteland of Téte.

In 1968 FRELIMO moved to Zambia and sought a new front in the Téte district of Mozambique. By mid-1971, FRELIMO had moved deeper into the colony and established a number of well-concealed bases.[2] These FRELIMO bases also hosted Chinese-backed ZANU insurgents, who were suggesting a similar flanking movement in the assault on Rhodesia.

Until that point, the Rhodesian military front with Mozambique had been largely quiescent, but this was to change. ZANU insurgents began entering northeastern Rhodesia and intimidating the local population with the ultimate aim of exploiting a classic insurgency strategy. Their freedom to attack randomly forced the government to defend everything, everywhere, creating the ultimate strategic dilemma. In the case of Rhodesia, the country's weakness lay in its small settler population, with which it was to defend a country the size of Montana or France. The shift in insurgent strategy—from a frontal assault to infiltration through a native population that they traumatized and cowed by abductions of their youths, intimidation, torture, and politically motivated murder—marked the turning point for Rhodesia.

It was into this cauldron that Hubbard arrived in early 1974, intent on serving rural Africans in the bush as a district policeman. Largely unaware of the undercurrents of change sweeping the country since his 1971 visit, Hubbard entered the British South African Police, completed training, and accepted an initial assignment at the Salisbury Central Police Station. Soon after, he accepted the position of instructor at BSAP's Support Unit and began training several hundred black African recruits to counter the emerging insurgent threat.

Hubbard immersed himself in the role of training a band of motivated, young, rural black Africans into a credible fighting force. He found the experience challenging, rewarding, and, at times, reminiscent of his service in Vietnam. In prosecuting the counterinsurgency strategy, Hubbard noted patterns of intimidation and torture of African peasantry by Chinese-trained insurgents identical to those he had just witnessed in Southeast Asia. Both the Viet Cong and ZANU shared ideological roots, based on the teachings of Mao Zedong.

A successful April 1974 coup in Lisbon by middle-ranking Portuguese officers heaped further burdens on Rhodesia. Portugal aimed to extract itself from the fight and withdrew from Mozambique in June 1975, profoundly altering the political and military balance in Southern Africa. Rhodesia now had its entire 1,300-kilometer eastern flank exposed and was left with only 222 kilometers of a total frontier of 2,964 kilometers with South Africa free of infiltration. In 1975, Hubbard's last year in Rhodesia, an estimated 400 insurgents roamed the country and about 5,500 threatened externally.[3] By April 1977, as many as 2,350 insurgents operated in the country and another 10,000 trained in Mozambique and Tanzania.[4] Militarily, Rhodesia seemed to be ahead, but it was gradually losing the political dimension of the war. Extraordinary tactical achievements were no longer contributing to any strategic success, because the national strategy, mired in the confusion of the times, was fundamentally flawed.

South Africa had seen the political liability of Rhodesia as early as 1974 and pressed Smith to fashion a peace settlement. Over the next few years, Rhodesia's minority government endured overwhelming diplomatic, military, and economic pressure—particularly from Britain and the United States—to implement a peaceful, political solution. In the end, Smith acquiesced. Meanwhile, Hubbard, like much of the world, watched the country's political and social transformation with uneasy intensity from his new home in Australia.

In March 1978, Smith and three conservative black leaders, The Reverend Ndabaningi Sithole, Bishop Abel Muzorewa, and Chief Jeremiah Chirau, crafted what was known as the "Internal Settlement." The four formed an executive council that would serve as a transitional government until elections could be held the following year. Mugabe and Nkomo were invited to join but refused, because collaboration would jeopardize their ultimate aim of gaining absolute control. Nearly three million voters turned out at the polls in April 1979, and, in spite of ZANU and ZAPU intimidation, overwhelmingly elected Muzorewa as the first black prime minister of the newly named country of Zimbabwe Rhodesia.

Muzorewa's government lasted a matter of months, because both the West and opposition African dictatorships vilified its new leader as a colonial stooge. With the insurgent armies of Mugabe and Nkomo preparing to fight again after the election, Muzorewa dispatched four envoys to offer an olive branch in May 1979. In response, Mugabe's forces seized the delegation, displayed the emissaries before two hundred tribesmen, and executed the men as an example of what would happen to those who negotiated with the new government.

The failure of the Internal Settlement both with the West and African nationalists ended hopes for replacing the insurgent movement with a moderate government. By mid-1978, insurgents had amassed large armies, fueling the storm of war. Amid the blood bath, international crisis diplomacy pressured all parties, including those led by Mugabe and Nkomo, to agree to a cease-fire in December 1979 and to attend British-sponsored negotiations in London, which yielded a modified constitution.

With ZANU and ZAPU participating in the February 1980 elections, the scale of intimidation intensified. Political observers reported at least one political murder daily and concluded that conditions for a free and fair election no longer existed in five of eight electoral provinces. Under the shadow of Mugabe's threat to resume the war should he lose, the ZANU party captured 64 percent of the vote in a 90 percent turnout. The international community and media toasted Mugabe, Zimbabwe's new prime minister, as a new sort of African leader. And with this support, Mugabe called for a referendum on single-party rule in August 1981, declaring that the Zimbabwean African National Union would rule forever.

In retrospect, Smith and the Rhodesia Front failed to grasp that a successful counterinsurgency campaign is 80 percent political and 20 percent military.[5] They were too late with too little in their efforts to achieve a political solution that might have enabled pioneering white settlers to develop the nation in cooperation with the native black majority population. Instead, Rhodesia—a nation that once fed much of southern Africa and boasted a remarkably developed local manufacturing base—would be condemned to a grim fate and would be remembered as a modern economic, political, and human international tragedy.

Hubbard's story is a compelling personal account of a nation shaped both by its internal struggles and the unrelenting dynamics of the Cold War.

NOTES

1. Michael Evans, "'The Wretched of the Empire,' Politics, Ideology and Counter-Insurgency in Rhodesia, 1965–80," in *An Art in Itself: The Theory and Conduct of Small Wars and Insurgencies*, ed. Peter Dennis and Jeffrey Grey (Canberra: Australian Army History Unit, 2006), 143.

2. Henrik Ellert, *The Rhodesia Front War: Counter-Insurgency and Guerrilla War in Rhodesia 1962–1980* (Gweru, Zimbabwe: Mambo Press, 1993), 88.

3. L. H. Gann, "Prospects for White Resistance," *Africa Report* 22 (September–October 1977): 9–14, at 10.

4. Anthony R. Wilkinson, Introduction to *Black Fire*, by Michael Raeburn (London: Julian Freedmann, 1978), 47.

5. David Galula, *Counter-Insurgency Warfare: Theory and Practice* (New York: Frederick A. Praeger, 1964), 89.

Bound for Africa

CHAPTER 1

Africa Introduced; Vietnam *Fini*

THE AFFAIR BEGAN in July 1971. I was twenty-six years old and had survived two years of the cataclysm that was the Vietnam War. My two years of service had earned me a month of home leave—and although it was my intention to find my way to the United States during the time allotted, I wanted first to see Africa for myself.

There was not much time—but there was enough for an introduction, perhaps a longing stare. When finally on that first journey I watched quietly in the shimmering heat of the Zambezi Valley, surrounded by a multitude of life in its many forms, my heartbeat slowed, I breathed deeply of the potent ambrosia, observed with amazement army ants and dung beetles at my feet, heard the weaver birds, and focused on a large msasa tree, where a lone male elephant stood watching me, chewing a late breakfast and fanning his enormous ears. This was a defining moment. I felt a part of it. I was not fully smitten, but I knew then that I wanted very much to learn much more—and really to experience Africa.

I had then served in Vietnam for two years as a special agent of the U.S. Naval Investigative Service (NIS), which had recently changed its name from Office of Naval Intelligence. The possibility of having a full thirty days away from Vietnam had been on my mind for a long time. During quiet interludes—which were few enough in the wartime environment—I would dream and plan how I might travel and spend a month-long holiday. I studied maps and calendars together, trying to estimate how much I could reasonably expect to do in the time available, and began writing letters to establish contacts who might advise me about travel in their countries.

Africa was at the top of my list of places I wanted to see. I established contact with a young constable in the South Africa Police Drug Squad in Johannesburg, who agreed to host me. In Rhodesia, the inspector in charge of recruiting and public affairs wrote me a detailed letter about the force and the country, saying he would be pleased to see me in Salisbury. And in Kenya, a British police officer extended a welcome to me. The itinerary started to take form over several months.

My supervising agent—the man every NIS special agent in Vietnam answered to—was a remarkable leader, as well as a scholar of the world. Alan Kersenbrock was a son of Hawaii who had served as an infantryman in Korea before joining the Honolulu Police Department. Later completing his degree after hours at the University of Hawaii, Al had come to the Office of Naval Intelligence at Pearl Harbor. A seasoned and very capable investigator when he joined, his talents quickly saw him promoted. He had been the senior resident agent at Camp Lejeune, North Carolina, when selected for promotion and assignment to Saigon.

Al had an enduring curiosity about Pacific literature, a subject we never tired of discussing over a bowl of lunchtime noodles at various Cholon *pho* (noodle) kitchens. He said that my early studies in the emerging South Pacific nations and my current vicarious explorations of Africa via the mail were of genuine interest to him too. Al talked to me often and encouraged my curiosity and initiative.

Supervising Agent Kersenbrock's year-long tour was coming to a close before I finalized my leave itinerary and purchased the ticket from Pan American Airlines in Saigon. He was replaced by Special Agent Dick McKenna, a former Ohio state police trooper promoted from the Special Operations squad at NIS headquarters. Dick McKenna quickly realized that he had very big shoes to fill, and I think he rushed to get up to speed after his predecessor's departure.

It was left to me to deal with Dick about my home leave. I had annual leave accumulated on the books as well as the thirty days of home leave, and I naively assumed nobody would object if I took an extra two weeks off to give myself about six weeks for the journey. I needed the time off, but Dick made it clear he thought six weeks away from the command was excessive. It was pretty clear to me that he wouldn't approve a leave period longer than one month.

I became aware of two things: I had obligated myself to a third year of service in Vietnam by accepting home leave and thus had to work with McKenna for another year in the close confines of the Vietnam office, and

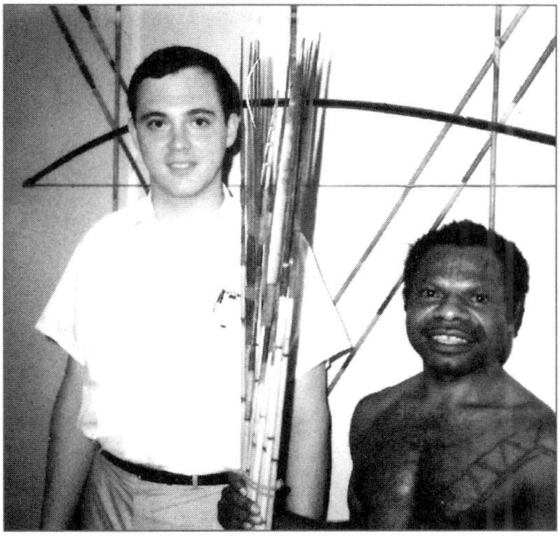

En route to Vietnam via Papua New Guinea: A Chimbu man from the Highlands displays native weaponry seized as evidence. (Author collection)

he plainly could not comprehend what twenty-four months of service in a war zone meant and why I needed a decent interval away. In the final analysis, I came to realize that he didn't want to risk criticism from superiors in Washington for authorizing "excessive" leave at a time of command transition when every agent seemed to be needed.

I shoehorned my itinerary into a thirty-day package and prepared to go. Whatever the obstacles, I was now determined to do this trip around the world.

* * *

When finally my travel day actually arrived, I carefully locked away my credentials in our Saigon office safe, put a final coat of oil on my rifle and handguns, stowed them, and headed for the airport with one suitcase and with friendly gibes from envious comrades echoing in my ears. The next morning at dawn, I was touching down in Port Moresby, Papua New Guinea, after an uneventful changeover in Manila.

Ian and Jean Bullock, the young couple who first had sparked my interest in Africa, hosted me at Bomana Police College, outside Port Moresby. Both were excited to know I was on my way to Africa. Jean's parents, Don and Eleanor Holmes, in Salisbury, Rhodesia, had extended an invitation for me to stay with them at Epping Cottage. It was reassuring for me to know there would be familiar, friendly faces there on my initial trip to the Dark Continent.

There was still a lively social scene in Port Moresby, and I missed few opportunities to join with the international contingent of Australians, Scots, Welsh, English, and Africans of European decent. They were deeply interested in my news and impressions of the Vietnam War. I was able to tell them something about what I had been doing, what I'd seen and heard. It was anecdotal; in truth, I had a remarkably poor overview of the strategic war situation, though I had completed two years of service there.

From Port Moresby, I flew to Melbourne, Australia. There, my good friend Leo Newport and his lady took me into their home for several days. It was the southern winter, but we managed to entertain ourselves outdoors every day with crates of Carlton Draught in quart bottles and cases of fresh oysters on ice. Undoubtedly, the neighbors in quiet, suburban Elsternwick wondered what or who had descended on the Newport residence. It felt very good to be with such warm, genuine friends. I was dreaming of Vietnam every night but was also rejoicing in my changed circumstances as I awoke in the morning.

I had managed to book an airline reservation from Melbourne, Australia, to Johannesburg, South Africa. Leo dutifully drove me to Tullamarine Airport on a cold, foggy morning—neither of us feeling particularly bright from all the social activity. There we were told that my aircraft would not be landing in Melbourne that morning but that they had a seat available on a flight to Sydney, which would allow me to make my connection and get through to South Africa. As he waved me off, Leo uttered a rude gibe about it being a good thing I was going.

It was a very long trip, made worse by my hangover and cramped three-abreast seating on the Boeing 707. There were fuel stops at Perth and Mauritius, the latter a tropical island of verdant sugarcane fields and forests.

My aircraft landed in the rarified atmosphere of Jo'burg at 10:00 PM local time. It was too late to try to call anybody, so after cashing a traveler's check at Jan Smuts International Airport, I made my way to the taxi stand. There it was that I heard Afrikaans spoken for the first time when I attempted to engage a driver in conversation. A country boy from Transvaal, the blond cabbie had virtually no English. But he understood "Hillbrow," the Johannesburg suburb I considered my destination.

Contemporary Hillbrow now is one of the most dangerous areas of modern Johannesburg; in 1971, however, it was a rather cosmopolitan neighborhood of ethnic shops, restaurants, and clubs reflecting the flavors of the multitude of new (mostly European) migrants. The Hillbrow Hotel was situated in the center of it all, an old white building of several stories. A black porter with a huge smile came out to the curb as I paid the cab driver and thanked him. The porter, overhearing our attempts at communication, told me in near-perfect English that the young Afrikaner driver had never met an American before; I grasped the driver's hand and shook it, saying *danke*, the word for thanks that my porter coach prompted me with. Exhausted, I wasted no time checking in and falling into a deep sleep in the midst of the sounds of a large, modern city.

I awoke for my first look of Mother Africa in the daylight. Pulling the old lace curtains aside, I looked up into a deep, blue sky. But there was no doubt that I was in Africa's most modern city. Multistoried apartment buildings arose in nearby blocks, and a steady stream of cars passed under my window.

Johannesburg was really a transit point for me for onward local and international travel. I learned that Detective Constable Alan Jack, with whom I had corresponded, lived in a nearby flat. I met him later that morning with his drug squad partner, Alec Holmes. Alan lived in a ninth-floor single-bedroom flat with views overlooking sprawling Johannesburg. He was young and personable, did not look like a policeman, and dressed in modish clothes. I quickly learned that drug squad duties were as fraught with dangers as they might be in a large American city. Alec and Alan joked about shots being fired through Alan's door during a recent altercation with a Lebanese smuggling suspect.

Later that day, in a Johannesburg watering hole, I met John Richard Ormonde Power, lately of the Royal Papua New Guinea Constabulary, where he had secured legendary status in a short time as the trainer of the police riot squad. Ormonde had served in the Northern Rhodesia Police before accepting the New Guinea assignment; now he was on extended leave, looking for opportunities in Africa. That day he was carrying a .45-caliber Colt automatic, doing a private investigation that appeared to have overtones of narcotics violations.

Ormonde was to become a very close friend of mine in the years ahead.

Despite the friendly camaraderie, it had not been my intention to spend any more time in South Africa's cities than absolutely necessary. I wanted to see the bush.

While I was still a high school student, our family home in Yosemite National Park had been visited by a large, jovial Afrikaner named Rocco Knoble. He rose to become director of South Africa's National Park Service, and my father and he had maintained contact over the interim years. Rocco had extended an invitation to me to see Kruger National Park. I needed to go to Pretoria, the nation's capitol, visit him, and make the necessary arrangements. There was regular train service between Johannesburg and Pretoria, so I decided to travel there as soon as possible.

The next day, armed with a crude map, phone numbers, and the name of a hotel described to me as "okay," I left Johannesburg station.

The train station was a legacy of Johannesburg's past, a gold-mining boom town whose city center contained a number of early examples of Victorian architecture. This was my first real exposure to the realities of apartheid, South Africa's segregation policy, and I felt distinctly uncomfortable at the signs stenciled on benches and other amenities to designate who could lawfully use them. Carriages at the rear of the train were labeled *nie blankes*; these were for native Africans and mixed race persons, called "coloured" in the South African parlance of the day. As our express train sped through lesser stations on the way to Pretoria, I watched groups of poor blacks standing on their station platforms. I had thus far liked all the South Africans I'd met, both whites and blacks. The concept of legal separation was against every tenet of civilized behavior I'd been taught, but I promised myself that I would make an effort to understand the forces that had brought it to be national policy.

The next morning in Pretoria, Rocco greeted me in his government office. He had arranged for me to spend time at Skukuza, at the southern end of Kruger National Park. Because my time was limited, an airline commuter flight was suggested as the best way for me to get down to the low veld.

It was always a pleasure to fly in a Douglas DC-3, the venerable prop-driven airliner that began service in the United States during the early 1930s. The ComAir aircraft I flew on that next morning was equipped with comfortable seats, unlike the military versions I knew so well from Vietnam. I relaxed with a cup of tea and enjoyed my first daylight aerial view of Africa, starting with a takeoff at Jan Smuts International, Johannesburg.

Johannesburg is one of Africa's higher cities, at more than five thousand feet elevation. The old aircraft's big Pratt and Whitney radial piston engines roared comfortingly as we took to the skies, overflying the massive tailings dumps of deep gold mines over which the city was built. Far back in the distance were the towers of the central city—but ahead I could see nothing but open country, the South African veld. It had the look of ideal cattle grazing country; dams, barns, and fences—tiny dots below—confirming this.

We were flying almost due east, toward Portuguese Mozambique. Though it was difficult to see from the air, the high plains of central South Africa were tapering downward, losing elevation. With that, the vegetation changed also. Later, instead of the open savanna grasslands around Johannesburg, the country had many more large trees—and as we finally began to lose elevation near Skukuza, I could see rolling hills covered with banana plantations and even the occasional red blossoms of towering African tulip trees. By New Guinea standards, this was far different than the equatorial tropics. As we landed, taxied up to a small building, and shut down, the doors were opened and a rush of warm, heavily scented air rushed in, redolent with traces of dust, grass, and even, I thought, animals. This was what South Africans called the low veld. The immense Kruger National Park had been carved entirely out of this country to save South Africa's rare flora and fauna.

Up to this moment, all I had seen of South Africa was city and high veld grasslands. I had been told that Kruger was very well managed, and my experience with South Africans prepared me to expect this. I wondered then if South Africa's national parks were so overwhelmed with visitors, much as Yosemite was, how much it would feel like my composite vision of "real Africa."

I need not have worried about warm hospitality, in any event. Standing on the apron next to a Land Rover emblazoned with the kudu emblem of the park stood ranger Fritz Fourie, my host. His two African laborers alighted from the back of the four-wheel drive, picked up my gear, and stowed it according to instructions issued by Fritz in Afrikaans. He greeted me in good, accented English—with a large, muscled hand of a working man and athlete. I had one night and portions of the two remaining days; he would be glad to have me accompany him on his ranger duties around the southern end of Kruger.

Fritz particularly delighted in the bird species native to the park. We stopped just a short distance from the airport in the middle of a river crossing to watch a pair of kingfishers search for food. With the 300-mm lens on my camera, I captured images of the bright-blue birds among the reeds and shallow rapids.

The country changed once we passed through the fences and barriers of the park perimeter. I saw topped trees, more downed timber. Fritz, noticing my gaze, said, "It's the jumbo; they go where they like, and if they see tasty

Inspector Ian Bullock. (Author collection)

foliage in a treetop, they simply push the tree over." The management of migratory elephant herds had clearly been a challenge.

There were thousands of square kilometers of bushland within the Kruger fence. Visitors were restricted to driving at slow speed on the well-maintained paved road that ran north to south. To leave one's car was absolutely forbidden because of free-ranging natural predators who wandered indiscriminately, unperturbed at the sight or smell of a motor vehicle. A pedestrian human was a likely candidate for an evening meal. Most visitors, my host reassured me, paid attention to the rules.

In Africa, I learned that water availability had much to do with animal behavior. Park designers, knowing that animals actually migrate to find water, sank deep wells at strategic points along the roadway. The windmills for these were favorite congregation points for animals, as was the shelter of surrounding trees and vegetation. Motorists were provided parking vantage points at the water holes from which the daily microdrama of survival in Africa could be seen: kills, ambushes, sedentary socializing, and the non-hostile interaction of some species. All observations were from cars.

My first views of the African bush were from Fritz Fourie's Land Rover as he patrolled and carried out routine tasks. I saw various species of native

Police recruits at morning parade, Bomana Police College, Papua New Guinea. (Author collection)

antelope, watched hippos surface abruptly in the river, and saw the skulking shapes of crocodiles under the surface.

That night I was safely ensconced in a thatched *rondavel*, a distance back from the tall fence that protected guests from the nocturnal depredations of Kruger's animals. Tired after an exciting day in the heat and dust, I lay between the crisp, ironed sheets of a double bed after a refreshing shower, staring up at the open, peaked ceiling of the thatched roof—marveling at the African artisan's painstaking work. In the distance were night sounds, most of which were totally foreign to me then: male hippos challenging, a jackal's yip, and faintly, a large cat. It was a new experience—and even a little exciting—but it felt somehow as though fences, amenities, and modern facilities made it less real. What would it be like to stand alone in the expanses of the African bush, to walk and even sleep out there? I soon drifted off to sleep.

Two days later I was again airborne over Africa, flying north to Rhodesia. Using the map in South African Airways' in-flight magazine, I attempted some dead-reckoning navigation to get a glimpse of the "great grey-green greasy Limpopo River" that Rudyard Kipling wrote of, the border between South Africa and Rhodesia. The country below looked brown and burnt, but it seemed wild and natural. The Limpopo, far from being a raging torrent at that time of year, was a ribbon of reflecting water in the holes and eddies of the ancient river bed.

A little over an hour later, we were landing on a spacious runway at Salisbury. From my window, I could see that Salisbury Airport was also New Sarum Airbase. Rhodesian Air Force Canberra bombers and helicopters stood ready, carefully sheltered back from the airstrip, which I was later to learn had been constructed by the Royal Air Force as an aircrew training facility during World War II.

It was a brilliantly clear day, a cool late winter morning on Southern Africa's high veld. The white plastered brick terminal was old, but in excellent repair—a reminder, I thought, of air travel in more genteel times. Customs officers were neatly attired in the traditional white nautical uniform of the service. My passport and luggage were carefully, but politely checked—and I was soon walking into a noisy lobby, where Don and Eleanor Holmes greeted me. "Welcome to Rebel Rhodesia," Eleanor quipped. It felt nice to be among good friends.

This friendly reunion was actually the culmination of a friendship that began six years before in 1965 when the Holmes' daughter Jean and her husband, Ian, recently settled in Papua New Guinea from Northern Rhodesia, had befriended me and introduced me to law enforcement in the environment of a primitive South Pacific colony. I had participated in my first homicide investigation alongside Inspector Ian Bullock of the Royal Papua and New Guinea Constabulary. Later—en route to Vietnam in 1969—I was introduced to the senior Holmes at Bomana Police College, where they were spending a holiday with Ian and Jean.

The Bullock police college residence was a three-bedroom frame structure elevated about eight feet above the ground on concrete pillars. The design made for dryer times during the monsoon, and it promoted air circulation in a location mere degrees off the equator in a country where air conditioners were unknown. The space under the home was also a favored place to set up chairs for sundowners and talk. An old, rusting refrigerator was always kept fully-stocked with New Guinea's own brew, South Pacific (SP) lager. Clutching a green bottle of SP, I learned that Don Holmes had served in the British army during World War II in a variety of African locales. I heard hair-raising tales of flights in aging Dragon Rapide aircraft into obscure dirt airstrips in Abyssinia; I learned of wartime exploits in ports such as Dar Es Salaam and heard about the gentleman existence of British planters in Kenya.

Over supper later, with Eleanor and daughter Jean present, through their descriptions and stories, I vicariously met other members of the family, Jean's brothers. Businessman, miner, farmer, pilot—and all were naturally rugby players as well. Theirs seemed colorful lives—perhaps riskier than what I was accustomed to, but certainly very full.

Don and Eleanor had farmed in what was Northern Rhodesia until 1965, when it became the independent nation of Zambia. A successful farmer, Don had sent his children to South African boarding schools. One son remained in Zambia; the other two had migrated south to Rhodesia, where the senior Holmes had also made their new life after selling their land holdings.

Dinner yarns were peppered with interesting anecdotes. Don, suffering an imperious stare for his indiscretions, regaled us with a story about one of his new farmer friends who had attended a weekend-long party at the Holmes Farm many years before. Feeling the need to answer a call of nature after overindulging both in a fiery curry and a number of quart bottles of beer, the guest made his way to the outhouse carrying a kerosene lantern to light the way. The country was still wild, and artificial light would normally deter roaming animals from excessive inquisitiveness. Settled comfortably on the plank seat, the young man was beginning to relax, when he suddenly experienced a sharp pain on his exposed buttocks. Jumping up, he saw a pair of red marks on one cheek—and panicked. Yelling as he made his way up to the house that he had been struck by a venomous viper, he encountered the corps of serious drinkers in a cluster of chairs on the veranda. None offered to suck venom from the snake bite, but one farmer, sensing an embarrassing lack of concern about the victim's plight, stood and walked to the farm gun cabinet and removed a huge double-barreled rifle, truly an elephant gun. Stalking out to the outhouse, he thrust the muzzle down the hole and pulled a trigger. There ensued a huge, messy blast—from which fluttered a shell-shocked Guinea fowl, which was quickly identified as the real bottom biter. The young farmer, naturally enough, was never allowed to forget the incident.

It had been bedtime before I had an opportunity to ask Eleanor about her family history in Africa. Sitting next to me, she related a fascinating story about her grandfather, a Scots engineer engaged to fabricate and erect bridges for the railroad that was central to British development plans for central Africa. The challenge was to measure, design, and assemble a steel bridge to span the Victoria Falls cataract, a railway bridge over the mighty Zambezi River. In 1903 careful, methodical British engineers had precisely measured the distance from the south bank to the north; that information was forwarded back to England, where factory engineers did their sums and began fabricating pieces of what was to be a prefabricated bridge. In the meantime, at the position chosen for the span, work went ahead over the dizzying chasm, preparing with great exactitude abutments to which the spans would be secured. When, much later, all was in readiness, the bridge members and all necessary hardware arrived by rail, and workers began assembling crafted pieces of the arch, until both sides of the structures touched—but did not fit together. There was, Eleanor related from childhood recollection of this favorite family story, much consternation when builders were unable to drive the final clevis pins that would marry the bridge sides into a solid arch. They sweated and worried for several days trying to find a solution. Then one unseasonably cool predawn morning, her grandfather was awakened by groaning noises from the bridge site. Steel members were moving. This, they soon deduced, was because lower temperatures had allowed the massive 470-foot steel span to cool. The two sides had contracted, dropping neatly into place exactly as they had been engineered to do, albeit in the cooler climes of Northern Europe. Relieved workmen soon drove the pins that completed structural unity. There was plenty of work for a talented engineer in developing Southern Africa; Eleanor's family elected to remain and take part.

* * *

There was no shortage of animated conversation that day in 1971 as Don and Eleanor introduced me to the well-laid-out, carefully maintained boulevards of Rhodesia's capital city, Salisbury. We drove past median strips planted with trees and shrubs; lawns were manicured and the atmosphere was one of order and organization. Soon after leaving the airport parking area, we were driving past the barracks of the Rhodesian Light Infantry. A squad of new recruits attired in battle dress and carrying rifles were double-timing down the highway under the watchful eye of a lean, seasoned colour sergeant. Dark blotches of sweat soaked through their dark-green shirts, and I heard both the squeak of rubbing packs and webbing meshed with the clatter of combat boots striking the tarmac. These, I was told, were most likely young Rhodesian men fulfilling their national service obligation. Rhodesia had a draft, at least for the population of European descent.

This did not feel to me like a country at war; rather, a nation in prudent preparation for a potential conflict. When I arrived in 1971, the country had been subjected to United Nations sanctions for several years in response to the Rhodesian Unilateral Declaration of Independence from Britain. Rhodesia had been self-governing since the 1920s—a parliament government, made up mainly of white farmers and settlers whose forefathers had pioneered with Cecil John Rhodes. Unwilling to accept a "one man, one vote" formula in an independence formula, the minority white government defied the world and declared its intention to find its own formula for equitable power sharing with the predominant African populace—in the full knowledge of what immediate universal suffrage had meant in the remainder of Africa. Apprehensive Rhodesians particularly remembered the violence and mayhem that accompanied Belgium's departure from the Congo less than a decade before; neither were there any examples of functioning democracies—or even near-democracies—in the newly independent African nations to the north.

Rhodesia's unilateral declaration of independence from Britain had not been a popular decision, particularly among those African British Commonwealth members who had exclusively taken the reigns of power from former white administrators. Zambia, formerly Northern Rhodesia, was overtly hostile to Rhodesia, as was Tanzania. Rhodesia, rightly or wrongly, was mindful that it had unfriendly neighbors to the north.

Don and Eleanor Holmes did not seem to be the sort who lived for the day's political events, but as Don and I later sat on the front *stoep* sipping tankards of Lion Lager, his conversations reminded me that most of the Holmes family had migrated to Salisbury after Northern Rhodesia became independent. The decision to sell the family farm that he had built from nothing had been based not on racial grounds but on economic and personal safety issues. Zambia, under its first president, Kenneth Kaunda, was not a good country in which to be a white farmer, I was told. Moreover, Tanzania's Julius Nyerere and Kaunda had forged alliances with Communist China. The Chinese were then building a railway from the Indian Ocean to landlocked Zambia.

From my front porch position with Don, I gazed over gardens to the tall hibiscus border hedge and the mature trees of Epping Cottage. I was at the time confounded at why such a spacious home might be called a cottage, except that it had only two bedrooms. Robustly constructed of plastered brick, the floor was laid out in magnificent parquetry patterned from African hardwood, kept always in a state of high sheen by the family servant, who skated around using polishing rags over bare feet. The living

Don Holmes spins yarns about Africa from the front porch of Epping Cottage, Salisbury, Rhodesia. (Author collection)

room was a repository of family memorabilia and rare African furniture. Pride of place went to an ancestral Indian army campaign chest, which stood imposingly next to the fireplace.

Bedrooms were furnished with antique stinkwood four-poster beds that in their early service had been transported around southern Africa in wagons pulled by teams of oxen. Each had a story to tell, and my hosts knew them all.

Meals were served at an English dining table under the watchful eye of my hostess. Their African young manservant, who lived in his own quarters, was attending university. He served meals in a starched linen jacket, signaled by the tinkle of a small dinner bell when each course was complete.

This was an altogether foreign experience for me. Don, sensing my curiosity one evening, turned to me and said, "You know, we are old people and set in our ways; we could not change and learn to live without servants now." But an air of caring and compassion was apparent between the young man and his employers.

There were three grown Holmes sons, one who had married an English lass employed with the British High Commission in Zambia. Reg and his wife remained in Lusaka, Zambia. The other two boys also resided in Salisbury. The youngest, Alistair, took an immediate liking to me. Married

A spirited game of rugby at the Police Club grounds, Salisbury, Rhodesia. (Author collection)

with a young family, he found time to introduce me to the world of masculine Rhodesia—at the Salisbury Club. A keen rugby player with a reputation for fisticuffs on and off the field, Alistair had a circle of colorful friends at the venerable club, situated with its polo field in old, central Salisbury in the Avenues. With soaring white Cape Dutch gables, manicured lawns, and sweeping verandahs, this was one of the more prestigious social and athletic clubs in Rhodesia. Alistair escorted me into the bar area, where we were served by a graying African barman who didn't need to ask what we were drinking. With pints of chilled lager in hand, we circulated among clusters of Rhodesian sportsmen where the latest news was shared—and I was introduced.

Later, we drove past through the leafy, broad streets of the Avenues past Government House and into the police training depot—the home of the British South Africa Police. The police rugby team was playing a match against a provincial team from Matabeleland. After my vicarious introduction to the game via Alistair and his rugby mates, I was excited at the opportunity to see what promised to be a vigorous contest.

It was a cool winter afternoon at the Morris Depot police grounds, the low sun casting shadows as we settled into the plank seats of the bleachers, surrounded by police supporters and families there to cheer their team on.

They were a friendly crowd, not unlike a large family, and many knew Alistair, speaking a few friendly words until their attention was snatched by the two teams running onto the playing field.

Well-played rugby is a flowing game, characterized by determined rushes downfield by runners intent in getting past opponents' tackles. There were few time-outs. I was quietly amazed at the stamina and fitness of the players engaged in such unbroken vigorous team athletics at more than five thousand feet elevation. In particular, I came to notice one of the police forwards, a huge man in dark blue who seemed to be omnipresent in the team plays. "Who's that?" I asked Alistair. He turned and grinned. "That's Billy Coetzer, the police farrier." Chief Inspector Bill Coetzer, at age forty-five, was still playing first-string rugby. His was a name I would hear much more of in years ahead.

My introduction to the police force itself came the following morning when Inspector Brian Cullingworth of the British South Africa Police appeared at Epping Cottage, turned out in an immaculate winter uniform patterned after Britain's army uniforms of World War II. Brian had answered my letter when I wrote from Da Nang to Rhodesia's International Police Association chapter in Salisbury. He was then assigned to Police General Headquarters (PGHQ), in charge of recruiting and public affairs.

Don and Eleanor had never met Brian before that morning, but in what turned out to be a regular occurrence in the small, friendly social circles of Rhodesia, they knew that Brian's son had undergone radical heart surgery in South Africa several months before. We chatted amicably in Epping Cottage's living room; then Brian drove us down Mount Pleasant's broad boulevards to central Salisbury.

Inspector Cullingworth was clearly an intelligent man, with a keen interest in international affairs. He asked me something about my job in Vietnam, curious as to the nature of criminal investigation in a war zone. He explained that Rhodesia too had experienced limited incursions by armed terrorists trained by nations of the Communist bloc. Perhaps I would be interested to meet the forensic scientists and musketry staff at the BSAP armory?

After a short visit to Police General Headquarters, where I walked through the towering hallways of a classic colonial headquarters and admired heraldry and historic photographs, we drove the short distance to Morris Depot. The armory was a fortress-like brick building behind an eight-foot security fence topped by barbed wire. While we waited at the gate to be allowed in, a squad of recruits dressed in gray shirts and dark-

Inspecting captured Eastern Bloc weaponry at the British South Africa Police armory. In the author's hands is an AK-47, showing signs of gunshot damage inflicted against its previous owner. On the wall behind is an SKS rifle and RPD light machine gun. (Author collection)

blue combat trousers practiced drill on the hard stand opposite. Their drill instructor, attired in uniform shorts and boots with leather leggings, was carrying a pace stick and bellowing out cadence to his charges. Brian chuckled. "Square bashing was never much fun."

There was far more to the police armory than the name implied. Here the firearms forensic experts worked, identifying weapons, projectiles, and spent cartridges discovered at crime scenes. There was a full-time team of gunsmiths at work maintaining the force weapons. The explosive ordnance disposal team worked from there, as did the depot weapons instruction staff, known simply as the musketry staff.

We were escorted through the perimeter fence, past steel doors, and into a large room where several hundred 7.62-mm FN assault rifles stood in long, neat racks. There we were met by Chief Inspector Don Hollingsworth, a shottist well known in Southern Africa because of his prowess on the one thousand meter rifle range. Don asked me several questions about the varieties of weapons then being captured in the Vietnam War. "You would be interested to see what we have captured from terrorists here in Rhodesia," he said quietly, then escorted us upstairs to a small display room. This was the sort of exhibit one often encounters in police laboratories, but instead of gruesome photographs of murder investigations, the armorers had secured captured weapons and equipment to a panel: there were AK-47s of East German manufacture, a Chinese SKS assault rifle, and a Russian RPD light machine gun. Some bore evidence of damage caused by the rifle fire that had killed their insurgent owners.

These were the weapons I saw almost daily in Vietnam. Of more interest, perhaps, were the captured diaries of the deceased insurgents that described in considerable detail their recruitment and training in Soviet and Eastern Bloc training camps. Of more strategic value were recollections of the encampments and farms in neighboring African countries, where they had been supplied with weapons and food before being dispatched to Rhodesia on missions of intimidation and assassination. I noticed particularly a copy of Mao Zedong's infamous *Little Red Book*, with the late owner's name neatly stenciled inside the front cover.

I learned then that most insurgent activity had been subdued several years earlier, largely because of a very effective intelligence collection program managed in the tribal trust lands by police Special Branch detectives. There were strong incentives for the populace to report strangers or evidence of their presence, and loyalty was strong—especially because tribal elders were recognized as government officials. I did not sense an air of complacency about the terrorist threat that day in 1971. My impression was that they felt they had met their enemy once, had prevailed, and somehow would do so again if necessary. That day did not then appear to be anywhere in the immediate future.

We were joined by Section Officer Eric Kennelly, soon to be promoted to inspector, in charge of the musketry staff that refined weapons handling skills of new recruits. Personable, astute, and very interested in my lessons from Vietnam, Eric was later to become a fast friend.

Eric was dressed in his winter uniform rather than the more usual utility uniform worn in weapons classes. There was a medal parade scheduled that morning; would I like to attend?

Here was an opportunity to see some of the heraldry, tradition, and splendor of the British South Africa Police's more than seventy years of service in Africa. I said I would be pleased to attend. Saying good-bye to Don Hollingsworth and the armorers, Eric, Brian, and I walked down a quiet street shaded by massive trees, past the historic camp hospital, where the police doctor and staff treated the day's sick parade, to the Montague Avenue entrance gate and the depot parade ground.

The BSAP's origins were rooted in Cecil John Rhodes' British South Africa Company, established before the turn of the century under a royal

With the author, left, at a depot medals parade is Inspector Brian Cullingworth, center, and Section Officer Eric Kennelly. (Author collection)

charter signed by Queen Victoria to develop the country north of South Africa that was later to bear Rhodes' name. Raised as a regiment of mounted infantry to protect the pioneer column of settlers that came north in wagons to establish Fort Salisbury, the British South Africa Company Police later fought in the Boer War and in East Africa during World War I. "Company" was eventually dropped from the regimental name, and the force continued to have full responsibility for national defense and policing through World War II, when an army and air force were created.

The traditions of a British mounted regiment had been carefully preserved, much as it has in the Royal Canadian Mounted Police. The parade square at Morris Depot, the regiment's "home," was a large rectangular lawn bordered by tall hedges and a variety of soaring, carefully maintained tropical trees. Men marched on the lawn, but the square was really the domain of the mounted ceremonial guard, senior recruits who paraded in formation on chargers with names like Dreadnought.

That morning, bleachers had been erected on either side of a large stone plinth, on either side of which stood flag poles. The green and white

A Morris Depot parade. (Author collection)

Rhodesian national flag fluttered from one; on the other was the BSAP flag—the gold emblem of a male lion leaping over a shield and spears on a blue background. The bleachers were filled with police medal recipients and their families, there to see the honors.

There was an interesting array of different uniforms. Depot training staff wore the Number One dress uniform—the winter tunic, breeches, Sam Browne belts, leather leggings, and boots, all polished to a mirror finish. Several senior officers, wearing colored collar tabs, were attired in "patrols," a dark blue tunic and trousers trimmed in regimental gold. The parade was also very much a social event, where colleagues from outlying districts were temporarily reunited. Eric and Brian were greeted by many passersby.

A police bugler in dark-blue band uniform, a fez on his head, marched out of the guard room as the minute hand on the regimental institute clock swung over its zenith. His hobnailed drill boots clacked down the footpath until he reached his assigned position, and, smartly driving his right foot down to assume the attention position, he brought his instrument up and blew a cavalry call to attention. The crowd hushed. After several addresses, recipients were called forward to receive medals. Most were in recognition of long service and good conduct, but there were also bravery awards bestowed that morning.

As I listened and watched, it occurred to me that the force was run in the manner of a British military organization, but it also had the feel of a large family. Blacks and whites mingled and greeted each other. Men who had completed six months of recruit training together at Morris Depot had been particularly bonded by their common experience. It seemed an apt mixture of people and experience to police an emerging African nation.

My time was very limited. With only two more days available to me on my far-too-rigid timetable, Brian later suggested that I make two day trips into the low veld. He telephoned the police station at Kariba, then spoke to a former policeman at Victoria Falls on my behalf while I bought air tickets from Air Rhodesia.

The following morning I boarded a turbo-prop Viscount at Salisbury Airport for the hop to Kariba. It was a short, but interesting flight that took us from high Salisbury down over the edge of the Zambezi escarpment to an airport a short distance back from the edge of the mighty river. While it had been pleasantly fresh and cool that morning at takeoff, when I stepped from the aircraft door onto the passenger ramp, I was enveloped in heat and brilliant sunshine. Trees and foliage were altogether different; I noticed distinctly shaped flat-topped acacias in the tree line. It felt like I thought Africa should feel. Quickening my pace across the aircraft parking apron, I cast my eye to the terminal fence for a friendly face and noticed that one man was watching me intently. This, I would soon learn was my host for the day—and eventual lifelong friend—Section Officer Angus Rufus.

Angus was dressed in what might best be described as "civilian Rhodesian": a tan safari suit, shorts, long socks, and the ubiquitous *veld-skoen* shoes favored by the country's males. This seemed eminently practical as the low veld heat began to draw perspiration through my shirt.

He greeted me carefully, not knowing what to expect, I'm sure; relieved me of my camera bag; and pointed me to the parking lot, where a small car sat under a shade tree. I could see movement in the back window and, as we got closer, the outline of a very large dog. This was Sheba, the Bull Mastiff that was Angus' inseparable companion. Very well mannered, but ever vigilant, her body mass occupied the entire rear area of the small car. As it was obvious to her that I was a welcome passenger of her master, my place in the front passenger seat went uncontested.

Kariba, I learned, was a settlement originally created for the crews who built the colossal concrete dam across the Zambezi gorge to dam one of Africa's mightiest rivers. In earlier days, the top of the dam had been a well-used highway to Northern Rhodesia; now—with tensions heightened between the neighbors—traffic had dwindled to a trickle. Because Kariba generated a majority of Rhodesia's electricity, it was strategically valuable. There was a company of army infantry in the area, and the Rhodesian air force had aircraft on standby ready to defend it.

As we leisurely drove away from the airport, I had started to ask Angus about his job and what policing in Kariba was like, when he suddenly looked ahead and said simply, "Jumbo. Want to have a look?" He drove the car well off the road and stopped, not more than fifty yards from a Mopani tree, under which a young bull elephant stood gently waving his ears, checking the scent of our vehicle with his raised trunk. The windows were down; it was perfectly quiet. Sheba breathed quietly behind me, and there was the occasional drone of a passing insect, punctuated only by the tiny noises of the elephant's ears moving the air. We sat wordless, and then I began to feel Africa just as I smelled the deep, pungency of the shrubs and the animals that were sharing the moment with me. I knew in that instant that this would be a moment that would remain with me forever—and even sensed attachment, as though I somehow had a place in this vast continent.

Angus and I had known each other but a few minutes; he was, however, a skilled bushman who knew Africa's animals and people very well. He sensed the significance of the moment and savored it with me, only starting the motor after the bull had grown bored and shuffled off down the hill.

We drove on, chatting about Kariba. I learned that an important part of the job was patrolling the vast wilderness along the banks of Lake Kariba, the hundred-mile-long lake created by the dam. The police carried out regular boat patrols, but more often drove Land Rovers or carried out prolonged tours on foot. Rhodesia was ever mindful that their Zambian neighbors on the north shore were hostile and that they had a history of harboring insurgents who might cross over to attack its people.

These things I contemplated as I stood on a hilltop vantage point looking westward, where the massive body of water seemed unending—and where directly north the brown rocky hills of Zambia rose from the waters edge. Later, on the dam wall itself, with the lake to my back I stared far below into the rugged Zambezi gorge, as released waters coursed over and around massive boulders, and wished that I could have seen the Zambezi Valley before man had felt the need to alter its craggy majesty. A troop of curious baboons reminded me that I really was witness to a day in Africa, despite the distractions of man's influences.

Angus quite naturally enjoyed a close relationship with the Rhodesian army. It was more than a professional liaison; he had previous army service and shared much in common with the men who lived on a hilltop base not far from Kariba police camp. We called in to the officer and senior NCO mess in time for morning tea. Perhaps six hungry young junior officers were filling mugs of sweet, strong tea—and grabbing handfuls of sandwiches. This was the day's first work break, after several hours of intense training activity; everybody was hungry and thirsty.

The men were dressed in carefully tailored dark green shirts with rank epaulettes, the Rhodesia Regiment patch neatly stitched to one shoulder. Shorts, long socks, and boots completed the uniform.

It was already growing very hot; electric fans shifted the air within. But because the mess enjoyed an unequaled view across the lake to Zambia and westward to the lowlands of Matusadona National Park, an occasional zephyr blew through the open doors.

I was warmly greeted. These men, whose job it would be to find and attack insurgents, were keen to know how we fought the Vietnam War. I explained how U.S. forces always tried to use mobility advantage, artillery, and air cover in their contacts with North Vietnam Army (NVA) and Viet Cong elements—and I learned that these things were not normally available to Rhodesian soldiers. Their advantages were a very high state of physical fitness that allowed them to pursue and catch their quarry on foot in difficult terrain, tracking and bush field craft, and superior weapon-handling skills.

The army personnel were impressive: intelligent, curious, loyal—obviously motivated junior leaders. Later, after farewells had been said, I watched a squad of young white troopers doing punishment dispensed by the company sergeant major for a disciplinary infraction. Rather than face formal charges from their commanding officer, all had agreed to spend an hour or so scrambling up a near-vertical hill at the camp and carrying full packs. There was no doubt in my mind that all were extremely fit; I hoped it would be enough for them if the war returned to Rhodesia.

Back at Kariba police camp, I sat and watched with real interest the routine of the indigenous African constables. These were the men who did the basic policing of Kariba, much of it on foot or with a bicycle. Constables assigned to districts (as opposed to towns and cities) wore carefully starched gray shirts, khaki shorts, leather leggings, and boots. A pillbox helmet and chin strap was worn on a near-shaven head. A prisoner in handcuffs was brought in and booked by a seasoned African noncommissioned officer (NCO). Two constables prepared equipment for an impending boat patrol, which would be under the command of a young white patrol officer. In the background was the faint clatter of a manual typewriter behind the doors of the camp Criminal Investigation Department. It seemed a very pleasant place to be.

I had a reservation to return to Salisbury on the late-afternoon flight. There was, Angus said, as he strode into his office, time for a beer at the police canteen. This was Kariba's infamous Jam Jar, a large, open-thatched *rondavel* constructed of stone and concrete among boulders on the slope above the police camp. A refuge for thirsty patrons from Kariba and environs, Jam Jar was a favored local social venue. I was glad to go—to meet a few more Rhodesians.

Seated under a soaring thatched roof before a carefully polished solid concrete bar, I sipped a cold Lion Lager and listened to Angus Rufus tell me of his early days in the Northern Rhodesia Police—of time spent in the Congo during the rebellion, and of interesting patrols in the Zambezi Valley. Several years my senior, his had been an interesting life steeped in African history and events. He had a demonstrated affinity with Africans and clearly liked and enjoyed their company. This was facilitated by an intimate knowledge of their languages and dialects.

I flew out of the Zambezi Valley that night wishing I had the time and means to learn more, experience more.

There was a fresh experience the next day, as I flew to Victoria Falls and was met by Peter Nicholls. Here the Zambezi was a broad, surging river on which boats navigated until the entire, enormous river plunged into a long cataract. It was an international tourist venue, with fine hotels and a nearby national park.

Angus Rufus and Sheba at Kariba's infamous Jam Jar canteen. (Author collection)

Peter met me at the airport, which was situated eight kilometers below the river on a broad, brown plain. I was again back in the low veld, where the men wore shorts and long socks—and women wore light cotton sun dresses. As we drove toward the township of Victoria Falls, we chatted about my Kariba adventure the day before. The conversation reminded me that people knew each other in Rhodesia. Peter was naturally curious to hear the news of people and events from downstream Kariba.

We stopped at the Victoria Falls Hotel for lunch. Surely one of the finest examples of colonial architecture in Africa, the old hotel had been constructed by Rhodesia Railways at the turn of the century as a place of rest for travelers on the rail journey north. Sweeping white masonry arches, towering ceilings, glowing parquetry floors, and a large attentive staff in immaculate white uniforms greeted me as we walked into the lobby, where my host had agreed to meet his schoolteacher wife. The old African major domo greeted Peter by name, advising us that his wife had preceded us and was seated on the outside veranda.

Walking out onto a broad terrace shaded by massive African hardwood trees, I was greeted by my first view of the famous railway bridge that crossed the river chasm immediately downriver from the point where the Zambezi made its plunge. The hotel designers had sited the building in a perfect position, where the single arch of the bridge span framed the clouds of mist and white waters of Victoria Falls.

Mrs. Nicholls greeted me warmly. She had ordered lemonade, a thirst quencher for the hot African afternoon, and she was curious to hear about my trip: where I had been, whom I'd met, and, of course, what I thought of Rhodesia. I told her quite simply that I had had a wonderful time in their country and that the warm hospitality of the people had been the best part of my experience.

A troop of Africans played marimbas fashioned from dried gourds while we ate a leisurely lunch, enjoying the view and the international visitors, many of whom were obviously having their own first experience in the continent. There were Dutch, British, and French tourists and also several stunningly attractive female French backpackers who had put on their best outfit for tea.

Peter told me that neighboring South African had deployed a detachment of Special Branch detectives to Victoria Falls. They had been sent to augment Rhodesia's stretched resources and perhaps also for training purposes. In any event, their Rhodesian counterparts were impressed with the fine equipment their southern neighbors had brought with them, including a new fiberglass launch. Would I like to meet them and take a trip up the Mighty Zambezi? Of course I gratefully accepted.

My South African hosts were Afrikaners of the old school, quiet and courteous. A few years older than I, they were dressed in casual civilian clothing and, as the fashion was in Rhodesia, carried no sidearms. The South African Police (SAP) boat was a spacious civilian cruiser with inboard motor, both fast and comfortable.

The Zambezi River carries with it the vast drainage of a large portion of equatorial Africa from the Congo southward. After the rains, it swells to a swift, wide torrent. That day, the mighty river was quieter, its waters crystal clear with the deep blue African sky above. There were small islands in the river upstream and some pristine bush where the Victoria Falls National Park bordered the water. I sat, fascinated as a pair of white-headed fish eagles caught prey from the waters below their nest, situated high in a dead tree. Farther up, there was evidence a small herd of elephants had been frolicking on the beach. The river was clearly the lifeblood of a vast community of animals that called the region home. As we quietly drifted, listening to the sound of water, birds, and mammals, I felt privileged to have shared it, albeit briefly.

Late that afternoon, Peter introduced me to a colleague who operated a scenic flight service from a short airstrip near Victoria Falls town. He offered to take me up for an aerial view of the river and its waterfall. I had by then walked out onto the bridge, seen the statue of explorer David Livingstone, and stood in awe on the edge of a precipice opposite the river as it plunged into the chasm, soaking all with billowing spray and mist. So, I gratefully accepted the offer and climbed into the rear seat of a small twin engine plane with camera and lenses poised. A few minutes later, we were hurtling down the strip toward the Zambezi chasm, pulling up over the trees and banking away from hostile Zambia to gather elevation.

From the air, both sides of the river appeared to be quite flat, with gentle undulations and occasional stream courses. My pilot host pointed to the north to a distant community, shaded by many large trees. This was Livingstone, Zambia—once a thriving small city from which the three Rhodesias—North, South, and Nyasaland—had been administered before the winds of change had swept over British Africa. That day there was no sign of vehicular traffic in sleepy Zambia.

Rhodesian aircraft were not welcome in Zambia's airspace, and my host kept us safely back from the imaginary medium in the river center that separated the two countries. Victoria Falls and its clouds of mist and bridge were captivating, even from 1,500 feet. The sun was getting low in the sky when we touched down several minutes later, casting a deep golden glow over land, trees, and water.

As I bade my new friends good-bye that evening, I was certain the images of these people, the river, and its animals were permanently affixed in my brain.

They certainly were fresh in my mind as I said good-bye to Rhodesia and headed north to Kenya, my first look at "independent Africa." I had corresponded with a British expatriate from Nairobi who had kindly offered his hospitality for the three days I had available. Ted Casey was employed by the Kenya Police. Soon after my arrival, I learned that he had been a Special Branch detective for most of his service. He and several British colleagues were conspicuous by their white skin in independent Kenya's national police force. I was soon to learn why.

Ted Casey had been single for many years. He lived in a modest two-bedroom flat, overseen by an irascible old African manservant who had been with him for decades. I settled into the spare bedroom—and also into Ted's social life, which centered around the venerable old Nairobi Club. A vestige of colonial times when Britain's gentlemen farmers, most from the officer class, settled the high plane to grow cattle and tea, the club was then central to the social lives of the dwindling British population. Ted and his mates gathered alongside the long bar at noon, or sometimes earlier, signed chits for drinks and meals, and shared innumerable stories and anecdotes.

The business of being a Special Branch officer was, after all, centered on the ability to gather useful information. The Kenyatta government had been subject to a number of attempts to illegally seize power. Experienced British detectives maintained information networks that had efficiently diffused the coups. The perpetrators, I was told, had quickly been flown to remote detention facilities near the Sudan border, where there were few opportunities for future plotting.

While my host was doing his office work, others took me to visit a nearby national park and something of the city. One detective's wife—whom he had met while serving in the Palestine Police soon after the end of World War II—was a particularly skilled negotiator who helped me shop in Nairobi's bazaars.

The Nairobi Club had a growing African membership, particularly including government administrators—and some army officers. As my available time in Kenya drew to a close, I sat next to a young Kenyan officer, listening to him tell me of his life in the army. He had attended a social event that afternoon and so had been drinking for many hours. Despite this, he was good friendly company. As the evening drew on, he invited me first to join him in a visit to a favorite private club where there were many friendly Kenyan girls. When I politely declined, he invited me to attend his regiment's officer's mess.

We drove to a nearby army cantonment, clearly a former British army facility, and entered the bar area of the mess. I was the only white present. He ordered us large bottles of Tusker Beer; I paid. The mess was buzzing. There were several clusters of drinkers at tables, some in advanced stages of inebriation after an afternoon of drinking. Several came by to speak with me. The conversation was convivial, if not particularly cogent, and after a while, I managed to excuse myself and leave.

The next morning, my host asked me some sharp questions about where I had been and who I had met. He knew the identity of the lieutenant with whom I had been socializing; could I identify others at the officers' mess?

I wasn't a great deal of help to Ted. I soon learned that the session I had attended the night before had been used to hatch a plan to overthrow the government. Even as we spoke, the perpetrators were being loaded on aircraft for desert detention. I knew nothing about any plans for a coup, and I said so. Ted let it be known that he had concerns that people in the U.S. embassy might get wind of the fact that I had been present; in fact, I had been the only non-African in attendance that night. I allowed myself to say that the last thing I needed was a hassle with the State Department and set about confirming my reservation on the next British Airways flight to Europe. I made it to the airport that night after a particularly heavy session at the Nairobi Club with fifteen minutes to spare. The Special Branch saw to it that I got aboard, and I found myself seated in first class.

What a way to leave, I mused, as I saw Nairobi's lights fading in the distance. My brief visit had clearly been a tantalizing sampler of Mother Africa. I wondered then at the expression: "You may leave Africa, but one's heart never entirely does."

America felt like a changed country when I finally arrived during that 1971 summer. Africa's memories remained fresh in my mind. My parents were no longer living in suburban Virginia. After his work for President Lyndon B. Johnson to establish what was to become a national historic park at the president's Texas homestead, my father had retired from the

U.S. National Park Service. They had chosen to live in the Texas hill country, where Dad accepted the directorship of a new museum named in memory of Fleet Adm. Chester Nimitz. Nimitz was born in a modest stone cottage opposite Fredericksburg's Nimitz Hotel, where the museum was to be housed.

The thirty days of leave was galloping away. My parents and young brother picked me up at the San Antonio Airport and drove me into the hills to the new family homestead, a hundred-year-old stone farmhouse they were restoring after previous owners had suffered a disastrous fire. It was wonderful to be back with my family again. Mother spoiled me with my favorite recipes, Dad asked a few gentle questions about my life and my plans—but there wasn't much I could bring myself to talk about other than the thrill of my first look at Africa. I'm certain my mother sensed my anxieties—and both parents must have wondered what it was that was driving decisions I was making about my life. They knew I had then done twice the amount of Vietnam service I had agreed to do: why then another year? They did not ask me these questions, but I myself was spending more time worrying about my return to Saigon as I sat out under the pecan tree sipping long neck bottles of Lone Star beer while a gang of Texas-German carpenters finished the homestead roof. I eyed my calendar, conscious of my due date back in Vietnam, and realized that I was probably more unsettled than I had been in the weeks before my departure.

A few days later I was in the air bound for San Francisco. It was a wrench to leave my family again, but I also felt as though I really couldn't have stayed much longer. My mind was elsewhere.

I was cheered at the prospect of having a few days in San Francisco with Judy, my girlfriend since Yosemite days. It had been two years since she put me on the plane to Vietnam at Travis Air Force Base, two years during which we had relied on letters to share thoughts, plans, and love. In a long-distance call she told me she had arranged a few days off from her Berkeley job and would pick me up at San Francisco Airport. I wondered what it would be like to have three or four days with her. We were twenty-six years old and had never had that much private time exclusively for ourselves, though we had been sweethearts since age sixteen.

It all seemed surreal as, later that day, we drove across the San Francisco Bay Bridge together in Judy's faithful old Ford Falcon, chatting shyly at first about our respective families that had come together ten years earlier in Yosemite National Park. So much had happened in our lives in the preceding two years. Yosemite and our childhood together seemed a comforting point at which to begin.

Judy lived in an old, spacious second-story apartment in a hilly part of Oakland not far from her Berkeley job. Her father, a talented tradesman, had recently painted the interior in light colors. There was an airy living room, simply decorated, a row of open casement windows, and a small balcony overlooking a tiny front yard. It was remarkably quiet; I enjoyed the fresh scents of the bay and of gardens and flowers.

I was introduced to her Airedale-Labrador cross, a precocious, highly intelligent dog that saw his mistress' protection as his role in life. Known simply as Black Dog, he was Judy's constant companion.

It was a magical time, this first private visit of several days. We were together constantly except for my visits to the Navy travel office at Treasure Island, where a commercial return ticket to Saigon was arranged for me. Judy was a positive distraction from the foreboding that lingered in my mind. I told her about my job, but never in any specific sense; I had not yet been able to explore what the Vietnam experience meant to me—so I could not share those all-important things with her.

I did know that I wanted to continue working overseas, probably for another several years, because I truthfully felt that I was good at it—and I enjoyed it. I explained my decision to work another year in the Vietnam environment by describing the changes that were occurring in NIS, in particular the Far Eastern office closures. It was important to me that I land in a duty station where I could work independently, as I had done almost continuously in Vietnam.

Judy was intuitive enough to sense the subsurface anxiety in me as I faced leaving her and another tour. Sadly, neither of us could bring ourselves to talk about serious things in our respective lives that may have detracted from the sparkle of this tiny interlude together.

When the departure day finally came, tall, blonde Judy dressed in a light-blue minidress with boots. She was so beautiful, and I was leaving. I patted Black Dog on the head and carried my gear down the staircase and out to the old Falcon, wondering whether I would see him again in his well-guarded apartment, where I had spent those idyllic days.

We both were intentionally cheery during that drive across the Bay Bridge. It was a cool but very clear summer day in San Francisco. But my stomach churned and my throat was tight. I told Judy how special the days had been for me, how wonderful the experience of having time exclusively with her and to share the magic that always seemed to surround us. What I didn't say then—because I had not yet thought it through—was how and when we could do it again. It was in the back of my mind, but was but not yet an idea that I thought I could share.

At the airport, I easily checked my belongings through at the Pan American Airlines desk—then we walked through the corridors to a lounge, ordered drinks, and sat awaiting my boarding call, chatting, ever conscious of the minutes flitting past. It came all too soon. There was a final hug, Judy's admonition about being careful—and my promise to write. Then, she was gone and I was on my way back to a country America was then showing its determination to leave. I had an overpowering sense that I had probably made some very bad decisions, and I wondered what form my punishment for those ill-considered choices would take.

As we approached Saigon to land more than eighteen hours later and I speculated about whether the previous thirty days were actually real or merely reverie, I considered a well-worn Vietnam legend: that despite overt appearances, one could never actually leave. Men taking off in their Freedom Bird on their 365th day of service never actually returned to The World; a tiny fairy flew around the aircraft moments after liftoff, touching every man with a magic wand and transforming him into a new guy who would momentarily be landing to begin all over again his first day of a whole new year-long tour in Vietnam. Africa was fresh in my mind, and I found myself wondering if I would ever be allowed to visit again. My travels were over: I was staring at another full year of Vietnam service to perform and survive.

Saigon had changed considerably since my arrival two years earlier. There were fewer American vehicles, fewer soldiers, airmen, and sailors to be seen on the street. President Richard Nixon's Vietnamization program, designed to turn over military assets to Vietnamese fighting units as quickly as possible, had begun to work. The U.S. Marines were finally leaving the northern I Corps tactical zone after nearly six years fighting the NVA and Viet Cong. Army infantry, artillery, and armor were also drawing down.

There were fewer sailors in Vietnam, and Naval Investigative Service Office (NISO) Vietnam was reducing its agent numbers, too. Some agents were not replaced, particularly as the Da Nang office reduced to a single-agent posting. Remaining Navy personnel were more likely to be assigned to advisory tasks, teaching their South Vietnamese allies how to use and maintain vast numbers of vessels and quantities of materials that were being signed over to them as a part of Vietnamization. These petty officers, many

The author in field uniform, Saigon, 1971. (Author collection)

of whom were volunteers, seemed far less inclined to engage in the sort of activity that would require the attention of an NIS special agent. This was a pleasant development for the agents of NISO Vietnam.

The NISO office was smaller now. The U.S. Army had given up its Cholon compound earlier in 1971, and because NISO Vietnam had shared the premises with the closing Army post office and PX facilities, we had searched for a new home. Fortunately, the U.S. Army Criminal Investigation Division (CID) in Cholon was reducing staff. They had turned over several floors of an aging nearby Vietnamese hotel to us, enough room for offices and billeting for all except the commanding officer and supervising agent, who remained in the villa.

In that autumn of 1971—with Africa fresh in my mind—I had returned to share a small, very plain room with Special Agent John Morgan on the fourth floor of the CID hotel. The nearby Five Oceans BOQ (bachelor officers quarters) had been closed also; this meant that we were without messing facilities. Agents did not have commissary privileges, but commanding officer Commander Gene Moore was very good about shopping for us. Morgan had been a commissary man cook in the Navy, which was particularly good fortune for me. He cooked on the floor of our room with a purloined electric frying pan, frequently blowing antique electrical circuits in the process.

I found myself being sent to the field again almost immediately, command making best use of my knowledge of unit deployments and talent for finding them. I started several letters to Judy, wanting to thank her and affirm all my good feelings but could not seem to complete the task. When finally I did, I said that I would like to see if we could start making plans to see each other and be together regularly. It didn't matter where, so long as we did it.

More than a month had passed since my return—and I waited many weeks for a response. When her response came in mid-November, Judy told me she had agreed to marry the brother-in-law of a previous roommate—a former naval officer intending to make a career in California forestry. Now I know that when she made the decision to marry someone else, she had not yet received my letter; for her, after our lovely days in the Bay Area, I had simply disappeared, with no mention of coming back.

Sitting in Vietnam, receiving news that she would marry someone else, I was stunned. Then I began to realize that I had probably taken Judy far too much for granted. Why should she pin her hopes on my suggestion that maybe we could find a way to spend more time together? She had an offer from somebody who was there now, somebody who could care for her; I was in Vietnam, again, and there were no guarantees as to where that decision might lead.

After several days, I had sadly talked myself into believing that my love had made a carefully considered and wise decision. I wrote her a letter in which I told her that I hoped she would be very happy in her new life—and that I hoped we would never lose track of each other.

As I handed the duty yeoman my letter to Judy that morning in Saigon, my heart was heavy and I felt more dislocated from my country than ever I could have thought possible. My brief time in the United States convinced me that few really appreciated the sacrifices and dedication to duty of so many who had served in Vietnam. America wanted out. President Nixon had promised to deliver on that promise, but what did "out" really mean? If Vietnamization could be made to work, the United States would find ways to stabilize and prop up its South Vietnamese allies against the North, I reasoned. But I was too far down the ladder to access the critical pieces of information together that might form a future picture of Vietnam's fortunes.

For nearly a year, the important news stories in Vietnam had related to troop withdrawal plans. Everybody wanted to know when they would be going home. The rumor mill suggested that ultimately, NIS headquarters too would take the opportunity to pull back agents to the Philippines. But it seemed unlikely to happen before my third year in-country ended in March 1972.

I found myself seriously considering the changes I had seen in my more than two years of Vietnam service, contemplating what I had seen, who I had worked with, and where it all might be leading as I considered my future in the organization. I became more conscious of negative aspects of the Vietnamese exposure to American culture and often sincerely wished that the United States could devise a way to help South Vietnam through more low-profile assistance. The United States military presence in the cities of Vietnam brought with it negative factors in equal measure to the positive effects. I soon understood that the Navy had planned its activities without considering long-term factors. Our people began to reach full potential in the last half of their year-long tour; continuity was always a problem as most people seemed to be learning their jobs. Little was done to encourage good people to remain longer than twelve months.

My contacts with State Department officials were not regular, but I noticed that they operated and oversaw programs that were delivering better infrastructure to the country: roads, bridges, schools, and communication. I came to believe that in some areas of the country these changes were reducing the influence of the enemy, actually making the country more secure. I took hope in this. Perhaps policy makers in Washington really were instituting a development program that might ultimately bring peace, even in ten years—like the British experience in the Malayan counterinsurgency campaign. I consciously tried to maintain a sense of purpose and optimism. The State people I met were dedicated professionals; the CIA personnel even more so. They had language skills and the best support facilities, and they impressed me with their long-term approach to Vietnam. These people did not leave after one year in-country.

My special agent colleagues and I grew into a smaller but even more close-knit group that came to know each other more intimately than most people know their own families. They were an interested and varied group. In the late 1960s, the Naval Investigative Service had assimilated more agents with law enforcement background. In the Vietnam offices, former police officers accounted for between a third and half of the agent force, which never exceeded twenty-three for all of South Vietnam. Those in another clearly defined group were the former military officers, naval officers in particular. These men often found the transition to civilian special agent status relatively easy because of their familiarity with the ways of the Navy.

Most agents were married. A year tour meant that husband and wife would be separated for twelve months, except for a five-day R&R leave in Hawaii. Home leave was not an option. There were no telephone facilities available—and this was well before the days of fax machines and e-mail. There was a group of married agents who came to Vietnam for the opportunity to save money—and because the NIS transfer policy favored duty station assignments for returning agents. For some, this meant they could return to their previous post without immediate concern about a disrupting family transfer.

There were some men in the latter category who shunned field duties in Vietnam. Just as often, good family men shared the most dangerous assignments, particularly in Da Nang, where agents traveled and lived with Marine field elements. Each man developed methods for coping with the Vietnam experience—always focusing on surviving 365 days in a war zone that offered so many ways to die.

NIS special agents in Vietnam had a difficult job even without the added factors of loneliness, stress, fatigue, and poor communication. Soon after my arrival I had noticed that morning mail call was the most important moment of the day for virtually everybody in the command. It was difficult to get agents to leave the office until the yeoman returned with the day's letters. Then the office became quiet as each lucky man opened envelopes and became lost in a reverie of distant wives, lovers, and children. Mail was delivered daily. Husbands who missed a letter might become sulky and introspective. This was also a time when one more day was scratched off each man's short-timer calendar.

We worked every day. On some Sundays, there would be a barbecue, where men drank beer and perhaps played volleyball. There was very little dissension between agents. They were a remarkably dedicated and mature group—and most helped me unreservedly to achieve professional competence.

Before 1970 NIS agents assigned to Vietnam were in a remarkably precarious, undefined position of uncertainty. The Navy hired them under a contractual arrangement. In 1970 special agents were designated as excepted civil service federal agents—but there remained nagging questions as to what a seriously injured agent might expect. The Navy's hospital system had no obligation to treat civilian employees outside of Vietnam. Agents were ineligible for assistance from the Veterans Administration. Indeed, reserve officers who served as special agents in Vietnam were not even authorized to wear theater campaign medals in recognition of their war service when they later donned uniforms back in the United States.

Special Agent Mike Nagle's Da Nang cartoon captures one of the dilemmas of civilian agents serving in Vietnam. (Courtesy of Mike Nagle)

The men managed stress in many different ways. There was a good deal of individual banter, biting humor, often deprecating, aimed at self. All of us who worked alone in the field worried about capture, knowing our credentials and issue weapons would give us away as intelligence operatives. There were animated conversations about the best way to eat leather-bound, laminated credentials.

Marriages generated both comfort and anxiety. Husbands who left the little lady at home with a checkbook and new-found wealth learned of new purchases and important financial decisions at least a week after they occurred. A response would require a further week to reach the States. There were infidelities discovered, patchwork solutions evolved—but there were far more instances of steadfast women who shouldered solo responsibility for self and family, including a cheery daily letter to their man.

I cannot definitely measure the cumulative effect of Vietnam on those who served, but two of my closest agent associates committed suicide: J. F. Washko, a former Marine officer with previous service in Vietnam killed himself in Colorado while on emergency leave from Da Nang; Anderson T. Lambert developed psychological problems and substance dependencies that led to his suicide some years later.

Others I'm sure noticed the transitory commitment of NIS to the organization's Vietnam presence. To my knowledge, there was only one visit by senior command in the years 1969 to 1972, that being the inspection by the staff of the Pacific Area Command, Naval Investigative Service Pacific. Special Agent Clive Roach, a calm and highly respected senior civilian traveled to Saigon accompanied by his assistant, retired Navy captain Jack David. Jack David had been a career intelligence officer. He was a wise, dynamic leader, and I respected his counsel immensely. Roach and David visited Da Nang, Cam Ranh Bay, and Saigon. They inspected offices and quarters of agents and support staff—and upon their return to Pearl Harbor, they shipped some basic furnishings to us to improve the comfort and morale of the Vietnam crew.

In retrospect, it seems likely that the Naval Intelligence Command had become ever more confident that the U.S. commitment to South Vietnam was transitory and that shrinking budget dollars were better spent elsewhere. From my perspective on the ground at the time, it began to feel as though we could be doing a better job had there been a valid long-term management strategy that began with identifying the best way to accomplish counterintelligence and investigative duties and to use manpower.

Also behind the daily challenges and stresses of serving in Vietnam at the time were the bitter tensions surrounding continued diplomatic efforts to reach a negotiated settlement with the North Vietnamese—the so-called Paris Peace Talks—and protestations about the war in the United States. Neither helped individuals to validate our mission or our personal efforts in the service of our country. Even to an untrained observer, it seemed obvious that the North Vietnamese were not negotiating in good faith; rather, they were trying to outwait increasingly impatient Americans. While never denying the right of America's citizenry to speak out, I could not help but think that antiwar protesters carrying North Vietnamese flags in our nation's capital were providing regular reinforcement to our enemy's strategy of delay, obfuscation, and denial. To me and many of my colleagues, antiwar protesters—in particular well-publicized activists who traveled to Hanoi—were overtly disloyal to those of us serving in Vietnam. Moreover, although protesters professed their desire to halt the war at any cost, the fact that North Vietnam found comfort in their activities seemed likely to prolong the agony. In 1970 it was impossible for me even to contemplate the possibility that the United States might walk away from a faithful ally; thus, encouragement of the enemy translated directly to more unnecessary deaths in Vietnam. By then I knew too well that those would likely be poor, disadvantaged Americans and Vietnamese. It was bad enough to contemplate being killed in Vietnam; far worse was the possibility of being the last man to die in a war not supported by mainstream America.

We did not like antiwar protesters, nor did we respect them. More than a few considered them collaborators of the enemy, particularly when material sent by American student activists was discovered in enemy supply caches. Those feelings were reinforced by reports of young uniformed servicemen returning to the United States being abused or attacked by like-age countrymen, who were often women.

As I reflected on my time in Vietnam and considered my future, I found myself observing that there had not been as many opportunities for professional interaction with Vietnamese as I would have wished. Although there was much I didn't understand about the people, there were many things that I enjoyed and respected. In truth, there was often mistrust, both by Vietnamese and Americans. Older Vietnamese, parents in particular, did not like to see the effect of a half million Americans on their social mores, the national economy, or traditional values. Americans, conversely, were inclined to think of Vietnamese as a nation of thieves, who lacked the will to vigorously prosecute the war against their aggressive northern neighbors. There was truth in both positions.

I had come to understand also that South Vietnam was a country struggling with a largely dysfunctional judiciary, a civil service that relied on corruption and nepotism to survive, and leaders whose decisions were not always in the best interests of the people. These were not pleasant revelations, but they were what we had to work with. I wasn't alone in my belief that our patient assistance could eventually bring about positive changes for the Vietnamese.

* * *

At NISO Vietnam in late 1971, our daily life in Saigon had changed radically from even a year previous. There was no longer a military mess to provide regular meals. There were no recreational facilities other than those we created for ourselves. It was a very good thing that the small agent corps was so tightly knit.

Our hotel home and office was situated on a broad avenue in Cholon. A few tamarind trees had survived the deprivations of war and drought. These provided shade to broad, tiled footpaths along the boulevard edge. Cholon's citizens walked on the sidewalks, held animated conversations there, bought their groceries there, and even ate evening meals under the trees. Though I knew good security practice dictated against establishing consistent movement patterns, I began taking pleasure from spending time on the sidewalk with the Vietnamese. I bought delicious French rolls from an old woman's cart, where she set up near the traffic roundabout; even more often, I squatted on a low stool a few yards from the hotel at a food stand operated by a middle-aged widow and her children. Their specialty was steamed mussels, a recipe from the coastal regions of France and Belgium. Accompanied by warm French bread and a quart of also-warm Tiger beer, I considered her meals a connoisseur's delight.

My fellow agents occasionally joined me. We were always heavily armed, but I think some of them concluded that I had finally "Gone Oriental." They were probably right. We were a constant source of entertainment to the Vietnamese, who were always delighted for an opportunity to laugh at big Americans trying to ride bicycles after too many beers.

The work days now finished with a stop in one of the office rooms that had been designated as a bar to replace Room Four at the Five Oceans BOQ. The Sears Roebuck couch and easy chair that Jack David and Clive Roach had sent out from Honolulu for our comfort were carefully maintained, the source of some envy from occasional outsider visits. The bar area was a normal venue for planning important after-duty activities that included visits to Cholon's Chinese restaurants. And then, of course, there were a few favorite bars.

Despite reduced numbers of Americans in 1971, there was a strip of bars running in the rabbit warren that was Cholon. Agents occasionally gravitated toward a favorite watering hole for beer and banter with the working girls. There was a bar along one wall with an aquarium behind it where *mama san* lorded over her cash box, the distribution of beer, and the pseudo drinks of the girls, the so-called Saigon Tea. Opposite the bar against the wall were a row of booths. These were where the girls did most of their maneuvering against potential soft touches, an activity we considered legitimate viewing sport. With time and familiarity, there was a good deal of teasing and kidding the girls about their devious ways—which were always denied good-naturedly. It was not a particularly salubrious venue, dimly lit, with primitive plumbing and a large population of rodents and insects firmly in residence. But it was a welcome diversion from the tension and angst of a difficult job in a dangerous land.

The face of Vietnam was changing. Our office and living quarters were now a small, isolated enclave in the country's largest city, identifiable by the barriers and sandbags that occupied the sidewalk in front and protected two portable military diesel generators that roared twenty-four hours a day, providing us with electricity. The Vietnamese walked around us, accepting the inconvenience with typical good humor.

We were encouraged to work with our Vietnamese counterpart agency, the Vietnamese Naval Security Bloc. This agency, which was capably led by a clique of Northern-born officers, focused as its mission on ferreting out potential spies from VN navy ranks, but they were committed to countering criminal activity if asked to help. I suspect that some of the investigative techniques they employed were designed more with spy catching in mind than criminal justice—but they could be effective, and I took hope that their presence would serve at least as a deterrent to the criminal elements. We quickly grew tired of burglary investigations, fuel thefts, and material thefts that had obvious links to Vietnamese military personnel.

Visits to other Navy outposts required more ingenuity—and often some sort of an aircraft ride. By 1971 roads that once carried fairly regular U.S. military traffic no longer did so, and I was less inclined to drive to the bases south, into the heart of the Mekong Delta.

I often used the U.S. Navy aircraft at Tan Son Nhut, a small detachment from the Naval Air Facility at Cam Ranh Bay. I rode their fixed-wing C-117 to Bangkok to work cases; more often it was the helicopters that got me to ships and outposts in the Mekong Delta. I could normally count on the Navy CH-46 Sea Knight helicopter that the troops had named *Ha Tien Hattie* to get me to a regular destination in one day. I would typically alight aboard an LST (tank landing ship) or APL (non–self-propelled barracks ship) anchored in the Bassac or Mekong Rivers as mother ships and repair facilities to a flotilla of river patrol boats, what was known as the Brown Water Navy. The helicopter would take on passengers and be gone.

In earlier days, shipboard operation staff could often request that passing aircraft stop for a passenger. By late 1971, we were no longer hearing much of the ubiquitous Huey helicopter's distinctive "whup whup" rotor beat in the skies of the Mekong Delta. The Army medevac choppers—long our most dependable ride source—were going or gone. So too were the Navy Huey squadrons based at Binh Thuy. Particularly if I had other work elsewhere in the field, it became necessary to hitch rides on Vietnamese navy riverine flotilla boats, the very same Swift Boats and PBRs (river patrol boats) that our own Navy had prosecuted the war with until recently. Although there were often U.S. Navy advisers aboard or around VN navy vessels, they were not in command so there was no guarantee when I would be put ashore, or where.

I worked alone, usually attired in U.S. Marine camouflage utilities, carrying a Smith and Wesson Model 19 Combat Magnum on my waist under the shirt, and often a CAR-15 assault rifle. There were always those credentials and ID cards in my pocket that we all worried about, not to mention the plastic briefcase with documents from the Office of Naval Intelligence. I had to be very certain that I was inside a secure compound by nightfall. I had no means of communication with my superiors in Saigon, and thus they had no means of knowing where I was. They just knew where I intended to go—not how or when.

At about the same time I was coming to realize that these field trips were involving too many risk factors (that I could not plan for and which many of the tasks did not justify), most of the work stopped.

I had managed probably two R&R leaves of five days for each year of my service. I opted for Australia twice, visiting Leo Newport, whom I'd met in New Guinea in 1965. He was in the process of setting up a small physical security operation in Melbourne, centered on the transportation industry there. There were road patrols and static guard operations, the business was growing, and the future looked bright. Leo had made me a standing offer that I could join him as a business partner at any time.

My fellow agents in Saigon were not bailing out of NIS—but there was plenty of concern about the organization's future as reductions in force took place back in the States. Offices were closed, and finally the Department of Defense established the Defense Investigative Service to manage the entire background investigation function that had previously been the responsibility of each service branch. Some NIS special agents suddenly found themselves working for another organization, with a permanent diet of background investigations.

I was tired. Very tired. I had survived nearly three years in a war zone via a combination of good fortune and determination. I needed probably six months off to regroup. With Judy now planning a life with somebody else, there was no lady in my life to help me reorganize and consider the best decision for the future. NIS headquarters had promised me a one-man posting at Kao Hsiung, Taiwan, but that seemed tenuous because of drawdowns. I began to seriously consider taking Leo up on his offer in Australia.

There were not many moments for peaceful, serious contemplation in my Vietnam environment. While assigned to Quang Tri Combat Base in 1969, I had snatched a few moments to sit and think during the monsoon at an old temple near the river. Never far from an armed sentry, the perimeter wire nevertheless took on an entirely different atmosphere when sheets of rain swept across the paddies and over nearby Vietnamese fishermen. Drumming rain drowned out every sound of war, cleaning the atmosphere of dirt, diesel, and conflict. I sat there under my poncho, absorbed in Mother Nature's spectacle of renewal—and thought about my life.

Now, as my third year was drawing to a close and I faced momentous decisions, there came another time when a monsoon storm blocked out the humdrum static of daily routine and gave me pause to consider my life: where it was, what I had done, what my future options might be. I was at a small base in the Mekong Delta, relieved that I had walked through the gates only moments before large raindrops began plopping in the dust. My day's work was done, and I was in no hurry. After dropping my gear in the transit quarters, I found a quiet position under cover, overlooking a tributary of the Bassac River. In the background, Vietnamese maids at work chattered over the ever-present hum of diesel generators. I sat and watched intently as rain approached me, a distant wall of gray mist moving slowly across the countryside preceded by bustling sheets of rain that lashed bamboo groves and far-off fishermen in small boats. Moments later the storm was upon us, rain drumming relentlessly on the corrugated iron roof—blocking out every vestige of the clatter of base life.

Mist rolled up to the nearby bamboo groves, the torrent of rain all but blocking the microcosm of Vietnam in my immediate view. It was as though Mother Nature was forcing my attention to the peaceful beauty on hand. I began to relax, to allow my senses to absorb the gentle, washed breeze that accompanied a cleansing monsoon.

There is more to life than Vietnam, I reminded myself; there is a life out there in the future for me. It is too easy to focus on the miasma brought on by a diet of war. Would it be possible to step away from that existence? Could I relearn the simple, important pleasures of nature and life?

Beyond those esoteric questionings of what I had become in Vietnam, I admitted to myself also that I was becoming disenchanted with the leadership qualities of my superiors, even though I felt certain they were experiencing many of the same anxieties about NIS and the war that I was. Of course, there was always the option of transferring to another federal agency—as a number of my colleagues had done—but I couldn't imagine myself as an FBI agent or Customs special agent working the streets of some large U.S. city. In retrospect, I probably should have made the effort to reexamine opportunities at the State Department. But on that day in the Delta, I found myself challenging myself to make a courageous decision. Was I brave enough to leave and forge an entirely new life for myself?

That afternoon on a small backwater of the mighty river, I decided the time had come to act decisively. I was tired. I knew I had cheated death more than a few times; the memory of nearby enemy rocket and mortar round impacts—the snap of a too-close errant bullet on those long, lonely drives in Northern I Corps—were fresh in my mind. One more silly mistake might mean there would be no other quiet dates with Mother Nature, anywhere.

I later wrote to Leo Newport in Melbourne, explaining that I would accept his offer to buy equity in the new security company—and I would join him there once my contracted third year in Vietnam was complete.

My spirits rose a little once I decided to make a new life in Australia. Known as the Lucky Country, it was a huge nation with a population then of only about thirteen million souls. If the Australian soldiers in Vietnam were representative, Aussies were good, solid citizens—friendly, and largely pro-American. I had always enjoyed my short leave periods in Australia. I knew people there. It seemed a near-perfect refuge in which to begin a new life.

With the reality of an imminent departure from Vietnam upon completion of my third year came powerful personal feelings. It was easy enough to rationalize the reality that every American serving in Vietnam one day reaches the end of his tour, but I was particularly aware that in almost every instance that meant the departing individual took everything with him and severed all local ties with the full knowledge future communication would be impossible, those friendships virtually voided by circumstance. After three years, I had Vietnamese friends and colleagues, most of whom were politely accepting of my decision to go. But one or two privately asked, "What is to happen to us?"

I started to feel intermittent guilt pangs, both about myself and the country I represented. In my heart, I was no longer completely convinced that the United States in its apparent haste to leave could honor its commitment to keep South Vietnam free of the avaricious northern communists that so many had fled from. Moreover, I was leaving too—and it began to feel more and more like I was running away from a lot of good people who needed support. It was not enough that I had stayed so long.

My agent colleagues understood my decision to go. We were a small, tight group whom circumstance had placed very close together in a hostile, foreign country. John Morgan and I shared quarters; Ted Cauble and I an office. Ted Hicks and Marshall Whidden shared an office with Morgan. In Saigon, we worked together, planned and initiated investigations, shared report-writing ideas, and talked incessantly about leave plans and various planned and unplanned adventures that seemed to occur almost daily. And some of us caroused together after work.

I knew I would miss the daily dose of irreverent banter that characterized the agent team. I suspected that I had grown closer to this small band than I realized; certainly the agents treated each other more as brothers than colleagues—but adversity and danger can do that. As the time to go neared, it felt a little as though I might be leaving an extended family, but I was not acknowledging to myself that the group was unlikely ever to reunite, once I left.

The destinies of my brother agents—and Vietnamese friends and colleagues—would prey on my mind in no small degree in the months and years ahead.

The afternoon before my departure from both Vietnam and the organization, commanding officer Gene Moore convened a medal parade on the third-floor catwalk that connected modules of our hotel/office. Gene had been a steadfast friend the previous ten months. A Naval Academy graduate, he was a career intelligence officer of unusual intellect and scope of knowledge for whom I had considerable respect.

The agents, officers, and enlisted support staff lined up in front of the office doors as the CO began by speaking about my service to NISO Vietnam. Then he pinned the Civilian Service Medal on my jacket. Finally, quite unexpectedly, he opened a leather-bound citation from Commander, U.S. Naval Forces Vietnam. This was personal recognition from Admiral Robert S. Salzer in the form of a formal commendation. Gene Moore read it to those assembled, who stood by quietly, shook my hand, and said simply, "Well done, Doug." We all retired for a cold beer.

The Civilian Service Medal was issued by the American ambassador. Mine was accompanied by a citation signed by Ambassador Ellsworth Bunker. As other agents before me, I appreciated that we received a form of recognition for our unusual service, but it never truthfully felt appropriate. Vietnam special agents were an integral part of the U.S. Naval service who wore uniforms in the field, carried rifles, and in many instances, shared dangers in the field with Marines and sailors. The medal could not be worn on the U.S. Navy uniform by those agents who were also officers in the Naval Reserve, nor was there authorization for them to wear the military campaign medals that were issued to all of the military support at NISOV. So, that afternoon as we slaked our thirst with cans of beer after the medal parade, there were some good-natured digs about how nice my Saigon secretary's medal looked. I had made the same observation at parades of other agents who had preceded me, so there was not much I could do but smile.

I said my final good-byes the next morning and, with Lt. John Klampfer and Special Agent John Morgan, took my last ride through Cholon to Tan Son Nhut airport. I had purchased an air ticket from Pan American Airlines and was scheduled to fly to Manila. Saigon seemed especially tired, dusty, and sad that morning. I wondered if was merely a reflection of my own state of mind, or really a fair observation of circumstance after several more years of conflict. So much seemed to have changed since 1969; finally, now, I was leaving too. I was unsettled and disquieted—but I knew it was time.

At the airport, checking in was especially simple, because I was on a regular commercial flight, not a Military Airlift Command charter. In ten minutes, I had my boarding pass. Not wanting to drag out the farewells even more, I stood to one side of the crowd and removed my leather-bound agent credentials from my breast pocket, took off the distinctive money clip, and handed them to Lieutenant Klampfer. I was no longer Special Agent Douglass Hubbard, U.S. Naval Investigative Service. I didn't know how that felt yet.

But thirty minutes later, as the landing gear on the Pan Am jet clunked into the wings and a stewardess asked me whether I'd like a drink, I felt as though an immensely important chapter in my life had just closed. I had made it. I was alive after three years of madness and the angry scarred mountains of Vietnam were nearly behind me.

* * *

I arrived in Port Moresby, Papua New Guinea, early the next morning. I'd told my business partner in Melbourne that I would be taking leave on the way to my new life in Australia, planning to wind down a little after Vietnam.

My father was now well established in his new position as executive director of the Admiral Nimitz Center in Fredericksburg, Texas. Well aware of the critical role New Guinea and the Solomon Island campaigns had played in World War II, Dad had an enduring interest in my casual explorations. Now he encouraged me to look for battlefield memorabilia that might be used in museum exhibits. I was glad to do so and had decided weeks before to use my leave for this purpose.

Ian and Jean Bullock had returned to Rhodesia. Inspector Ilid "Taffy" Evans, a good friend from earlier stays at Bomana Police College, met me at the airport. I would be the houseguest of Taffy and Ruth while in Port Moresby.

On our way down the now-familiar Bomana gravel road through the tropical countryside, Taffy said he had recently received a letter from the Bullocks announcing that they had arrived safely in Salisbury and had already bought a home with a swimming pool. Ian had landed a civilian job almost immediately; Jean seemed to be very happy to be back close to her family. There was further news: Ormonde Power, late Bomana riot squad leader, had elected to settle in Rhodesia. He and wife, Tanya, had jobs; Ormonde was trying to get an appointment to the British South Africa Police.

We stopped at the police camp boom gate, where one of Taffy's officer candidate students was standing sentry duty. Determined to make a favorable impression, the young man came smartly to attention, crashing his right heel down and snapping a smart salute, fingers quivering above his brow and beret badge. "Good morning, Sah!" he bellowed, staring straight ahead. Bemused, Taffy replied, "Thank you, Tambu. Good morning." We drove through the gate and into the police facility that I would consider home, off and on, for several weeks.

Bomana's officer's mess remained the social epicenter of the camp. With a staff numerically dominated by British expatriates accustomed to the friendly institution of a neighborhood pub, this was not surprising. There was always time for a game of pool or good conversation accompanied by a cold South Pacific lager. When my interest in World War II relic recovery became known to mess patrons that first evening of my stay, the stories and leads started coming in.

Most of the stories were just that: unconfirmed sightings of wrecked aircraft or artillery, often in extremely remote regions of one of the world's wildest countries. One lead seemed far more promising: there were tanks and artillery said still to be standing on the battlefield at Buna.

The next day I spoke to a pharmacist named Chapman in nearby Boroko. An Australian with an enduring interest in New Guinea's wartime history, Mr. Chapman told me he had explored the Buna battlefield on foot and found that there were three knocked-out M-3 General Stuart tanks present that had been operated by troopers of Australia's 2/6 Cavalry Regiment during the Christmas 1942 battle. Moreover, he had found the Japanese three-inch naval gun on the now-abandoned Buna airstrip—the very weapon an Australian military historian had credited with hitting the M-3 on the airstrip. Chapman was enthused about discovering both the tank and the gun.

I was not a museum expert, but the Buna tank story, if true, seemed worth following up. It was an important event in Australian/American history. As they had done in World War I, seasoned Australian veterans had fought alongside newly arrived U.S. Army soldiers, who had not yet heard a shot fired in anger. There were enduring stories of bravery and camaraderie from both allies. I decided to go see for myself—and after locating the rusting relics, I wrote a report for my father. The battlefield relics seemed well worth salvaging for posterity; the question was how?

I had been away from Vietnam only a matter of weeks. It still felt as though I was taking leave from the country and my special agent vocation. The reality of change had yet to fully sink in, and I found myself listening carefully to regular news broadcasts beamed to New Guinea by the Australian Broadcasting Commission, where Vietnam War dispatches were carefully detailed almost every day. I was quietly anxious about the country—its destiny, but most especially about people still embroiled there.

On 1 April 1972, I became twenty-seven years old. Also on that day, North Vietnamese armor and infantry burst across the demilitarized zone (DMZ) in an all-out assault on Quang Tri, the very place I had been stationed in late 1969. This time there were no Marines and very few U.S. Army troops to halt the tide as they always had done. The news presenter said it would be up to South Vietnamese troops to defend the province.

As mid-April approached, news from Vietnam continued to seem desperate and grim. The North Vietnamese Army had overrun Dong Ha and were besieging Quang Tri city. News descriptions suggested there were artillery duels being fought and massive air strikes by B-52s staged to break up communist attacks. I wondered about the small monastery I had visited many times, thought of the monks who had always treated me with courtesy, and was forced to admit that all had likely been reduced to dust and rubble.

On 17 April 1972, I mailed the report of my relic findings to my father in Fredericksburg and caught the flight to Sydney, where my business partner would meet me and I would begin my new life as a businessman in Australia.

* * *

I discovered that life in Australia was pleasant and easy, for the most part; but after several months spent building up and selling the first business—then trying another on an island in Queensland—I became increasingly aware that it was going nowhere. I was not settled, nor was I genuinely happy. Vietnam was never far from my mind, the news seldom if ever good, and I was starting to feel guiltier about leaving. I knew better than to engage young Australians in conversation about any aspect of Vietnam. In my mind, they just didn't care—and I found myself resenting it.

After a good deal of thought about what I wanted to do, the idea of returning to Africa recurred more often. I had felt very much at home there, enjoying its people and the unique wildness of the bush. Perhaps I could actually live and serve in rural Africa. I finally wrote to Brian Cullingworth at British South Africa Police General Headquarters in Salisbury expressing my interest in learning about an appointment to the force. When the response came back, Brian's reply made it clear to me that I would be welcomed; application forms were included.

My father and I had maintained our usual, regular correspondence in the months I had been in Australia. The Texas museum dedicated to Admiral Nimitz and the service personnel who served with him in the Pacific War was taking shape. I offered to return to New Guinea in 1973 if funding and support was available to actually recover war relics for museum exhibits.

Given that we were using airmailed letters to formulate a plan, things began to move quickly. In mid December, I received a note from Dad with an important enclosure—a copy of the letter U.S. Navy Chief of Naval Operations Admiral Thomas Moorer had dispatched to his colleague and counterpart in Australia, Chief of the General Staff Admiral Sir V. A. T. Smith, RAN. In it Admiral Smith was asked whether it might be possible to extend assistance to me in Australia and the Territory of Papua and New Guinea in order that historically important World War II relics might be recovered for museum display. Dad's note explained that they had limited funding available to support my operations as the Admiral Nimitz Center's representative; the timing was up to me.

Dad's letter was a milestone. I had decided to leave because of general dissatisfaction with the direction my life was taking, but I had not decided how to effect the change, or when. The letter changed everything. I decided to wrap up my affairs in Australia and go to New Guinea to facilitate the relic recovery project. This, I knew, would be a temporary assignment of several months during which I could consider my future more carefully. But Africa seemed more attractive the more I considered it.

To get the relic recovery under way, I knew that I needed to pay Admiral Smith a personal visit in Canberra. As I had already settled my partnership, this would conclude my Australian business.

My appointment with Admiral Smith had been arranged some weeks in advance. At the appointed time, I presented myself at Russell Offices, the home of Australia's Ministry of Defence. Soon, I was being escorted through the hallways to a spacious waiting room that served the chief of the General Staff. At a desk, dressed in civilian business attire, sat a tall, carefully groomed officer whose desk tag identified him as an army lieutenant colonel—obviously the admiral's aide. He greeted me warmly, poured me a cup of tea, and announced that "the chief" would see me momentarily.

I had just drained my cup when the aide stood, announcing that "the coast was clear" and opening one of a set of double doors that opened into a spacious office. Behind the desk, a graying man, apparently in his late fifties and possessed of natural military bearing, arose and held out his hand to shake mine. Dressed in a brown tweed suit, "Vat" Smith, as he was known in military circles, could have passed as a Melbourne banker—but his voice and conversation were almost exactly what I would have expected of a senior flag officer.

We chatted a few minutes, Admiral Smith obviously genuinely interested in our plan to recover relics that might be enjoyed and appreciated by common citizens for many years to come. He then spoke in warm terms of his experiences in the U.S. Seventh Fleet, where he had cemented an enduring friendship with Admiral Tom Moorer. The chief naval officer's (CNO's) original letter was on the desk; Admiral Smith announced simply, "I think we can help you. Here is a copy of the letter I dispatched to the commander of the Papua New Guinea Defence Force, Brigadier Jim Norrie, at Murray Barracks in Port Moresby. Go see him when you get up there." He said also that army landing craft operated in New Guinea waters, operated by the engineer squadron based at Middle Head Barracks, in Sydney.

That was my exit cue. I'd had ten convivial minutes with the most senior military figure in Australia. I thanked my host, rose, and minutes later was outdoors in the cool morning where I admired a tall column capped by a statue of an eagle. This monument was an expression of gratitude by the Australian people to the United States for the role they played in staving off the Japanese invasion in the early days of World War II.

On the way back to Queensland, I stopped in Sydney to pay a courtesy call on the Australian army engineers. There I was cordially greeted by Lieutenant Colonel John Hughes, Royal Australian Engineers, a recipient of the Military Cross for valor while serving with the Australian Army

Training Team, Vietnam, during the Tet Offensive of 1968. The engineer officers that night held a dining-in night at their mess, at which I was the commanding officer's guest. Seated at a grand old mahogany table bedecked with the regimental silver, I sat next to my host who, after some coaxing, told me he had been in a small compound in Quang Tri overrun by the enemy; badly wounded in the attack, he had been left for dead. His rescuers had him flown to the U.S. Navy Hospital Ship *Repose*, then steaming off the coast. Emergency surgery had saved his life.

It was a very pleasant, even mellow evening, where I much enjoyed the fellowship of John Hughes' officers. Our business—confirming that army LCH (heavy landing craft) *Balikpapan* would be in New Guinea waters later in the year and would carry basic recovery gear and material for transporting and preserving relics—had been completed in a matter of minutes.

I had by this time mailed documents to the British South Africa Police to determine what they might offer me. I had not received the formal response that would spell out their offer and potential dates for training induction. Nevertheless, with the New Guinea project progressing well and apparently certain to happen in the next month or so—and my growing confidence that the BSAP would make an acceptable offer—my life began to take on much more direction. It felt good. Once again there seemed to be a path ahead toward new, worthwhile things.

* * *

The months that ensued in New Guinea were happy ones. Soon after my arrival, I received a written offer from the British South Africa Police and accepted it. The way of life and challenges of the people and environment all helped convince me that my plans to work and live in Africa were well founded. Not only did I have my old friends in the New Guinea constabulary, but I also met a whole set of new ones at the army barracks. Most were Australian army infantrymen, all of whom had served in Vietnam—and many in the Korean War as well. These men all ultimately assisted in the major logistic effort that resulted in the recovery of several tanks, artillery pieces, and aircraft from remote areas of Papua New Guinea.

After LCH *Balikpapan* finally sailed out of Port Moresby harbor loaded with three recovered tanks, artillery pieces, and two recovered Japanese military aircraft, my time in Papua New Guinea quickly drew to a close. My mission was accomplished. Had the fledgling Texas museum had at its disposal a substantial budget, I might have remained to investigate more of the reports of exotic war relics that were now coming to me regularly; but the available funds were spent. It was time to say my good-byes to many good friends.

I was sad to be leaving Papua New Guinea once again. Many expatriates were choosing to leave as independence loomed, but I had grown to appreciate the varied peoples and ever-changing political scene in this emerging nation. But there was simply no place for me, and I had come to realize it.

I was bound for Africa at last.

CHAPTER 2

To Africa

ON A BRILLIANT, clear morning in January 1974, I arrived in Johannesburg after an overnight flight from Heathrow. In London I'd had a very pleasant reunion with my last Vietnam commanding officer, Cdr. Gene Moore and met his wife, Betty. Gene was then assigned a liaison post at Whitehall with the Defense Intelligence Agency; he had not remained in Saigon much longer than I, but he knew where many former colleagues were—or were not. It was a chance to exchange news about people we had been very close to in that strange environment. I left our dinner realizing that I missed many colleagues and the sense of duty I had felt in Vietnam, but not the job.

Even bustling Johannesburg was like a breath of fresh air after the dour, dark streets of winter London. Alan Jack met me at the airport. It had been three years since we met, and he greeted me like a good friend. Then we drove to his Hillbrow flat, which I intended to use as a base while I got myself equipped with necessities, most especially a car.

I had not slept well on the flight. We sat that morning in Alan's tenth-story flat, having a cup of coffee and making plans for the day, when there was a loud knocking on the door, followed by colorful epithets directed at Alan, delivered in a thick Scots brogue. My host opened the door and in walked Warrant Officer Leo Tumilty of the South African Police (SAP). He was dressed in civilian attire: shorts, long socks, and a fulsome shirt to cover a well-developed girth.

I had known Tumilty in New Guinea, where he had served at Bomana Police College, but I was virtually speechless at this unexpected meeting. He and Alan were police colleagues, but I quickly learned that I was the reason he was there: he was now in Special Branch. It had taken my friend and his colleagues perhaps three hours to identify me from South African Customs records and to come calling.

I never considered that the visit might signal a problem. Leo simply said that his colonel would like to meet me and that he was there to drive me to police headquarters at John Vorster Square in downtown Johannesburg. We left the flat promising to catch up later with Alan and wended our way in an unmarked police car to the central city.

The Special Branch offices were situated in a highly secure upper floor of the headquarters. After passing through various locked doors, Leo took me through the detective's work area directly into his commander's office, where he introduced us and left the room.

The colonel was a small, very alert man in his fifties, who was clearly a well-educated Afrikaner. With impeccable manners and twinkling blue eyes that were obviously sizing me up, he offered me refreshments, asked how my flight had been, and spoke in general terms about South Africa. I was interested to hear his observations, and I asked several questions. Finally, he said that he understood from my host that I was intending to accept a police appointment in Rhodesia. I told him that was correct and let him know that I was hoping for a chance to work in a district where I could experience rural Africa.

"I could use you in this organization," he said. "You could expect to come in as a warrant officer; your promotional possibilities would be bright." Tumilty had briefed the colonel well, certainly about my experience in Vietnam as a federal agent.

"Sir," I replied, "I've got my heart set on rural Africa. I hope you will understand. I am honored by your interest in me and your offer."

"Think it over. Here is my card. It was a pleasure to meet you, Douglass."

Perhaps thirty minutes later, my Scots friend and I were walking in central Johannesburg, going to one of his favorite watering holes—where the beer was cold and the service friendly. I knew very well what to expect. Leo and I had shared some long nights in the mess in New Guinea. Over an excellent South African steak and several cold Castle beers, he told me of his decision to settle in Johannesburg, though he was uncertain how well his Australian wife liked it. And he reiterated that the colonel meant what he said to me about working for the SAP. I said simply, "I don't think I could handle living in Jo'burg."

The next morning Alan and I pored over the newspaper classifieds, searching for a suitable car. Ian Bullock had told me that good cars were expensive when they were available at all in Rhodesia. Buy in South Africa, he counseled, and drive it across the border. As luck would have it, Alan spotted an ad for a near-new Volkswagen sedan being offered at an attractive price. We phoned; the owner said he was selling because his doctor would not allow him to drive a manual transmission postsurgery. That afternoon, I bought the right-hand-drive car. It had fewer than a thousand miles on the odometer and had been carefully maintained in a garage. I felt very fortunate.

After a further day in Johannesburg, I began my solo journey north to Rhodesia very early—intending to drive across the Transvaal to Messina, on the Limpopo River, and then across the bridge to Rhodesia. It was well that I started when only a few service vehicles were on the streets. I managed to solo navigate out of the city without mishap and began a long, tedious drive with the speedometer on fifty miles per hour. In the wake of fuel shortages, the South African government had lowered the national speed limit as a measure to curb gasoline consumption. The road was dotted with traffic police speed traps. In between, I absorbed the changing landscape as the highway descended from high Johannesburg to the close warmth of the low veld. There were country towns along my route, Afrikaner dorps with red brick Dutch Reformed churches, and country businesses. The parks were planted with jacaranda trees, lawns were well tended—in the main by a workforce of African domestic servants. At a service station where I stopped for fuel and refreshment, there were the signs of apartheid. In the Northern Transvaal, it was obviously embedded in the way of life. Still, it made me uncomfortable. I chatted a little with the young African man who filled my tank and checked the tires. He was cautious but guardedly friendly—perhaps because my accent identified me as an outsider.

At the mandated reduced speed, I had plenty of time to think as I drove across the open spaces of northern South Africa, past pastures of fat cattle and eucalyptus tree lines. I had been cosmetically flattered by the SAP colonel's approach, and I reasoned that the offer had come because of Tumilty's endorsement and recounting of some of my background. But I also wondered how my friend could so seriously have misjudged my personal ethics; I simply would not consider doing internal security work for any government other than my own. And, although I listened sympathetically to reports of Soviet-backed attacks against South Africans, I did not wish to work for the government. Rhodesia did not have apartheid. It was not a pluralistic society; it would need to change, but I felt comfort in the basic British values and law that governed the country.

I watched my speed carefully and in the early afternoon cleared South African customs at the southern end of Beitbridge. Driving slowly across the silver span, I looked curiously down at the pools that were the Limpopo, remembering Rudyard Kipling's poem. At the midpoint, I crossed into Rhodesia.

Though it had taken nearly two hours to complete entry formalities, I was again under way by midafternoon. Rhodesia's roads were beautifully maintained, rest areas were frequent, and the countryside was greener than South Africa had been. I crossed the Nuanetsi River, noting a small hotel placed back in the trees. I had decided that even at fifty miles an hour I could reach Fort Victoria by sunset.

It was even more difficult to resist stopping at the Lundi River. This looked like the Africa of my imagination: acacia trees, yellow-barked fever trees, all fully leafed and green. When I descended to the bridge crossing the Lundi, my spirits rose as I watched the water dance past on the way to Mozambique. I felt glad to be there, perhaps even reassured at my decision to live in Africa for a time and experience what she had to offer.

It was late afternoon when I slowly entered the broad main street of Fort Victoria, designed, I thought, with the pioneer bullock teams in mind. To my right appeared a period brick structure, the Fort Victoria Hotel. It looked a good place to spend my first night in Rhodesia; I swung the VW into a parking place in front and walked into the lobby.

The Fort Vic Hotel was an icon from an earlier day when weary travelers had found refuge from the dirt and dust of horse and wagon. I was shown down the attached hall to a high-ceiling room with a single bed and dresser in it, then the bath and toilets farther along. The claw-footed bathtub bore the manufacturers mark of a British firm, and I noted with satisfaction that it was more than six feet long and quite deep. I wasted no time soaking a long day's travel grime off, dressed, and made my appearance in the dining room. A graying African waiter attired in a white linen coat and ancient black shoes from which his ample feet were bursting, greeted me politely and seated me at a table with an outside view before handing me the day's menu.

Over a meal that could have been served in the British Midlands, I noted with interest the dining room furnishings: old cutlery and glassware, tables and light fixtures all looked as though they had been used since turn of the century—but all were neat and clean, if somewhat worn. Rhodesians had learned to make do, I was to learn.

After supper, I walked around Fort Vic, even inspecting the police station. A neat, white-walled structure, it bore a highly polished brass emblem—that of the British South Africa Police (BSAP). All was quiet. Trees shaded the station, and I thought that the thick arched walls had been well designed for the high summer temperatures of Rhodesia. I briefly considered entering the station and introducing myself; but it was growing late and I was already thinking about the morrow's drive to Salisbury.

Back at the hotel, I telephoned Ormonde Power in Salisbury, telling him I expected to reach the capitol the next afternoon.

Ormonde and his wife, Tanya, had successfully settled in Rhodesia following his contract with the Royal Papua and New Guinea Constabulary. They had accepted the New Guinea assignment after Northern Rhodesia became Zambia; now they were back, this time on the south side of the Zambezi River.

He was a good friend and would become a valuable mentor in the weeks and months ahead as I underwent a sort of cultural acclimatization. Despite being nearly ten years my senior, he had been accepted by the BSAP, which had retrained and promoted him after training.

Armed with Ormonde's verbal directions, I started out the next morning on the final leg of my journey. Rhodesia had reinstituted gasoline rationing. I had been given coupons to purchase fuel for my trip—small green pieces of paper that authorized the holder to purchase a set number of liters of gasoline. These I carefully counted out with the currency I was also getting used to—and then I started northward. My near-new VW purred steadily along as the road gradually ascended from the lower climes where tetse flies and malaria were concerns to the high plateau and Salisbury at nearly five thousand feet. I passed through the town of Umvuma, noticing that each small town had a central police station. All were neat, and well-cared for. At Enkeldoorn, there was also a picturesque hotel and general store; otherwise, just open grazing country and herds of fat Hereford cattle. I drove onward.

I sighted the tall buildings of Salisbury's central business district from a good distance out. Perhaps twenty minutes later as I neared the metropolis, the road widened into gracious avenues and I entered the city. Boulevard medians were well watered, lawns and gardens were carefully manicured, and I was delighted to see scores of trees shading avenues and businesses. With Ormonde's directions handy for ready reference, I drove to the suburb of Belvedere and on shady Mull Road found the home of the Power family.

As I pulled up to the gate, the family maid ran out from the kitchen to let me in. She was young and shy, very dark, and neatly turned out in a carefully ironed uniform dress, but shoeless. Both Ormonde and Tanya were at work, but they and baby Lucy were expected home soon. She showed me to a small, bright bedroom, where I stowed my gear. Then I called Inspector Fred Mason at Police General Headquarters recruiting to let him know I had arrived and was ready to complete final screening. A very friendly Fred Mason told me that he had a target date for my interview and induction for training that was a week away, in the final week of January. I promised to pay him a courtesy call soon.

Soon after, Ormonde arrived, riding a Honda 55 scooter designed to help the family function with their monthly gasoline allocation. He welcomed me warmly, and we sat down in the family living room with its New Guinea memorabilia to chat about his assignment and the force generally. He had recently been promoted to section officer (sergeant) at Police Support Unit. Support Unit, the Black Boots, in force parlance, was the successor of the BSAP Askaris. After World War II, there had been an influx of veteran African soldiers from the Kings African Rifles (KAR), many of whom had served with distinction in the Burma campaigns. The Askaris were tasked with military duties, particularly counterinsurgency, and while a part of the police force, it was run in the manner of a military organization. Ormonde's background of British army service suited him well in Support Unit; he had been given command of G Troop, the Presidential Guard Detail, and had been serving in the field on a regular basis.

Support Unit operated from the African Police Training Depot adjacent to Morris Depot. Morris Depot, the home of the regiment, would be the venue of my recruit training, as it had been for Ormonde. Because his duties took him to visit the drill instructors and instructional staff at Morris Depot every day, he was well versed in their affairs and even knew which instructor would be taking charge of my recruit squad at the end of the month.

It seemed likely that I would be the oldest man in that squad, just as Ormonde had been several months previously. Runs and physical training in the high elevation of Salisbury would be difficult, I knew. I would have to learn the drill of the British army in daily sessions on the hardstand under the watchful eye of drill instructor Section Officer Mike Lambourne,

Rhodesian hammer-throw champion and reportedly possessor of the biggest voice in the country. I was quietly pleased to be doing an abbreviated six-week course as opposed to the six months my squad peers would endure. My training and experience had qualified me for this—and would place me also on an elevated pay scale. The only drawback that I could discern was that I would not train in military equitation because of my relatively short stay at Morris Depot.

Tanya and Ormonde made me feel very much at home. I used my preinduction week also to visit Brian and Jo Cullingworth at their Mandara home. Brian had been transferred from recruiting and public relations from headquarters to Salisbury Central Station. Jo nursed at Andrew Fleming Hospital and cared for three young children. These good friends introduced me to more good Rhodesians, the sort of people whose friendship endures.

I reported to Inspector Mason at Police General Headquarters in the Salisbury Avenues. Fred welcomed me and explained that the next part of the process would be a screening board appearance before a group of senior officers that would include the Morris Depot commandant. They could be expected to ask questions about my professional experience, strengths and weakness, and perhaps about my aspirations in the BSAP. I was given a date to report for interview, two days hence.

I arrived early that day for the interview and waited with several other potential recruits. Most appeared to be recent secondary school graduates, shy, eighteen or so, and a little overwhelmed by the authoritative atmosphere of the high ceilings and cavernous hallways at PGHQ. We spoke little, each man absorbed by personal thoughts and perhaps doubts.

I had endured screening boards before and had come to expect that at least one of the panel would play devil's advocate to see if I would rattle. This did not occur. The questions were respectful and well considered. Several officers wore World War II campaign ribbons on their summer uniforms. Only the depot commandant, Chief Superintendent G. B. Dunn, put forward that I could expect training to be arduous, perhaps not unlike the United States Marine Corps. What I had heard thus far did not convince me that I was facing Parris Island, but I supplied a respectful answer that seemed to satisfy my interrogators.

Inspector Mason let me know that I could expect to return early next week for attestation. After that, with a new regimental number, I would report to Morris Depot as a recruit patrol officer.

The following Monday I gathered with a small group of men in a large office at PGHQ. Inspector Mason handed out documents to each man, then said: "The oath I am about to administer stipulates that you promise to fairly administer and uphold the law; it says nothing at all about supporting any particular brand of politics, and nothing about supporting Prime Minister Ian Smith." Recognizing what we had heard as irony, we raised our hands, and the oath was administered. We were officially patrol officers in the British South Africa Police. As the papers were collected, Fred nodded my way and wished me good luck. Soon after, the new recruit squad passed down the gracious Avenues to nearby Morris Depot, where each man would face the challenges of a radically different lifestyle in his own way.

The first step in that process was the introduction of the squad's new mother, Section Officer (S/O) Mike Lambourne. Then only twenty-four, Lambourne was a man who already possessed an imposing command presence. Perhaps six feet two with the physique of an athlete, he had an enormous chest and the ropy muscles of a hammer thrower. With a particularly erect posture, a carefully set-up guardsman-style uniform cap and leather leggings and belt that glistened and shirt and shorts without so much as a misplaced crease, he successfully communicated to each trainee the clear message that they had a long way to come before they would be entrusted with the privilege of membership in this proud regiment.

His voice was clear, his manner distant, as men were assigned to training quarters. We were allowed several minutes to find the two-man rooms—and to learn the identity of our new bunky.

I was lucky enough to draw Gavin Rabie, a twenty-year-old who had come to serve from Windhoek, Southwest Africa. Blond, muscular Gavin was quiet and unassuming—the sort of roommate who seemed unlikely to draw unwanted attention to our quarters or me. We had been told to expect rigorously thorough inspection of our rooms, each of which held two beds with suspended mosquito net overhead, two wardrobes, and two small desks. I could expect to live in the room for six weeks, but Gavin had a six-month training stretch ahead of him.

Our assembly location was to be a small paved square immediately in front of the recruit's mess and adjacent to the small accommodation wing that housed Gavin and me. We were together on the veranda our entry door faced and starting to walk toward the square when I first heard the infamous Lambourne voice bark: "All right, people! Let's have you out here!"

With those commands, all chattering ceased as men hustled onto the square. Section Officer Lambourne stood at attention facing the mess. He ordered us to form up in three ranks, facing him, with the tallest man to the right. That was me. In that moment, I became the squad right marker and thus under the immediate scrutiny of a drill perfectionist with little sympathy for the bad habits that had been engendered in me through experience with American military drill.

There was not then time to refine squad drill, but as Lambourne now needed to move us as a group, he had decided to do so in a basic formation. The finer points would come later. Now, we were on our way to the BSAP Quartermaster Store for our kit issue. We swung off down one of the narrow depot service roads behind a police service wagon drawn by a pair of mules, which left evidence of their disdain of new recruits over the roadway on which we maladroitly marched toward the rear gate.

I would eventually come to know the "Q Store" intimately. But that day it felt like a large barn, where row upon row of shelves supported boxes of clothing and equipment considered necessary to do the business of policing in Africa. Two crusty old civilians in white dust jackets served from behind the counter, scrutinizing every requisition with an expression that suggested the requester was stealing from his mother.

There were about twenty of us. S/O Lambourne spaced us out in an open area of the store, and the issue process began with gear that did not require individual fitting: blankets, duffel bag, mosquito net, brushes, and socks—a seemingly endless inventory that rose before each man. Then we were individually called up to receive hats, shirts, trousers, boots, and shoes. The old quartermaster knowingly sized uniform hats small, very small, in the knowledge that none of Lambourne's charges would have much hair in the morning.

Late that afternoon, the squad staggered back to depot in three ranks, because each man carried a full recruit kit issue. None had any idea as to how it should be cared for or worn, but those lessons were imminent.

As he dismissed us from what would certainly be the easiest day in training depot, Lambourne gave us orders: "You people get over to the recruit canteen tonight for a regulation haircut. Take some money. The Portuguese barber doesn't do it for free." I had noticed several young men sporting stylishly long locks; now they wore expressions of resignation.

My hair was short, but it hadn't been cut for perhaps a week. Gavin and I agreed to walk over for a haircut after the evening meal in the recruit mess.

There were several squads under training at any given time at Morris Depot. We were the newcomers, finding our way, struggling to assimilate as quickly as possible the routine of learning and surviving as recruits. We discovered the dining area to be a spacious, nearly square hall equipped with long tables, outside which was a drill square and the green lawns of the parade square. It was Spartan but very clean and far more pleasant than messing facilities I had known elsewhere. The squaddies seemed to dine by preference with members of their own group, who were identifiable by the type of uniform they wore at any given instructional period—that being dictated by the subject of the training. Behind the tables was a cafeteria line, where steam tables were carefully monitored by a matronly, cheerful English lady, who seemed to know many of the trainees by name. Gavin and I walked silently through the line, heaping our plates with helpings of cottage pie and vegetables that seemed to have been cooked a long time. We were hungry; it had been a long day.

Once seated at our table, we quietly ate and watched the senior recruits, curious as to who they were and how each was managing in the Morris Depot atmosphere. Gavin chewed his cottage pie thoughtfully, and I asked him if this was the sort of meal he was used to at home in Windhoek. He chuckled and murmured that the fire-cooked meat of the traditional South African *braaivleis* was far more to his liking.

We finished a traditional English desert of pudding and fruit, downed the dregs of the hot, sweet tea, and arose from our table. Several of the senior recruits nodded greetings, and I noticed that one group was exclusively new national service patrol officers candidates, conscripts training to serve their country for two years as policemen.

The nearby Regimental Institute was a fine old building with a clock tower overlooking the grassy parade square, the top floor of which housed the sergeant's mess. In far more modest surroundings were several small rooms on the bottom floor set aside as a social gathering place for recruits. A small sign emblazoned with "The Left Right Inn" pointed to Morris Depot's recruit canteen. We walked up steps carefully polished with red *stoep* wax and through the doors to an unpretentious room with a bar and several stools and chairs. An African barman stood behind the battered counter watching two recruits engaged in animated conversation over pints of local lager, while in the adjoining room Santo, the Portuguese barber, had set up shop and was making short work of the blond tresses of a recruit who watched apprehensively as his locks fell in his lap and on the floor. We joined the line and waited our turn.

Santo was a voluble young man who had migrated from Mozambique when the security situation there deteriorated several years earlier. He could address most topics of interest to a young Rhodesian: rugby, women,

The recruit's canteen, euphemistically known as the "Left Right Inn," was situated on the lower floor of the Regimental Institute, Morris Depot, Salisbury. (Author collection)

beer—but he always managed to let each customer know what evenings he would be available to cut hair as well as the location of his nearby barber shop.

My bunky seemed to be a quiet young man who had learned the value of listening. That was what we did that first night at Morris Depot recruit canteen, and after we had been appropriately shorn, we walked back to our barracks under a clear, bright African night, wondering what the first day of actual training would be.

I awoke a few minutes before 5:00 AM the next morning, stared up at the conical mosquito net frame suspended from the ceiling overhead, and listened to Gavin's deep breathing from the adjacent bed. Through the net, I watched a gecko scurry across the wall after an insect. It was very quiet, with only the first traces of dawn in the distance. I arose, reached for my shaving gear, and stepped out on to the porch just as the duty fire watch rounded the corner and began knocking on doors. The first into the communal showers, I began a hasty shave in the certain knowledge the area would soon be crowded with sleepy recruits hurrying to make parade.

Wrapped in a towel, I splashed water on my face and completed my ablutions in record time and then made my way back to dress for my first physical training (PT) parade.

The PT uniform consisted of white singlet, white shorts, and white canvas shoes called tackies. All were expected to be immaculate. After we had formed on the drill square, Lambourne demonstrated the correct way to fold our sock tops. The next morning, he explained, there would be no excuse for a less-than-perfect turnout. With that, he called us to attention, then screamed "Right turn!" to transform us into a three-wide column—and we started off running in cadence to repeated calls, "Left right left! Left right left." Soon, there were uniform footfalls as the squad followed lightly stepping Lambourne down the depot lanes and out the gates of Morris Depot.

Shortly thereafter, those of us not used to running at elevations of more than five thousand feet were breathing heavily in unison with our double-timing footfalls. As fatigue set in, some recruits had more difficulty staying in step. They earned growls from Lambourne, whose ears quickly identified a runner out of step.

It had rained overnight. Our instructor guided us around the edge of the army camp and into the national botanical gardens, now damp and verdant—feeling very much like unspoiled forest. We slipped on the muddy trails, and I noted that my PT kit was no longer spotlessly white as I struggled to stay in formation. I found myself envious of some of the recent schoolboys who had trained for athletics in these climates and who now loped effortlessly along behind Mike Lambourne.

I was relieved when two miles or so later we were led, still doubling, through depot gates and onto the drill square in front of the mess, where our forward motion was halted but our feet were not. We double-timed in place for what seemed like a long time, then were halted to listen to instructions about the next phase of the day.

"Listen up people. I want to see you back here after breakfast, turned out for drill. That means gray shirts, riot-blue trousers, drill boots, and hats, soft blue." Dismissed, we doubled away to our rooms and to shower hurriedly. I hoped that my newly acquired *batman* (manservant) had my drill kit in reasonable shape; but putting on the new apparel correctly—with all the various uniform accoutrements—was my job alone.

The choice of one's *batman* was a critical choice. Fortunately, mentor and friend Ormonde Power of Support Unit intervened to ensure that I was able to hire a choice *batman*. His name was Penny. He had served

Ormonde during his recruit training and had agreed to remain with him when Ormonde was posted to nearby Tomlinson Depot.

Penny was a graying old African gentleman who had cared for successive generations of depot recruits. He knew the trade tricks that could insulate a trainee from the unwanted attentions of instructional staff: how to fold the regulation mosquito net that we were all required to sleep under; how to block bed corners, how to apply red *stoep* polish to the floor of our shared rooms and, above all, how to keep our uniforms immaculate, creases razor sharp, and leatherwork polished. Even the best *batman* could not help a recruit who did not dress in his prescribed uniform with great care and attention. But without a skilled *batman*, the task of ensuring good military turnout became nearly impossible. So, learning how to manage clever, wise old Penny became an early test for this non-African. I had to make him understand that I expected his best at all times, but I was unused to the responsibilities of having my own manservant.

Penny did not disappoint me that morning. My single silver rank insignia bar and BSAP epaulette badges had been carefully affixed to the gray shirt, and the collar was perfectly ironed. But the heavily starched and ironed shirt was not comfortable, feeling as though it might crack at any moment.

Gavin Rabie and I carefully dressed in the drill uniform, checking each other to ensure that creases were aligned, belt straight, brass devices without smudges, and new boots brightly polished and dust free. A few minutes before time, we walked up to the drill square and stood in the shade, anticipating the arrival of Section Officer Lambourne. Precisely at the appointed time, our instructor emerged from his office. He was dressed in an impeccably tailored gray uniform shirt, khaki uniform shorts, and a brass-trimmed black web belt, and he carried a long brass-tipped pace stick precisely positioned under his arm. Now marching smartly onto the paved square, his steel-shod drill boots rapped out every step until he arrived at center stage and came abruptly to attention, crashing his right heel into the pavement and executing a ninety-degree turn to face us. Eyes nearly concealed under the brim of a guardsman-style cap brim, he glared across the square at his apprehensive charges and boomed out, "All right, you lot, I want you over here now, facing me in three columns, with the right marker here." He pointed to a spot on the square to his left. Without a word, the group doubled en masse, briefly jostling as they remembered rank positions.

Looking down at his charges, Lambourne began his lesson: "The purpose of this lesson will be to teach you how to correctly come to the position of attention, thus." From the at-ease position, legs apart with hands clasped behind his back, he smartly shifted weight to his left leg and brought his right leg up parallel with the ground, finally driving his boot precisely into position. It was one fluid motion. Some, I'm sure, even thought it looked easy, but it was not.

"On my word of command, you will come to attention as I just demonstrated." The ranks stood in anticipation, adopting an uncomfortable semblance of the at-ease position. "Look up!" Lambourne commanded by way of warning of the command to come. When it came, it did not sound at all like the "Atten-hut" I had heard many time in the United States. Rather, although the "Atten" part was intelligible, the remainder of the command was a pitched bellow that could be clearly heard three hundred yards away. The squad reacted instantly, fear being an instinctive reaction, but with varying degrees of success. Boots did not hit the pavement in unison, nor were the movements nearly as smart as our instructor would have wished.

"Pitiful! That sounded like a cow shitting on a flat rock! I want to hear those heels driving into the square at the same instant. We will do it again!" We did it again—and again. Sweat soaked through shirts and streamed from under the soft blue hats we wore. The senses of every recruit were keyed as tightly as possible, trying to anticipate and respond to the none-too-gentle commands. Seeing this, Lambourne would caution, "Wait for it, wait for it!"

Fatigue, spurred on by physical activity that seemed unnatural to even the fittest members of the squad, soon set in. After twenty minutes of our first lesson, our drill instructor sensed this too: "Listen up, you dozey pricks! I'll have you double around the barracks block and back here now-now—then we'll see if you're awake!" Lungs bursting, unused to running in heavy boots, we thundered off in a wild melee, thinking only that we didn't want to be the last man back in formation. Chests heaving, we reformed in front of glaring Lambourne, who ran us through the lesson for a further ten minutes or so. Those were long minutes for all of us.

Finally, our first lesson drew to a close. We were dismissed—and while Lambourne marched off the square in perfect, matched cadence, we doubled from the square to our quarters to change uniforms for the next instructional period.

None enjoyed drill, but few ever questioned its purpose or importance in the overall scheme of things. It was, we were told, a means of building a cohesive squad, getting men used to accepting and giving commands—and it was the accepted way for a uniformed group to move and maneuver. It

Nobody who ever heard drill instructor Mike Lambourne's parade square bellow would ever forget it. (Mike Lambourne collection)

was part of belonging to a proud regiment—and learning drill was part of the test of belonging and being allowed to wear the uniform and share in a century of tradition. We were, thus, in the main, grimly determined to learn—though there was an element of dread about the process of doing so.

There was a fairly distinct pattern to our training days. Each began with a physical training session, often a run or training on the obstacle course, interspersed with runs up and down the bleachers at the police football grounds. And always there were exercises and man carries and team activities to challenge even the most fit.

Fitness standards among the young Rhodesians were generally good. It was a sporting nation. Saturdays in Rhodesia were often given over to organized sport such as field hockey, rugby, and cricket, and within the police and army, Wednesday afternoons were often set aside for sport. "Fit body, fit mind" was a common philosophy.

BSAP training doctrine had evolved through several generations, but the origins were firmly rooted in the British army, at least in physical training, drill, and weapons. The BSAP had served as Rhodesia's sole defense force until World War II, the regiment having accumulated honors fighting the Germans in East Africa in the early days of World War I. In the early 1970s, the force shared responsibilities for counterinsurgency with the army and often operated in the field with them. Thus, Mike Lambourne's recruit fitness program aimed to instill stamina and strength in young men, such that they could successfully face the rigors of field operations, if necessary. From a diet of long runs, the squad graduated to Morris Depot's assault course—a series of obstacles, barriers, and pits that required rope climbing, swinging over water, balancing on logs, and wall climbing.

Besides sharpening coordination and building strength, the assault course taught young men to rely on each other. Every squad had members who were less capable, who struggled to overcome the calculated difficulties of the course. We learned to help each other. Still, there were injuries when muscles screaming for respite could no longer hold or when sweaty palms slipped on a rope swing; the wounded hobbled off to the camp hospital for bandaging, the remainder heading for a well-earned shower, grateful it had not happened to us.

In the first weeks at depot, I attended normal classes with my squad. These introduced us to diverse topics about the force and about the Rhodesian people. I learned where ethnic African peoples had settled, what their languages were, and something about their culture and traditions. I learned how Western law had been adapted to the Africans, and to Africa generally. This was presented by experienced instructors, often with an overlay of anecdotal commentary that helped me to understand the reality of law enforcement in the sometime-contradictory environment of Rhodesia—where it was quite possible to leave the carefully groomed civic center of Salisbury and, less than an hour later, be seated in a traditional African kraal that had changed little in centuries.

I was the only recruit in Morris Depot on a short, six-week training course. The administrators recognized that I already had many requisite skills, so as I reached the halfway mark, my training was concentrated toward learning law, and I was becoming impatient to leave and do the job. Nearly a decade older than most of my squad mates—and older even than many of the Morris Depot instructors—I often gravitated away from the after-hours activities at the Left Right Inn and eventually found my way to the nearby police reserve canteen, appropriately labeled "The Copper Pot."

Recruit training rules had not specifically prohibited me from the canteen. It was, I knew, located just off the hard stand square in front of the depot armory—so at the end of day on a Friday, I changed into civilian clothing and walked quietly up past the saddler's shop and into the cool, welcoming clamor of the club. Here I hoped to meet the Rhodesians and find some interesting people to talk with.

There I found a large, open room equipped with tall tables, a dartboard, and a bar. The late-afternoon drinkers were dressed in a variety of uniforms, most in the summer shorts and tunics of the BSAP—but intermixed were gray shirts and dark-blue denims of the traditional working dress and several members of a Police Anti-Terrorist Unit (PATU) in Rhodesian camouflage battle dress. There were no familiar faces, so I made my way to the bar, where the African barman served me a cold pint of Lion lager for twenty cents. It tasted wonderful. Then I noticed long sticks of dark dried meat in a jar behind the bar. My server patiently explained to me that this was *biltong*, the local version of jerky. I selected a piece, paid for it, and began gnawing at the salty meat and quaffing the beer. A cheerful soul standing down the bar noticing my newness and recruit haircut, told me the canteen *biltong* was supplied by Rhodesia's national park service. Animals necessarily culled in their wildlife management program were carefully butchered and the meat and hides sold to bolster conservation initiatives.

It was at the Copper Pot that I was reintroduced to Eric Kennelly, now an inspector, but still assigned to the depot musketry instructional staff as member in charge. He was standing at one of the tables when I noticed him and walked across. Eric recognized me immediately, at first expressing surprise that I was back in Rhodesia from Vietnam and now a depot recruit. That soon seemed to evolve into an expression of appreciation that I had made such a radical change in my life and was now in Rhodesia to serve its people as a policeman.

My meeting Eric was a defining moment, the start of a close and enduring friendship—despite differences in our ranks. He had soon determined that I was in depot on a short course, doing well, but also anxious to finish. One day he asked me whether I would like to work for him at the armory. Knowing full well that this would effectively shelter me from the attentions of other depot instructional staff, I accepted immediately. Working around firearms, ammunition, and ordnance seemed perfectly natural to me, and I was confident that I could do a good job. I reported the next day after morning PT and a stint of study at the law office.

If anything, I found the police armory fuller than it had been when I passed through as a visitor in 1971. The force was actively purchasing new FN-pattern rifles from their South African manufacturers; the new R1s with their black synthetic stocks stood in rows on wooden rifle racks, not unlike the ranks of a pipe organ. To one side, in rather more bedraggled fashion, were captured and impounded weapons from counterinsurgency operations. These were almost entirely AK-47s and SKS rifles of Soviet and Eastern Bloc manufacture. Many were scarred by rough handling from their previous owners, but a few were near new. All of this I took in as I came through the steel entry door that first day, before making my way upstairs to the musketry staff office.

There were four men working on the musketry training staff for Eric. Their job was to ensure that every recruit who passed out of Morris Depot was competent to fire each of the several standard weapons in every police armory. Members of the BSAP did not carry handguns, as is the custom in many of the world's police forces; their issue weapon was a rifle, just as it had been in the era of the Boer War—and that rifle normally stayed locked away unless the member was engaged in counterinsurgency operations. The BSAP was thus, by appearances at least, an unarmed force, and Rhodesia's citizens liked it that way.

Rifle marksmanship was stressed in depot training. There were also indoctrination classes covering the single-shot Greener police shotgun, intended for use as a riot gun, and the semiautomatic Browning shotgun. Each recruit also had to qualify with the P-1 pistol, an FN weapon in 9-mm patterned after the Walther P-38—and the force submachinegun, called the FNSMG, which was distinctly an Uzi.

That first day when I walked in, Inspector Ian "Chalky" White was preparing his training materials for an adjacent classroom, where recruits awaited the next lesson period. Eric gave instructions to other staff members and answered the phone while I waited for a quiet moment to learn what my duties would be that day. I stared out of the second-story window to watch two of the armorers who were preparing to fire an AK-47 into a bullet catch and in the distant background heard a drill instructor on the hardstand calling out cadence to marching recruits.

Eric looked up, smiled, and said, "Are you well?"—a distinctly Rhodesian greeting. I replied, saying that I was, and that I was present to work. He arose and walked back toward the stairs, and I followed back down to the weapon storage area.

"Things are in a bit of a shambles down here in my equipment store. You can start organizing it." I looked up as we walked into a large windowless storeroom that was permeated with the composite odors of canvas webbing, gun oil, and cosmolene—the scent of an old, airless armory. On the shelves were backpack radios, batteries, weapon cleaning gear, ammunition, and load-bearing webbing. I told Eric that I could sort through the material and organize it so that things could be found.

He saw me stare past him to shelves on the other side of the store, where a machine gun rested on its bipod—and where there were a number of deactivated Soviet pattern antitank mines and wooden ammunition boxes with distinctive Russian Cyrillic stenciling. I smiled, shook my head, and said, "The bastards are pushing here too, just as they did in Vietnam."

"Yes Doug. A lot has changed since you were here last, and it's not all for the best."

In the quiet of the store, my boss began to speak about events of the previous two years. He reminded me that Rhodesia had successfully fended off a series of attacks launched in the late 1960s from hostile neighbor countries, Zambia in particular. The attackers had been determined, hard-core insurgents who in the main fought to the death when eventually confronted by defense force personnel. Some groups had attacked and killed farmers in remote border regions.

Rhodesia responded by tracking down and attacking these organized bands. The Soviet weaponry and equipment I had seen in 1971 had been captured during these largely successful early operations. Later, strategic thinkers analyzed events and realized that much of their success had been because they developed essential intelligence about enemy movements and intentions that had facilitated the counterinsurgency operations. The BSAP refined and set in motion a primary information-gathering program in the African tribal trust lands, the Ground Coverage (GC) protocol. Coordinated in the main by young district policemen under the direction of Special Branch, GC generated a torrent of basic information from African sources that were largely cooperative and even enthusiastic about supplying information about goings-on in the bush. Traditional tribal law supplied much of the social fabric and rules of everyday life for most rural Africans; there tended to be recognition of the authority of the chief—and chiefs were formally empowered by the Rhodesian government. Tribesmen in the trust lands thus were often particularly observant and willing to share their observations.

"We were holding our own very nicely," Eric recalled. Terrorist forces pulled back, apparently to regroup, and Special Branch continued to develop information sources elsewhere in Africa. These initiatives in many instances identified key enemy operatives, where they had undergone training and where they were presently operating. Tanzania's Julius Nyerere was hosting not just cadres of Communist Chinese engineers; his government also hosted insurgents from Rhodesia—as did nearby Zambia. Rhodesians had an awareness of these activities; many possibly hoped that the nation's vigorous response to earlier attacks would be a deterrent to similar hostilities in the future. But after a spell, attacks had resumed the previous year.

"The attack in Centenary was different from earlier terr ops," he explained. Operational training had been far more thorough and enemy tactics more sophisticated. "We moved into a newer, higher-threat phase with this attack."

Eric paused, picked up a clipboard, and motioned me to follow him back upstairs into the armory workshop and forensic examination area. I realized that he intended that I see the case file about this event.

In a small, well-lit office upstairs sat Rhodesia's comparative microscope. These instruments are used by police forensic experts to match recovered bullets and cartridge cases with the weapon that had fired them. Much to its credit, the BSAP investigated every attack just as it would a domestic homicide; evidence was carefully gathered and preserved under appropriate legal protocols. Every weapon captured in counterinsurgency operations was turned over to the armory for examination by expert witness Chief Inspector Don Hollingsworth. Thus, police frequently were able to link particular weapons to a series of attacks—and as I was later to learn, this might be used as evidence against an insurgent captured with a weapon thus identified.

From a file drawer, Eric removed a sheaf of color prints that had been taken in the aftermath of the abduction and killing of a lonely miner in the northeast, Len Koenig. He said little as he shuffled through them, apparently in thought but in actual fact recalling the horror of the killings. He passed several 8x10 color prints to me, the first of which was an obscenity scarcely recognizable as a man's face—reduced to a misshapen pulp by multiple gunshots.

Eric began to speak, first explaining that he had been called to the crime scene from Mount Darwin: "The poor old guy was lying face down about thirty yards from his decrepit old hut, and the indications were that the terrs had dragged him out and then used a Tokarev pistol first and then the RPD machine gun. We recovered about seventy expended cartridges cases, three from the Tokarev and the rest from the one RPD. The gunner probably stood right over him and I guess about every bullet hit him. It was like ground beef. The most horrific part was the single eye in the middle of his face, the rest just bone splinters."

The Rhodesian Light Infantry (RLI) stick leader had made his men walk past the body before they began the follow up. "They were all very pumped up. If a contact had taken place, there would have been no stopping them," Eric recounted.

Then I heard the story of the Whistlefield Farm attack: how a brave man in the dark of night had sheltered his family as best he could after rounds from AK-47s began pouring through the windows and shattering fragile brick walls. There had been a desperate radio call for help to the police command post and attempts to fend off the attackers.

"They planned this attack carefully," Eric said suddenly. "Soviet land mines were buried in the dirt driveway where an Army truck carrying the SAS tracker team struck one of them. Corporal Neil Moore, seated in the rear, was killed, struck by a piece of brake lining from the wheel that rolled over the device."

We were interrupted before I could ask about what must have been a story conclusion. Had there been a successful follow-up with insurgents killed or captured? The conclusion would have to wait for another time. I returned to the armory store and my reorganization task.

My training days at Morris Depot took on a regular pattern. I attended physical training parade every morning before breakfast and often a period on the square under the watchful eye of drill instructor Mike Lambourne. Then I would walk to the small library and study room used by the depot law and police procedures teachers. Here Section Officer Dave Ward helped me prepare for examinations that would demonstrate my understanding of Rhodesia's criminal law; this would qualify me for "passing out" and assignment to my first posting.

Coincidentally, I found myself sharing the scarred old Mukwa study bench with Section Officer Angus Rufus, the very man who had shown me my first wild African elephant at Kariba in 1971. He too was studying law, but for him it was preparation for the impending inspector promotional examination. We grilled each other on common law definitions of various criminal offenses and discussed applicable case law and legal precedents, and I learned more about the changing situation in Rhodesia's northeast. Angus had been member in charge at Centenary, the very area of the 1972 farm attacks—until relieved by Dave Ward to take on a new assignment. Soon after the Wards' arrival, Dave was driving with his wife to a dinner at a nearby farm when their vehicle detonated a land mine planted in the dirt access road. The force of the explosion had blown the Land Rover on its side and trapped both Wards. Dave, although injured, managed to extricate himself and go for help. But his wife had been gravely wounded by the blast and could not be saved.

Hearing this story gave me added respect for my instructor, who always managed a cheerful demeanor despite what we all knew was a recent and terrible loss. Angus, it was clear, had searched his soul, wondering if somehow he might have done more to prepare the man who took over from him when enemy intentions still remained an uncertainty.

I had not fired a weapon since my arrival in Rhodesia. Eric had not seemed particularly concerned that I might need indoctrination and instruction in depot classrooms, clearly assuming that all would be evident when I received my counterinsurgency (COIN) training, a stint of training on the rifle range and in the nearby countryside under simulated operational conditions. As the time neared, I began to look forward to COIN; it would be my first chance to experience the African bush close up.

Salisbury recruits knew where Chikarubi and Goromonzi were. I heard these names mentioned as the frenetic pace of preparation for COIN training picked up, but no matter how strong my imagination, I could not visualize what lay ahead. As our training deployment date arrived, a modest convoy of dark-green Land Rovers and trucks was drawn up on the hardstand in front of the depot armory and loaded with ammunition, weapons, and rations. Finally, a recruit squad attired in newly issued camouflage uniforms clambered aboard the trucks, each man carrying basic gear and issued rifle and magazines. Inspector Kennelly had assigned me to be his communicator, which gave me responsibility for his vehicle and backpack radios. It also won me a seat in the back of his Land Rover, which towed a tank trailer loaded with drinking water.

Kennelly Force got under way early one summer day in January 1974. A ragtag outfit made up of bright new faces in new, unfaded camo transported in whatever transport was available that day from the Public Works Department. The faces of civilians we passed driving through suburban Salisbury clearly conveyed to all that everybody knew a new recruit when they saw one. Saviors of Rhodesia we were not.

Although charming and sometimes rustic, Salisbury was by anybody's standards a modern city. Streets were wide and well kept, and the traffic lights worked. With national fuel rationing in effect, one thus might have expected few motor vehicles to be out, but the road seemed busy to me as I sat under the rear canvas canopy while Eric wheeled us out of town, Inspector Ian "Chalky" White riding shotgun. With all the weight of ammunition, water, and personnel aboard, he drove carefully. We were periodically overtaken by Rhodesian families, which often waved, and farmers in their light trucks, who always did. That felt good to me—the genuineness and friendship of Rhodies always had endeared them to me.

Chikarubi, I understand, later became virtually a suburb of Salisbury. It was not far from Morris Depot—perhaps half an hour drive—but in 1974 the country had a pleasantly rural feeling about it. The attraction at Chikarubi was the rifle range, an impressive facility, with firing points delineated from seventy-five to one thousand meters. An open forest of native African trees girded the long, grassy open area of the range and its abutments. Opposite the range area was more bush. I didn't know it at the time, but that bush was to be where I would spend my first night out under African stars.

For me, the first day at the rifle range was largely uneventful. I didn't shoot. Others needed instruction; I did not and so was detailed to the butts with a small team to mark and patch targets. While standing in a pit below ground level and staring upward as bullets struck paper bull's eye targets, most recruits first heard the distinctive crack and thump associated with receiving small-arms fire. I explained that we were hearing the passage of the bullet overhead before the rifle report.

That afternoon, after all brass cartridges had been picked up and target frames returned to storage, we clambered aboard transport and drove away from the neatly mowed rifle range and into the bush opposite to make camp. For some, it would be their baptism to practical bush craft, the learning of skills for living on the ground in Africa. To me, Chikarubi was simply beautiful. It was then the rainy season. Trees had fresh, new growth; grasses were verdant; and on the narrow, dirt road crawling along in a Land Rover, I mused that we could have been just about anywhere in Southern Africa, let alone on the outskirts of cosmopolitan Salisbury.

An established training campsite was situated under trees adjacent to one of the low granite outcroppings that characterize this region of Africa. The instructional staff members had set up large military tents for sleeping and messing. For the trainees, it was a multifaceted lesson in how to live with basic equipment and ration packs while simultaneously defending against potential attack. We were not required to dig in; but defensive points were established and watches posted. It was all about building a sense of responsibility and awareness among young men who had not yet heard a hostile shot.

I set up my poncho shelter and sleeping bag on the ground within calling distance of Eric and the instructors, ensuring that radios would stay dry even if I couldn't. Another recruit would share radio watch duties with me. As dusk neared, a low hum of activity could be heard under the trees and in the rocks as men prepared meals from ration packs, cleaned rifles, and readied themselves for the night ahead.

I was spared from yet another meal out of a brown cardboard box. At the instructor's tent, a fire was crackling and preparations by an African servant under way for the evening meal. Eric invited me to join the staff for my meals, and I gratefully accepted. These men lived in the camp regularly.

They rightly saw no reason why life had to be any more difficult than necessary. There were folding chairs and tables, chilling beers, and steaks. Later, there would be visitors from Salisbury.

The tent that evening was my first opportunity to meet the man who would divert my career away from traditional police work. He was Chief Inspector Bill Coetzer, the BSAP's farrier, whom I'd seen play rugby with Alistair Holmes in 1971. Billy was a legend in the force, a huge man who had represented the police in many successive rugby seasons—but who was also known as a fair and compassionate leader. As he took my hand in greeting, I was reminded of a bear's paw—the great mitt that had wielded a smithy's hammer and the fist that was reputed to have knocked cold a misbehaving police mule.

There was spirited banter among the instructors over beers as meat sizzled over the coals. Bill Coetzer was perhaps the quietest of the group, but I sensed he was watching and listening to the few comments I offered up—and when later a carload of smiling women arrived from Salisbury, he retired. I sensed these were likely policeman groupies, a phenomenon I was not altogether unfamiliar with from earlier uniformed duties in California. Not beautiful, but certainly functional, I was certain—and they were not there for me. After some pleasant chat, I excused myself and stepped out behind the tent flap and into a very dark night.

I stood under a soaring msasa tree, its canopy blocking out a blanket of stars, waiting for my eyes to adjust. The outline of my shelter half tent became visible, and I walked carefully in that direction, testing my footing with each step. The radio crackled as I crawled inside. My sleepy offsider passed me the handset to acknowledge a communication check from one of the sentry posts. I settled into my sleeping bag, making myself as comfortable as possible on the bare earth, to take the next watch. Lying on my back, the radio handset cradled against my ear, I stared up into the heavens on one of those remarkably clear nights so unique to the high elevations of Africa. I concentrated on identifying the constellations of the Southern Hemisphere, particularly the Southern Cross—and marveled at the endless immensity of the heavens. The night was utterly silent except for a cricket and occasional polite laughter from the tent. I was tired, and I was at peace. My first night of so many spent out under the stars in the African veld was unforgettable in its simple beauty. War and conflict seemed so very far away.

Later, as my watch ended and I handed over the radio to my relief, my thoughts returned to Vietnam. What was happening there, I wondered.

Who was still alive; who was not? I could never be certain, the guilt returning again and seeping into my body. Troubled sleep finally came.

Even in the summer, a high veld morning can be cool. Fully clothed and alert, I awoke to a fresh morning, the demons of the previous night now far away. I enjoyed my sleeping bag's warmth as the first sunlight broke over the *kopjes*, standing dawn radio watch. As soon as I heard movement at the tent, I arose and walked across to make my report. The teapot was already hot over the morning fire. I learned that we would be returning to the range to shoot for the record, our formal rifle qualification. I would be qualifying too.

After a quick breakfast, I toured recruit positions with Eric. The men were cheerful, many of them cleaning up after a morning ration pack breakfast. Most greeted us quietly, even formally, but there clearly was a positive spirit in the air among the new patrol officers savoring the outdoors. Eric sensed this, engaging in gentle banter, all the while observing each man's demeanor, equipment, and attitude to the new challenges. "Would you be ready to march on a follow-up in five minutes without leaving half of your gear behind?" he asked one particularly disorganized young man who was probably used to having an African servant tidy for him.

Soon we were back in the trucks for the short drive out of the forest to the rifle range. Squads were dispatched in different directions to break out target frames; others hauled heavy wooden 1,000-round boxes of 7.62 ammunition, each clearly stenciled by their South African manufacturers. Twenty minutes after our arrival, the first detail was lying prone at the two hundred yard firing point firing warm-up rounds before shooting for record. I too was feeling prematch tension, wanting genuinely to shoot well and perhaps qualify as a marksman. Instructors walked behind the shooters, watching as the rounds were marked on the target by the detail working in the butts, occasionally suggesting last-minute sight adjustments before the real shooting began.

The BSAP's qualifying shoot was both demanding and practical; it included a final phase in which qualifiers walked back to the six hundred meter firing point, then began a timed shoot called a run-down. At six hundred meters, the qualification began by timed firing from the prone position, after which all ran to the five hundred meter point and again shot. The men were pressured both by time restrictions and the difficulties associated with accurate distance shooting while breathing heavily from the exertions of running. The course was completed at the fifty-meter mark where qualifiers were required to shoot very quickly.

Despite years of shooting experience, the run-down shoot would be a new experience for me, and I was uncertain how well I would manage. Moreover, I had not yet been issued a personal rifle. I was scheduled to shoot in the final detail; when the time came to form up, Eric turned to me and said, "My rifle is in the Land Rover; you may use it."

Inspector Kennelly's personal weapon was a heavy-barrel FN, of a design used by the Dutch army—perhaps the only one in the BSAP armory. I had never fired it, but during the warm-up phase I found that it seemed to shoot well. I had a respectable grouping with those first ten rounds. Then the run-down began. There would be nobody to spot my target strikes for me in this event; I would need to hope that my sight adjustments were correct and that I had truly mastered this new rifle.

At six hundred meters, the bull's eye target appeared to be almost the same width as my rifle foresight. I carefully adjusted the rear peep sight and tried to get my elbows comfortable in the grass as I lay on top of the low mound that was our firing position. On either side of me recruits fidgeted nervously in anticipation of the order that would signal the start of the qualifying shoot. Behind us, ever watchful for careless weapon handling by nervous shooters, roamed the instructors. Finally, the string of orders came: "Load ten rounds!" There was the distinctive clatter of magazines being inserted, followed by "Ready!" when weapons were cocked—and finally "Fire!" I took my deep breaths, held, and carefully squeezed the trigger, trying to set a regular rhythm in the time available. My last round boomed out just as Ian Chalk yelled, "Stop." We made safe rifles, then in an extended line, ran to the five hundred meter line, where the process was repeated. I concentrated on managing my breathing after the run, focusing on the target and a controlled trigger squeeze. I, like the others, had no idea where their rounds were hitting—and it was better not to think about it.

At the fifty-meter point, the men halted at the last leg of the run-down, quickly loaded fresh magazines, then fired as targets rose from behind the butts. There was little time for aiming in the time allowed. This was a test of instinctive point-and-shoot. Inspector Chalk was pushing his charges to shoot quickly and shoot well. As the final rounds boomed out across the range, the shooters cleared their weapons and began chatting quietly. Some shook their heads, certain the pressure of the shoot had undone most newly acquired weapon-handling skills, while others seemed pensive. The shooters walked together to a tree at the edge of the range and waited while final scores were tallied by the detail in the butts.

When Inspector Chalk returned to the group carrying a clipboard with the qualification scores, all attention focused on him. Eric Kennelly and Chief Inspector Coetzer stood behind us, well pleased that there had been no failures and several better than average scores. With a mischievous grin, "Chalky" left my score out of his announcements—adding it as an apparent afterthought. My score was the highest, more than qualifying me to wear the coveted crossed rifles of a marksman. There were several "Well dones" from squad members, then from one of the wags behind me, "He's been shooting gooks in Vietnam; he can do better I'm sure!" There was good-natured chuckling, but I noticed that Bill Coetzer was watching me.

The formal qualifying for record behind us, the training would move into a distinct new phase: counterinsurgency training. Back at the nearby camp, the men that night settled into their positions, cleaned rifles, and began preparing meals.

The BSAP had always played a direct and active role in the defense of Rhodesia, beginning at the turn of the century when internal insurrections evolved. As the senior service, the police continued to play an important internal security role even after an army and air force were raised. Police antiterrorist units were even then patrolling the bush constantly. Thus it was that every recruit was given training to permit him to function in an operational role if and when needed.

Inspector Kennelly's training program began by teaching basic skills each man would need to perform his tasks in a bush war. These were interesting lessons enthusiastically followed by all. The next morning we gathered into a group to learn observation skills—what to look for and how to understand the many clues to be found in the bush, including animal tracks and different types of human ones. Then we moved to the edge of a large open area with an upward slope. "How far away do you think that small tree is?" we were asked. There were a range of guesses, none correct. The instructor knew the answer exactly—it having been previously measured off—but he then launched into a lesson plan designed to teach each man the vagaries of estimating distance and the tricks the human eye can play when observing nonlevel surfaces.

Later in the day we gathered in a large tent, where patrolling tactics and formation lessons were presented. The African sun beat down on our dark-green canvas overhead, permeating the tent with a heavy musky odor that mixed the smells of the grass and men living in the wild without ablution. It would have been very easy to nap in the gentle torpor of the afternoon.

The men sat on hard wooden benches, trying to concentrate on a chalkboard presentation designed to be a theoretical precursor to the practical part. We were told how to position scouts and trackers out in front of a main patrol group; we learned the particular advantages of the V-shaped grouping in the open and semiopen country of the African savanna—and we were cautioned about the dangers of patrolling in line.

Never one to belabor theory for long, Eric soon had his charges out practicing formations. In groups of seven, we moved through lightly wooded country and open grasslands, while instructors observed and commented when men bunched up or lines straggled. Clusters of men presented easy targets; ragged lines would have difficulty with rapid response in the event of an enemy contact.

There was an underlying lesson in these patrol tactics. The men came to realize as they struggled to learn techniques for moving quietly through dense bush that the odds were very good that a chance contact with an enemy group would likely be at close range. Our instructors confirmed this and in somber terms explained that in a confrontation of this nature, the group with internal discipline would inevitably survive best. That discipline required the attacked patrol to react immediately by turning and launching a vigorous counterattack directly into their ambushers, the so-called Immediate Action Drill taught in the old British army field manuals.

"If you get hit, the command is either 'Ambush left!' or Ambush right!' The patrol instantly turns to the direction of the enemy and charges them while firing. Keep your rounds low, because it is likely the ambushers will be lying prone behind cover. If you hesitate even for a moment, you will remain in the killing zone—and you will die. Immediate action drills require constant practice, until they become second nature, but we will introduce you to them now."

Thus, the men were divided into groups of friendlies and enemy. Blank ammunition was issued, and all cautioned that even blank ammunition could be dangerous if fired at close range. Friendly patrols mounted up and moved cautiously through the bushland adjoining the camp, only to be set upon by a primitive ambush laid by the then-enemy. Urged on by close-following instructors, the attacked squads initially stumbled in the undergrowth, a nonaggressive performance that quickly earned the ire of their teachers.

"You pricks are dead. Dead. Even garden boys with rusty rifles would have given you a good rev in this ambush. They were only ten meters away.

You should have poured fire into them as you charged through. Now, we'll do it again!"

After initial lackluster performances, patrols began to rally together, attacking in line at a fast trot. Adrenaline levels rose, as did the aggressiveness of attacks. There were complaints heard from "enemy" ambushers about blank rounds being fired at close range. Finally, the first lesson complete, Inspector Kennelly called his charges together, by then a group of tired, dirty men in camouflage marked by grime and perspiration.

"Your lesson today was designed to introduce you to essential tactics for patrol. By now, each of you has realized that there is a lot more to learn. Much of it can be refined when you join a permanent patrol and start working together."

That evening after a ration-pack dinner, the patrols, called "sticks," reformed in the dusk to begin to learn the skills of movement at night. Each appointed squad leader was given a compass and a bearing to be followed. The men, understanding the necessity of silent movement, stepped off in V-pattern formations—but as dusk grew to darkness, increasingly they couldn't see those next to them. Gradually, the formations tightened, until each stick had to move in line formation, each man focused on the pack ahead lest he become lost. Some patrols tried to hurry; these were the groups most easily heard as men stumbled and loose equipment clattered in the darkness. It was a humbled group of recruits that stumbled back to the camp that night, most thinking about the lessons of the day.

Our initial training period at Chikarubi was drawing to a close. The next morning, a Rhodesian air force Alouette II helicopter landed in the *vlei* adjacent to our encampment to support the recruits in learning a well-defined drill for tactical loading and unloading patrol groups. There were a myriad of safety rules to learn and practice for men who had never flown in rotary-wing aircraft—as well as weapon-handling skills designed to prevent injury from personal weapons. A small helicopter, even compared to the ubiquitous Huey I had known so well in Vietnam, the Alouette was commanded by an air force pilot officer with an noncommissioned officer crew chief. The recruits were broken up into sticks of five men. Each stick sat together, awaiting a fast and exciting first flight together and watching with enthusiasm as a new group was given the "Embuss!" command to file with heads down toward the cockpit, rifles held low.

That afternoon, after completion of helicopter exercises, Eric let me know that we would soon be traveling into Salisbury with the Land

Rover to bring fresh water back in the tank trailer. We would also be doing an ammunition and ration resupply at Morris Depot. I assembled my gear and the backpack radio in the rear of the vehicle, and we were soon under way.

Instead of driving directly to the heart of Salisbury and the depot, Eric turned into the eastern suburb of Mandara, where good friends Brian and Jo Cullingworth lived with their three children. As we turned into Banchory Lane, he turned his head and spoke to me over his shoulder: "I got a message from Jo and Brian saying that 'your Aussie girlfriend,' Jennifer, has arrived from New Guinea and is staying with them. I'll be back for you in two hours."

This was an unexpected surprise, but a pleasant one. I had met Jennifer Harrison in Australia. She had written to me faithfully from Port Moresby, whence she planned to travel to Rhodesia; but the question of when and how was never very clear. For a time, she considered crewing on a French yacht that was bound for South Africa. When that didn't eventuate, she bought an open plane ticket with an itinerary that included Hong Kong, Singapore, Sri Lanka, and the Seychelles. Her postcards eventually found me, but mail delivery was not particularly timely or dependable—and I was never certain when or how she would find her way to Salisbury.

We parked alongside the Cullingworth's three-quarter-acre lot and I unfolded myself from under the canvas canopy as Eric alighted and strode down the driveway to where the sounds of an ailing washing machine could be heard. We arrived simultaneously at the rear door, where we were greeted by Jo and the domestic, a Shona gentleman named Peter.

Jo greeted us both warmly, turning away from her errant washing machine to wipe her hands and hug first Eric, then me. Hearing our conversation, a smiling Brian entered the room, saying he had left the messages at Morris Depot for Eric that found their way to our encampment overnight. As we conversed, a tanned and rather shy Jennifer appeared in the doorway, barefoot and dressed in a summer dress. Jo quickly introduced her to Eric, after which Eric took his leave, promising to return soon.

My two hours galloped away very quickly. I learned that Jennifer had talked her way through Rhodesian immigration authorities the day before. They had wanted to cite her return ticket; she said she had none—that she was intending to stay. Hearing her conversation, the Air Rhodesia captain who had just flown the Viscount in from Johannesburg stepped up and vouched for her and later delivered her to the Cullingworths, an address I had given her months before as a point of contact.

We were happy to be back together again. Almost immediately we began making plans for when my training was complete and I would be assigned police duties. In the interim, Brian and Jo Cullingworth would be traveling soon to South Africa and would be glad to have us care for the family home in their absence. Jennifer would retrieve my car and begin looking for a job.

On our way back to the encampment that afternoon, steering carefully with a loaded water tanker behind us, Eric said simply, "Pretty girl, Jennifer." My life seemed once again to be taking some form—not exactly as I had planned perhaps—but I now had somebody I cared deeply about who had traveled a long way to share life with me.

The final stage of COIN training began when the Chikarubi camp was taken down and the area carefully policed for litter and personal equipment. Trucks were packed first with packs and equipment, then finally the recruits boarded and Kennelly Force began moving toward Marandellas Road in convoy.

Our destination was Goromonzi, a tiny rural community about twenty miles east of Salisbury, where sympathetic farmers permitted their land to be used for training purposes. Here it was that initial lessons in marksmanship and field tactics would be practiced in conditions virtually identical to the less-settled operational areas of Rhodesia.

Inspector Kennelly had briefed the contingent before we broke camp, reminding us again to be aware of the dangers posed by the bush. The likelihood of bumping into an enemy cell was considered remote, but in some circumstances, live ammunition would be issued. There was always the danger of venomous snakes: cobras, mambas, and vipers were very much at home in Goromonzi. But it was the water we were warned of repeatedly. Rhodesia's water was widely infected with bilharzia (schistosomiasis). Exposure to the water put one in real peril of a blood infection brought about by a parasitic flatworm, the treatment for which was a dosage of arsenic. Some of us had seen bilharzia victims undergoing treatment at Morris Depot's camp hospital. Premature graying and hair loss were both obvious symptoms of a radical treatment.

The threat of bilharzia meant there would be no washing or impromptu dips in streams or dams. Seasonal rains meant more small watercourses would be available to entice men who had lived a week already without a shower.

"Don't be tempted," we were cautioned. "Furthermore, you should be aware that your adversary will smell some of the things you take for granted in your daily ablutions—things like soap and toothpaste. Your best defense will be to simply get grungy. After a week or so, neither you nor your mates will notice body odor or halitosis much."

There were chuckles and recriminating stares among young men who were becoming more conscious of their increasingly odoriferous state, but the bilharzia warning was taken seriously, particularly among the farm boys.

Our journey took us out on to the main highway to Rhodesia's eastern border, after which it transited Mozambique to the port of Beira. This was a well-maintained modern paved highway over which a passenger car could have traveled at speed; our progress was more modest, Kennelly Force being led by a laden Land Rover followed by two aging British diesel five-ton trucks. Soon we turned north off Marandellas Road onto a smaller paved rural road and progressed across increasingly hilly country. I peered over the passenger seat through the windshield to see tall, green stands of planted corn and tobacco along the road—but what most attracted my attention were granite domes and outcroppings in the distance. These were the distinctive geological formations I was always to associate with Goromonzi's beauty.

We stopped at Goromonzi police station just long enough to let the member in charge know that we were en route to a local farm and thereafter would be patrolling and exercising on foot in the adjoining properties. Then we set off down gently descending dirt road toward the valley bottom and the farm that would host our live-fire exercises.

Goromonzi was a sea of green foliage accented by the granite outcroppings thrusting up from cultivated fields. Around the high ground were stands of native timber. Seasonal rains ensured that even native grasses were lush. It was a mixed blessing; temperatures were moderate, but it was difficult to stay dry.

Our farm exercise area had geographic features that made it an attractive area in which to train. Notably, there were steep hillsides that could stop small-arms fire, small meadows across which we could maneuver, and forested reentrants—all in a short radius. Against a spectacular granite bluff, our instructors erected silhouette targets that were to serve as the enemy during an attack in which live ammunition was to be used.

Eric Kennelly had selected the location for the lesson with care. A grassy meadow extended back from the target site, the open ground affording good visibility—and thus control—of the recruit sections as they moved and fired. On the far side of the meadow stood a small stand of trees, a natural place from which to site supporting fire. Reckoning that it would be too dangerous to use recruits for this role, he provided me with an FN MAG machine gun and gave me orders and belts of ammunition. I would provide fire support to my peers.

This machine gun had an interesting history, it having been captured or stolen from a contingent of Royal Marines in Zanzibar some years before. It later found its way into the hands of an insurgent group whose temporary owners were killed by Rhodesian security forces. The police armorers had fashioned a new bipod to replace the one lost—and this robust, accurate weapon was returned to service.

As the first attacking party was preparing to advance over open ground, I picked the gun up with ammunition belts and moved to the tree line, where I quickly located a sheltered position that allowed an unfettered view of the targets ahead. I had cover from my right, should an excited trainee unleash a round in my direction instead of the "enemy" ahead. I threw myself down into a prone position, loaded a belt of ammunition, and tried to make my elbows comfortable as I pulled the butt up close to my cheek. It was not comfortable, lying on moist forest floor and exposed tree roots—but it was a good position—and in the distance I heard the attacking party ordered to step off. A group of about seven men moved in line and began to maneuver, taking advantage of low ground and cover while trying to score hits on the targets. I began to fire three- and four-round bursts into the far-left target. The little valley boomed with gunfire and rounds could be seen smacking into the damp earth, throwing up clumps of grass. After firing about fifty rounds, the attackers came into view on my forward right flank, moving at a trot in line, and I stopped firing just as they closed on their imaginary enemy and overwhelmed them to complete the final assault.

Eric and another instructor were close behind them. I cleared my gun and jogged forward to the targets to hear his critique of the attack exercise. The recruit section had performed well. They were muddy, panting, sweating, and mildly elated by the experience of delivering coordinated small-arms fire—and of having a machine gun firing from behind them.

The remaining sticks followed in turn, putting in spirited attacks, covering each other, maintaining fire discipline, as instructors trotted behind, watching carefully for sloppy weapon handling that could so easily result in a friendly injury or death. Each time, I fired a fifty-round belt from the gun, carefully aiming each burst. There were no mishaps.

Once the live-fire exercises were complete, there was an intense period of simulated patrol activity in which the men were given an opportunity to operate in the bush, carrying all their requisites with them in load-bearing webbing. They had studied the theoretical tactics of counterinsurgency: blocking forces, cordon searches, and tracking. Although rural Goromonzi was not then considered an active operational area, the exercises would be realistic both because of the environment and because of the pressure inherent in the instructional plan.

I was selected to join Eric to become the imaginary cell that my peers would track, pursue, and attempt to "kill." Late in the afternoon we left the main force in a Land Rover and drove some distance to a cluster of farm sheds. There we concealed the vehicle and found some dry ground under the overhang on which to place our gear among hay bales. We reasoned that, with the briefing they would be given, the students would probably conduct reconnaissance of nearby farms. For us, it would be a matter of waiting. In the meantime, we set up a stove and brewed tea, speaking in hushed tones as we made our camp site comfortable as well as unobtrusive. Then we concealed ourselves and waited.

Late in the afternoon Eric alerted suddenly, held his hand up to one ear, and silently gestured to a nearby field of mature maize. I did not hear what had alerted Eric, but I concentrated eyes and ears on the field and heard a soft, dull clunking sound, suggesting that a person carrying equipment was nearby. I nodded to Eric and focused on the corn. When stalks moved near the front rank, I raised my rifle and opened fire with blanks, while Eric bolted in a flanking move to get in behind the observer. With no avenue of retreat, the recruit quickly surrendered. While interrogating him about his intentions, we took away rifle, blank ammunition, equipment, and, ultimately, even his uniform. He eventually told us he had been operating alone, and a check of the tracks in the field he entered seemed to confirm this.

To make our point about the risks of being captured, our prisoner was ordered to sit on the hood of the Land Rover as we drove back to the main camp, past sentries, to the supply truck, where we "liberated" ammunition and pyrotechnics. Leaving our prisoner standing cold, damp, and naked, Eric wheeled the vehicle out of the camp as I threw thunder flash grenade simulators toward sentries and vehicles. We left the camp in an uproar, looking for an undiscovered position to lay up for the night, hopefully as dry as the one the conscientious recruit had just compromised.

It rained at least once a day for the entire duration of the Goromonzi exercises. Farmers rejoiced as their fields of corn burst forth from the rich soil, and there was speculation about a bumper tobacco crop. Despite sanctions, the Rhodesian tobacco crop seemed always to be in international demand, and it was an important source of foreign exchange for a country that prided itself on careful, pragmatic fiscal management.

By day, we were pursued by increasingly competent recruit patrol officers. Never actually cornered and caught, we were nevertheless chased relentlessly and forced to hide several times. I found myself hugging the reverse side of an ant mound while insects paraded over me and through my clothes as I lay as still as possible—trying to mask heavy breathing as my "enemy" walked feet away, scanning the surrounds for anything that might have given our presence away. We successfully evaded as they passed by, heading the opposite direction, in the hope there was no follow-up element behind the sweep. As the exercises progressed, I became ever more certain that I never wanted to be pursued like a wild animal frightened by a line of distant beaters.

Rhodesia's farmers typically built at least one large brick tobacco barn on their property. Many were constructed of homemade bricks by talented African masons. These barns were heated to dry tobacco, and they were a welcome refuge in which to dry damp clothing. The luxury of emerging from a barn with dry socks on and a partially dry uniform was not lost on me. The farmers and their families were invariably very hospitable; many were glad to have any security force presence in the area because of its deterrent value both to insurgents and potential criminals. We were invariably invited into the house or the veranda for refreshments and talk, though there was not often much time available to us.

Eric and I did manage to find our way into the tiny community at Goromonzi in the evening. This was a cluster of homes and offices there that provided services to the rural community surrounding it. There was a government forester, the postmaster, agriculture advisers, teachers—and, of course, the police. The Goromonzi Club was a gathering point for the community, much as the institution of the village pub exists in England. The club was the social epicenter of a community where there were no strangers.

With only an occasional downpour for ablution, we probably would not have been welcome in more genteel surrounds; but rural Rhodesians were used to receiving men into their midst fresh from a patrol. Our muddy knees and damp camouflage jackets caused not even an eyebrow to rise. We crowded up to the tiny bar, relished the first mouthful of chilled Lion lager, and looked around for friendly faces.

A spirited dart game was under way. A few couples sat at tables, while the remainder found places on stools and in clusters at the bar. A patient

African barman trotted back and forth with a metal tray crowded with frosted pint bottles of beer. Eric was well known at the Goromonzi Club, and I was quickly drawn into the fold of farmers, public servants, and bored wives looking for adventure. I was grateful for the opportunity to meet and enjoy these people, and I more than once reflected on the good fortune that had teamed me with Eric Kennelly.

As the COIN training neared completion, there were final map-reading exercises and cross-country marches. By its very topographic nature, Goromonzi is an excellent location to teach and learn map reading. The multitude of granite *kopjes* and ridgelines, many with visible trig beacons on the high ground, easily translated to understandable single-dimension contour lines on our government maps. My map courses took me through cultivated fields of maize or tobacco, but we also ranged into the wilder slopes and crests of the granite outcroppings that were real Africa: troops of baboons, the occasional native antelope, and even the distinctive pug marks of a leopard. Eagles soared overhead, and I reveled in the social activities of communal weaver birds nesting together in select trees.

Goromonzi was my indoctrination to rural Africa—and as luck would have it, my last night in the Rhodesian bush would be spent there, far sooner than I had imagined.

CHAPTER 3

Policing Rhodesia

RETURNING TO THE ROUTINE of Morris Depot was a letdown after the experience of COIN training at Goromonzi. My academic requirements for pass-out on the abbreviated training program were virtually complete; unfortunately for me, the depot commandant, Chief Superintendent G. B. "Dumbo" Dunn was on annual leave. I soon learned that my future was in limbo until he returned from a family holiday and could review and sign my service records.

Once again, my days began with PT sessions under the direction of Mike Lambourne, after which it was normally possible to take refuge in the law and police instructor's office for further study of the various laws and acts that would soon surround me. Then there were afternoons at the police armory working for Eric Kennelly. Eric found time for us to walk to the nearby miniature range to test fire weaponry and practice with handguns. The depot range was a tall brick wall with earth piled up against it to act as a bullet trap. It was possible to fire at ranges of about thirty meters with weapons up to 7.62 NATO caliber. Surrounded by stands of eucalyptus, we tested weapons in anticipation of musketry classes for new recruits. I was told I had potential as a weapons instructor, but I never seriously considered asking for assignment to the BSAP main training facility.

I would soon have to decide what direction my police service was to take. Though my ambition initially was to accept a rural posting at a remote police district, I wasn't certain the time was right to make that commitment. I did not feel that I knew either the country or the job well enough yet to make a good decision straight out of training. Moreover, Jennifer had arrived in Rhodesia to be with me. She had become a close friend and lover, and it did not seem to make sense to complicate our lives with an immediate rural assignment.

Brian Cullingworth was once more a fount of good advice, a man with more than a decade of experience across the country, who understood the unique ways of the BSAP and its corps of senior officers. Brian had been reassigned from PGHQ to Salisbury Central as duty inspector, one of a sequence of his previous commands that included stations at Stodart and Matchipisa. Why not, he suggested, take a posting to Salisbury Central? This option seemed more logical the more I thought about it.

In the meantime, Jennifer had found a job as a bookkeeper for a developer with offices in central Salisbury. We saw each other on Sundays and occasionally in the evening.

When Chief Superintendent Dunn returned to his desk at Morris Depot, I had decided to accept a posting to Salisbury Central, perhaps a mile away from training depot. In the small, old building that had housed successive depot commanders since the turn of the century, the commandant wished me well in my new posting, gave me the name of the station chief inspector, and told me where to report the next morning.

With orders in hand, I returned to my depot quarters and began packing my gear. Old Penny had done a credible job of readying my new leather leggings and belt for my first station inspection. Bunky Gavin Rabie and other squad mates gathered at my room to wish me well, most of them envious and mindful of more than four months more training before them. At the appointed time, Jennifer arrived in my VW to fetch me and my gear. Together, we drove past the old depot office and parade square, through Morris Depot's gates, and out into Salisbury. My career in the BSAP was about to officially begin.

Brian and Jo Cullingworth were then taking annual leave in South Africa. We had been entrusted with caretaking their home, a particularly useful arrangement while Jennifer and I made decisions about living arrangements. I arose very early the next morning and once again rechecked the summer uniform in which I was to report for duty. Creases on the shorts were sharply ironed, each shirt button securely fastened with metal keepers, and epaulette rank devices shiny and straight. I rebrushed my uniform cap for phantom lint, and then carefully rebuffed the leather cap strap. Finally, I carefully donned the uniform boots and leggings, polished to a high sheen, and my uniform belt. With Jennifer at the wheel, we set off through leafy suburban Salisbury to the central station.

The station was an imposing multistory structure in the old part of Salisbury, built on a corner in the 1930s on the pattern of a number of Rhodesia's government buildings. It was white, had pleasing lines suggestive of colonial architecture, and obviously was well cared for. The *stoep* was freshly polished, as were decorative brass plates and door knobs. Jennifer carefully double-parked the car so I could unravel myself from the passenger seat without marring my efforts at creating a smashing personal uniform turnout for my new officer commanding (OC). As I stood and turned to close the door, two passing patrol officers in summer uniform turned their heads, first in curiosity at who the new guy was, then more particularly to stare at tanned, blonde Jennifer in her white summer dress. I bade her good-bye and followed them to the main entry, asking for directions to the station chief inspector.

The chief inspector at Salisbury Central functioned in much the same way as a British army regimental sergeant major. It was he who screened visitors to Assistant Commissioner Terry Thorpe. Brusk, somewhat officious, he let me stand in front of his desk while examining my paperwork. I had not been assigned to a particular branch. He mused out loud that there were openings in the plain clothes Crime Prevention Unit (CPU), normally an entrée to the Criminal Investigation Division (CID). And there seemed to be a slot at the Enquiries Office too. He noted that I had not yet attended police driving school and thus could not drive official vehicles. Finally, he announced that the provincial commander would see me. "Wait here," he announced and strode out into the hall, his heels clicking down the polished passage.

Moments later, I was standing to attention in front of the assistant commissioner's desk, rendering my best salute. A fatherly figure neatly turned out in a summer tunic bearing several rows of ribbons indicating World War II service, the assistant provincial commander stood and asked me to take a seat. The chief inspector, clearly uncomfortable at this sort of familiarity between senior officers and recruits, took a chair on the side of the office.

It was a bright, unpretentious office. Casement windows stood open, permitting garden perfume from the courtyard below to waft in. I quickly took in a number of book titles and shelf memorabilia that suggested something about his background.

After assimilating the lessons and lore of the regiment at training depot, I was unprepared for a conversation in which the OC treated me almost with deference. He was interested to know of my experience in Vietnam, the nature of my duties as well as a general appreciation of the war situation. I spoke openly and frankly—and he listened, eventually telling me he had been a naval aviator in the Royal Navy. Clearly, he had seen a good deal of active service, and I sensed an understanding of my own feelings about the Vietnam War, which was even then grinding horribly onward toward eventual disaster, although nobody could predict when the end might come. Rhodesians clearly recognized a common enemy in the communist North Vietnamese and their allies—the Soviets and Chinese.

My next interview was with Chief Superintendent Jim Collins, who asked about my duty preferences. Jimmy Collins had grown up in a tough London neighborhood, answered the call to duty during World War II, and was awarded the Distinguished Flying Cross as a ball turret gunner on a Royal Air Force bomber over Germany. Would I like to return to criminal investigation eventually—perhaps I might like to work plain clothes at the Crime Prevention Unit, he asked? Though most new patrol officer coveted an assignment to CPU, I was certain it was not what I wanted to do. I wanted to wear a uniform, mix with the people, learn about Rhodesia and Rhodesians of all varieties—particularly native Africans. I wanted also to assume minor command responsibilities; despite my officer-like status in the Navy, I had never commanded men, nor was I trained to do so.

I accepted an assignment in the Enquiries Office, where minor crimes were investigated by uniformed personnel. It would mean day shifts only, and my office space would be in the central police station.

I soon learned that there was a trade-off for a permanent day job—the type of cases the Enquiries section handled. When offenses were reported and could not be resolved in the same shift, they were referred to us, unless the offenses were serious enough to spark the interest of CID, upstairs. From working complex espionage investigations for the U.S. government, my first cases were about stolen articles of personal clothing, or a case of alleged public exposure. The trivia in my case load might have been a source of aggravation, except for the leadership of my member in charge, Chief Inspector Dave George. Dave had come to Africa from the hard life of Midlands England and had the characteristic broad accent of that region. With a twinkle in his eye, he was heard to counsel frustrated subordinates: "Just remember; somebody has to do it."

Despite the simplicities in common investigative practice, the Enquiries section was an excellent grounding for me. I shared a sparse, high-ceilinged office equipped with several small wooden tables with a team of patrol officers and African constables. The BSAP remained in the mode of starting their young, usually well-educated members of European extraction as patrol officers—who were expected to quickly learn qualities of leadership and management in much the way a junior military officer does. Thus, I found myself working in a pool of African policemen who had vast street experience, linguistic skills, and procedural competencies that I did not. I was keen to learn from them. I watched them interview and interrogate; I offered to attend arrests and witness interviews in Salisbury and the nearby townships. I always learned something.

Rhodesians of different ethnicities seldom lived together or shared activities outside those of the workplace. While there was no active segregation practiced, economic factors in the civilian world dictated that most native Africans lived in townships designed for the workforce—or on their traditional land holdings. Government housing, particularly that intended for army or police personnel, was assigned according to rank. This was the way of the British Raj and the way Britain had administered its colonies around the world. Rhodesia was slow to change, but changing it was; both the BSAP and the armed services were moving to liberalize the rank structure to accommodate exceptional African members in the upper rank structure. To me at the time, Rhodesia felt like I had always imagined a British colony, perhaps thirty years earlier. I sensed no resentment whatever in the ranks of the Africans with whom I worked; but I began to recognize that Rhodesia's leaders would soon need imaginative solutions to help them realize their professional potential and recognized standing.

With the practical lessons provided by my African peers and patrol officers of European extraction, I began also to learn small lessons about leading Africans. I was older than most of my patrol officer companions at Enquiries. The constables were curious about me—where I had come from, what I had done, and most of all, why an American would choose to work in Africa. With that curiosity, several of my African colleagues gradually began to create opportunities for me to learn about them. I accepted it as a challenge to find out what they expected of a leader, even one with less experience in Rhodesian law enforcement than them.

My life settled quickly into a pleasant routine. High-altitude Salisbury enjoyed exceptionally fine weather. Jennifer and I enjoyed the banks of flowers carefully attended by gardener Fanwell in the Cullingworth garden and discussed the results of her daily house-hunting efforts. We were determined to find our own house to rent before the Cullingworths returned from leave. Chief Inspector George had fended off efforts by the station

Chief Inspector Dave George holds a morning inspection of the Enquiries section, Salisbury Central Police Station, while a bemused Section Officer John Sutton looks on. (Author collection)

chief inspector to assign me a room in Fife Avenue Hostel, where Salisbury's bachelor patrol officers were quartered in a large building reminiscent of an English public school. In a country with the moral standards of 1950, which prided itself on being more British than Britain, overt cohabitation was frowned on—and certainly not within the parameters of the discipline code known as The Police Act. We would be careful not to rub anybody's nose in our living arrangements.

Police shifts were typically begun formally each morning with a short parade and inspection convened under cover in the parking area behind the station. Longtime friend Section Officer Angus Rufus was leading a traffic enforcement team that often paraded next to us, where Angus checked each of the snowy-white visibility sleeves for smudges before his charges went forth to police Salisbury's motorists. Inspections were a convenient venue for our member in charge to address the section as a whole while also satisfying himself that every uniform was worn exactly as required. Standards of turnout remained high.

The only hitch to my new assignment was my inability to drive police vehicles. Recruits were normally dispatched directly from Morris Depot to the police driving school upon pass-out and before assignment to their first stations. That had not occurred when I accepted my posting to Salisbury Central. It was accepted that at some point, the Enquiries section would send me off for several weeks of training, but the dates for this remained open to conjecture. In the meantime, I became adroit at scrounging rides from other Enquiries members, most often on the back of a police motorcycle. Motorcycles had been a transportation mainstay of the force from the early days when they began to replace trooper's horses as a mode of rural transportation to effect police business. Patrol officers were exhaustively trained to ride their two-wheeled charges safely, and they were expected to do so even when weather was unkindly. Traditionally—and until sanctions took hold—British 650cc-twin Matchless motorcycles were procured for the BSAP. But in 1974 the Japanese had aggressively marketed trucks and motorcycles to Rhodesia; we were riding two-stroke 350cc Yamahas.

I suspect the sight of two large men in uniform on a police motorcycle must have been more a source of amusement than deterrence to crime.

On occasion, a gray Land Rover could be used—particularly if an arrest was to be made. These were equipped with stone guard grillwork over all windows and with internal weapon-carrying racks.

In those first weeks of assignment, I began to learn the layout of central Salisbury and appreciate the multitude of trees and well-tended parks and points of historical interest. The original pioneers of the British South Africa Company had carefully laid out streets to allow for the expansion of government and commerce together. Courts, parliament, and government buildings all were within easy walking distance of the central business district.

The BSAP maintained a domestic reaction force in Salisbury, ready to respond to public disturbance or disaster. Known simply as riot standby, it was a duty shared by personnel assigned to stations in the city and suburbs. My turn to serve came up soon after my assignment to Salisbury Central. For a week, I would be assigned to the police camp in suburban Cranborne. I carefully packed every conceivable type of uniform and equipment I might need: three summer uniforms, blue riot gear, boots, helmet, and so forth. On the morning my duty was to begin, Jennifer drove me to Cranborne and helped me move into a small, spare room.

In charge of my small group was Section Officer (S/O) Nigel Bothwell. A keen weight trainer, Nigel's imposing bulk had earned him national recognition in the Mr. Rhodesia titles. Then assigned to one of Salisbury's suburban stations, S/O Bothwell knew the riot standby routine well.

Section Officer Nigel Bothwell, left, gives assignments to his riot standby detail, Salisbury, Rhodesia. (Author collection)

Our shifts would normally start in the late afternoon and extend into the night. But we began the deployment with a refresher course on crowd control and riot management, turning out on the parade square in the uniform known as riot blues. We donned gas masks and helmets, practiced formations, and even practiced how we exited our vehicles. It was a clear, warm day. Though we were all fit and healthy, our uniforms were quickly soaked in sweat.

That evening, Nigel Bothwell's team set out in several gray police Land Rovers, with five or six men in each. Nigel drove the vehicle I was assigned to; I took a spot on one of the side-mounted rear bench seats behind the radio man. In the rifle rack were FN rifles, a Browning 12-gauge semiautomatic shotgun, and several single-shot Greener 12 gauges. I shoved my feet across the vehicle to stretch out, and we headed for Salisbury's main African township, then called Harare. If there were no calls for our assistance, we would show the flag and let the citizenry know we were close at hand in the event of trouble.

Nigel drove us patiently into the township's dusty streets, looking constantly for signs of trouble. There were none, yet, but there was plenty of evidence that the people of Harare were intent on enjoying their Saturday night. Wonderful, spontaneous African music and singing wafted out of *shebeens* and beer halls, and when we stopped for a closer look, I walked into huge beer halls where native beer was being consumed in enormous volume. Happy, smiling patrons lined up milk cartons of Chibuku beer on the metal tables before them and drank as though each sip might be their last. On an elevated platform, a band bumped out African melodies with a collection of guitars and percussion instruments. In front of them, appreciative patrons of both genders shuffled and swayed to earthy rhythms, sweating in the closed atmosphere. My colleagues looked around with a practiced eye. There was no trouble. There were drunks, but they were not bellicose drunks—although this was all subject to change on a moment's notice.

Harare township was normally policed by a hard-working team of constables and patrol officers who seemed to thrive on the regular diet of mayhem and death that typified the area. In 1974 it was not an overtly political environment and whatever violence that brewed up was normally of the domestic variety. When crimes occurred, victims—and often the accused—would take themselves to the nearest police station and there patiently await the next policeman available to hear and report the details. Arrests were made, statements taken, the injured interviewed—and the deceased transported to Harare Hospital's morgue. Nigel Bothwell was well aware of the extraordinary workload our compatriots at Harare station faced, and he did his best to position us to render assistance.

My first experience with a rioting African mob occurred late one weekday night when a traffic fatality was reported at one of the bus depots that serviced the people of Harare. We arrived a few minutes after a patrol officer from Harare station and his constable. A bus passenger, attempting to board an overcrowded bus, had slipped from the entry door and was run over by the bus. The body remained trapped under the vehicle, and a crowd quickly gathered. The crowd was restive, milling around, becoming noisy—and I sensed that somebody was agitating them. When the Harare policemen managed to extract the young man's body and place it in the back of their light truck, the crowd surged forward and the first stones were thrown. As the body-bearing vehicle pulled away, Nigel ordered us back to our vehicles, and with everybody accounted for, we drove a short distance away to regroup. There, one of constables explained that two older women in the crowd had been inciting those around them and had actually told people the police were responsible for the young victim's death. They would be arrested.

Stone throwing was simply not tolerated in Rhodesia—and the citizenry were well aware of it. Throwing a rock was akin to attempted murder; the rioter could expect to be shot.

Perhaps three minutes after driving away, the riot standby Land Rovers had regrouped and were back at the bus depot. The crowd knew we were heavily armed. There were no stones thrown, and no resistance was mounted as arrests were made. To me, it was yet another example of how the BSAP had adapted good British policing to unique African conditions.

I quickly learned that life in Harare was a lot more basic and potentially violent than in some of the more genteel suburbs of Salisbury. It was not that dissimilar to some of California's cities in that respect, but there was a uniquely African feel to much that I saw while assigned to riot standby. Harare Hospital provided modern medical treatment and facilities for its citizens, most of it altogether without fee. Rhodesia levied a hefty income tax on its workers, but those whose income was sufficient to attract tax were in the minority—and it was they who supported the less fortunate, largely without complaint. The hospital was one such example of this largesse, and its mixed staff worked long hours to treat African patrons.

Our business was in the morgue. It was perhaps 2:00 AM when we walked through quiet corridors past wards where patients slumbered under mosquito nets. The morgue was in a nearby outbuilding, old but clean and neat. Refrigeration compressors clattered in the background as I entered a large room lit only with several exposed overhead light bulbs. The morgue was fully occupied; it having been a weekend of the usual mishaps, accidents, and mortality. The attendant opened doors to the refrigerated areas where stainless steel trays held the deceased, and there was a tint of death in the air. I had seen it all before in other times; there was really nothing notable until the last door was pulled open. There, piled like firewood on the trays, were dead babies, the victims of a recent influenza outbreak. I wasn't shocked as much as taken aback. This was indeed life at its most real, without any pretence.

Our business completed, I thought about it more in the dark quiet hours of that night before the shift ended while the African constable sharing the bench seat dozed off as we slowly navigated quiet streets and laneways in the township. Vietnam, a memory I lived with daily, had been a massive, high-tech meat grinder just waiting to grab up the unwary or unfortunate victim. In many ways there had been a surrealism to that experience and the seemingly endless ways death was visited on both friendlies and the enemy. Conversely, Salisbury had not an inkling of the war zone about it—but I was coming to understand that Rhodesians lived a life much closer to hard reality than most cosseted Americans. It was perhaps this that forged much of the national persona I had grown to appreciate so much. These were people who were not shy about gripping life by the horns. The country played hard; they cared about each other—they drank and partied. And they treated me like one of them. The more I thought about it, the more I became certain that Vietnam had changed me indelibly—and in ways few Americans other than those who had shared the experience would understand. While Rhodesians could scarcely grasp the vast panoply that was Vietnam, there was often a tacit personal warmth emanated toward me, a sharp contrast to the indifference or hostility common in hometown America. I had no intention of settling permanently in Africa—but it was feeling a lot more comforting there than in the United States.

There was a further unusual experience for a new member of the force: we were assigned to provide extra security at the High Court of Rhodesia, where captured insurgents were on trial. I waited for my cue from Nigel Bothwell as he drove one of two Land Rovers into central Salisbury. We were amply supplied with weaponry, but I had learned that the BSAP were loath to display firearms unless there was an imminent likelihood of actually using them.

"We're not expecting trouble," he explained. "But the prison service would like to have extra people around when the prisoners are brought in—and there is the possibility of trouble from spectators."

Rhodesia's High Court was an imposing structure built many years before in the colonial style of the day, in much the same manner as nearby government buildings and the parliament. We had just walked up to the old building when a vintage dark green Bedford prison truck arrived at the alleyway and quickly wheeled into the courtyard. A smartly turned-out African warder hopped from the cab and trotted around to the rear doors of the steel truck enclosure and opened securing padlocks. The two doors groaned as he swung them wide and issued an order to two prisoners within. I heard scraping and the sound of rattling chains as two men helped each other from the enclosure and down steps to the ground. Both were neatly dressed in the tan shorts and shirts of Salisbury prison.

The prisoners were full-blooded native African males in their early twenties. The shorter of the two was missing a leg below the knee, the still-angry red scars of the amputation evident on a short stump that waggled below his shorts. A manacle secured his remaining ankle to that of his partner, who assisted him. With handcuffs on as well, the two hopped and shuffled in front of the warder and toward the chamber entrance.

There were a few curious onlookers on the sidewalk, all African, but no signs of a gathering or of possible unrest. Our vehicles, discretely parked nearby, were under guard. There would be no display of force in this instance. I had been preparing myself for a possible confrontation, but in their usual low-key way, my colleagues had avoided even a hint of trouble.

The prisoners, I was told, had been captured with their weapons after a firefight with Rhodesian security forces. The amputee's leg had been shattered by rifle fire in the contact. Although I did not hear testimony from the police forensics examiner, I knew that evidence about the captured assault rifles would be presented at their trial. If the weapons had been used in previous attacks, that would be verified by expert examination of spent cartridges and bullets and that evidence presented to the court. Thus, these two prisoners were facing capital charges and might be hanged if found guilty.

As the court session progressed under the tall ceilings of the somber chamber that was the High Court, I found myself staring at the accused, wondering what their stories were—where they had been born and what had lead them to take up arms and terrorize their countrymen. Both were quiet, even somber. They had likely become even closer by their shared adversity in prison. They sat quietly through the proceedings, as did spectators—many of whom were Africans.

I reminded myself that in many ways, 1974 Rhodesia was in a similar state to what postwar Britain had been. There were shortages, rationing, and a certain amount of adversity. The law of the land and social mores reflected this, as did the conservative, Churchillian attitudes of government leaders and many citizens. Premeditated homicide was punishable by hanging, just as it had been in Britain. So too were certain offenses associated with terrorism, which were prosecuted in much the same manner as a murder.

Sensing my pensive contemplation of the proceedings, Nigel Bothwell ventured a comment: "White offenders are hanged in Rhodesia too," he said.

As much as anything, the somber court with its scores of old memories and the pitiful amputee had made me introspective. There were fresh memories of captured, injured Viet Cong prisoners fresh in my mind too. These did not detract, I reminded myself, from the awful acts these people had committed against their people. It was the same in Rhodesia.

The riot standby experience ended at the end of the week. We gathered in the police canteen at Cranborne, where many of the BSAP bachelors assigned to traffic duties were billeted, and shared a few beers to say good-bye. Nigel Bothwell and I would soon be seeing much more of each other, although we did not then realize it. Jennifer met me to take me and my gear home—and she had news. We had a house to move to.

Jennifer had located and signed a lease for a modest three-bedroom home on about three-quarters of an acre in the northern suburb of Marlborough. The owners, a young family, had transferred to Bulawayo. The rent was $100 a month. We drove out after my shift ended to have a look at 1 Newstead Road for the first time. We found it on a corner, shielded by high hedges of hibiscus and a gated fence, much like every other home on the street. With young but maturing jacaranda trees and pines planted along the gravel driveway, it looked to be a very welcoming place to make a home. I liked it even before we put the key in the entry door. I had never really had a home to call my own, a private refuge, even if it my name was not on the title. I was ready to make a home, as I think Jennifer was also.

Built on a concrete slab with solid brick plastered internal and external walls, the single-level home stretched diagonally across a rectangular corner lot. There were small steel casement windows that gave it something of the air of an English cottage, a modest brick fireplace, and parquetry floors throughout. The kitchen was basic. We would need to find both a refrigerator and an electric stove—and we had not even a stick of furniture.

None of that seemed very much like a problem. I found the remnants of a vegetable garden that looked potentially viable, noted that there was a overhead cover for the car and servant's quarters in the rear. It seemed comfortable, friendly, and even a little palatial.

Between the two of us, we scraped together enough cash to buy a Rhodesian-manufactured refrigerator and electric range. There wasn't much left from our monthly paychecks, so I decided to see if a furniture store might extend us at least short-term credit on a bed. The next day, one of the senior patrol officers in the Enquiries section sold us a small table with two straight-back chairs. Flushed with success at this budgetary win, I walked into central Salisbury to a furniture store and spoke to management about the credit and finance plans they were advertising in their display window. Knowing exactly what a single-bar patrol officer made, the manager declined my application. I was offended. Ultimately, my bank extended modest overdraft facilities to me, but only after Ormonde Power acted as guarantor.

We moved in with our table, two chairs, and a bed—and with some basic crockery acquired at a trade store. My issue uniforms took up an entire hall closet. We were soon joined by an irascible old Shona domestic named Enoch. A friend of the Cullingworth's servant, Peter, Enoch was said to run a tight ship and understood how to launder and maintain uniforms. After long days at work, we could expect to arrive home to a clean house.

A final and important acquisition was the dog. Because I was often likely to be away from home, a watchdog made sense. Jennifer identified the candidate at Salisbury's Society for the Prevention of Cruelty to Animals refuge, a large young male Rhodesian Ridgeback that we promptly named Roscoe.

Roscoe seemed to settle in with us almost immediately. A great jumper, as one might expect a lion-hunting hound from the African veld to be, he was always at home for us in the evening, despite his disquieting habit of leaping the gate to pursue our bicycle-riding African postman.

Life was very pleasant. Rhodesians loved to gather at the weekends for long, lazy afternoons of cooking and socializing and swimming and storytelling. Ian and Jean Bullock, formerly of New Guinea, were close neighbors, as were Jean's parents, Don and Eleanor Holmes. All were very kind about including us in weekend festivities—and I was reminded how lucky I was to have day shifts with most weekends free.

It was only a matter of weeks before I received a summons to report to a senior officer upstairs at Salisbury Central. There a young superintendent asked me whether I would consider transferring across to the police Support Unit. By this time, because of my friendship with Ormonde Power, I knew much more about what the organization did and was impressed by the leadership opportunities such an assignment might bring with it. I told my inquisitor that I was favorably disposed to a transfer, and I asked him for permission to visit the unit to learn more about what was envisioned for me before providing a definite answer.

Support Unit was on the verge of enormous expansion. From a corps of about six troops, it was set to more than triple in size. This was, at least initially, designed so that new Support Unit constables could be used to provide security for the extensive road building and infrastructure improvements then under way in northeastern Rhodesia—where most insurgent activity had occurred. The enemy was not in favor of new roads and improvements that might be seen to curry favor with the native African citizens of the region; they had begun attacking road building gangs and mining roads. I learned that force farrier Chief Inspector Bill Coetzer had been ordered over to Tomlinson Depot to oversee training the vast new force—and Bill had asked me to assist him with that task. That made my decision simple; Bill Coetzer was a fine leader for whom I would gladly work.

Back at Salisbury Central, I told Chief Inspector George of my decision and began waiting for the transfer machinery to process me out, and into my new job. Administrators noted that I had not yet attended police driving school and decided that I should not be reassigned without a police driver's license. I was to be sent to learn driving in the mold of the Hendon System, the training doctrine of London's Metropolitan Police.

Jennifer and I took one of our weekends to drive up to Rhodesia's northern border at Lake Kariba. Although gasoline was rationed, we had carefully horded enough extra coupons for the drive, so, with Roscoe ensconced across most of the rear area of the VW, we set off early on a beautiful Saturday morning. I had not seen Kariba since my single-day flying visit in 1971 when Angus Rufus was my host; Jennifer had not yet experienced the heat, animals, and smells of low veld Africa, and I had not seen the country between.

We hummed along the well-maintained two-lane road northward, enjoying views across open fields, occasionally broken by forest groves. This was grazing country, typical high veld Rhodesia. A little more than an hour later, we were pulling into Sinoia. I turned off the highway and into the town center. We were both curious about rural Rhodesian towns: what there might be to see, what facilities and services were available, and what the town might be like to live in. We saw shops frequented mostly by farmers and their helpers—pickup trucks loaded with sacks of feed, tools, and Africans being driven by florid, robust-looking ranchers in khaki short sleeve shirts and hats. The district court was quiet, but there was ample activity at the police station, where we watched a rural patrol about to leave the vehicle yard. A gray BMW sedan driven by a section officer pulled in as we drove past, the highway patrol for the day.

We were restless to experience the warmth of the low veld and were soon driving northward again, and eventually, after the turn off at Makuti, the road began to descend into the great valley through which the Zambezi River flows. We rolled down the windows to take in the warm, rich smells of the bush and watched as the trees and foliage changed. As we rounded a corner, a huge baobab tree was a firm reminder that we had arrived in tropical Africa. So too was a roadblock manned by neatly uniformed government agriculture employees, there to ensure that passing cars were not inadvertently carrying tetse flies, a risk both to the health of humans and cattle.

Finally, in the distance we caught a glimpse of the azure shades of Lake Kariba, marking the northern border of Rhodesia. The brown hills of Zambia lay beyond. Soon, we were slowly driving through the narrow, winding roads of Kariba town, constructed on sharp, small hills that rose from the water's edge. Originally established as a hostelry for the mainly Italian artisans who labored several years in the 1950s to dam the waters of the mighty Zambezi River, Kariba had grown to accommodate a small tourism industry as well as various government contingencies. It had become a pleasant, small outpost where nobody was a stranger.

A small guest cottage was maintained at the police camp for use by force members and their families. The sleepy young African domestic was sweeping the veranda as we pulled up to unload. Our quarters were spartan but airy, clean, and pleasant. With the doors standing open, there were views of rugged, brown hills shimmering in the heat, and we watched a Martial Eagle gliding effortlessly in the updraft created by heat rising from the Zambezi River gorge below the dam. There were hornbills that came looking for our crumbs and evidence that wart hogs passed nearby in their daily migrations. We sat in the quiet of an early afternoon, when the only sounds to be heard were humming insects and the distant call of the eagle.

On that first late afternoon at about 4:00 PM, we walked the narrow path to the Jam Jar for sundowners.

There were already one or two early arrivals, propped at the stone bar with cold pints of ale. I introduced us to the two off-duty patrol officers, and we moved up to take our own refreshments. I looked around quickly, taking it all in and wondering what had changed. There was a massive pair of ivory tusks attached to stone support pillars that I could not recall having seen before; there were several framed photographs, a goat skull with ping pong balls for eyes—and behind the bar looking a little dusty was the silk banner I had sent from the Mekong Delta to thank BSAP Police Kariba for their hospitality in 1971. On it were words carefully embroidered in red, white, and blue. It said, simply, "Ho Chi Minh Kiss My Ass." I chuckled and pointed it out to Jennifer.

When my fellow drinkers realized that I was the source of the banner, some animated conversation ensued: What had brought me to Rhodesia? What was happening in the Vietnam War? Why didn't America realize that the same bastards were terrorizing innocent folks in Rhodesia?

Books could have been written about most of the topics these sincere young men raised in the best of faith. While they were both products of the excellent Rhodesian education system, neither had ever been outside of Africa, never been exposed to good foreign media or alternative ideas. I did my best to explain what I understood: America was trying to save a non-perfect South Vietnamese nation from communist aggressors who had not even admitted to the world that their national army was even then killing innocent southerners and attempting to overrun the South. Despite the open assistance of the USSR and Red China for the North, support for the conflict among America's citizenry was waning, with the South Vietnamese left to do more without direct U.S. military support. I hoped they could persevere; there wasn't much more that I could say to them, although conversation always seemed to stir memories and concerns about people and places I had left behind two years before.

There was even less that I could say to them about the U.S. attitude toward Africa—Rhodesia in particular. It seemed that Rhodesia's declaration of independence had given certain British elements enough political ammunition to rally forces in the United Nations and implement sanctions against their erring kin in Africa. British Commonwealth nations, many recently independent, were firmly against a white government in Rhodesia—no matter what might be anticipated from a black nationalist alternative—because Rhodesia's native Africans did not yet enjoy universal suffrage. My young colleagues reminded me that it was all well and good to take on lofty ideals; the fact remained that the Brits in the cozy security of their isle did not have to live with whatever a still-developing African population might vote into government, whether freely or under the sort of coercion the nationalists had already employed to gain support.

"Britain doesn't give a shit about us," one said. "They are just kissing black arses in the Commonwealth and the UN."

I had to admit that the evidence seemed to support what he was saying. But it was no solution to the problem. Hopefully, the world would give Rhodesia enough time to sort out its own problems from within—and allow more worthy Africans to take an active role in government and public service. I couldn't explain why atrocities by communist-trained insurgents did not seem to matter in the global forum.

As the conversation drifted away to more neutral topics, I reflected to myself over another beer. These were bright, well-intentioned young men who wanted to live normal lives—marry and raise children and educate them—all in the environs that they and their parents and grandparents had done so much to create. I could not see that a spontaneous handing over of power would be to the benefit of any segment of the population, except power-oriented ideologues. Moreover, I had spent most of my adult life exposed to the true intentions and methods the USSR and its satellites employed to expand power and influence. I hoped fervently that Rhodesia would be given a chance, would somehow find a way to achieve its own rebirth.

Jennifer and I had enjoyed our weekend away at Kariba. We'd made new friends, had been given promises of boat trips out on the lake on future visits, and had seen and enjoyed some of the smaller of Africa's natural menagerie. We drove back on a warm Sunday afternoon to our Salisbury home. The low veld had reminded me again of the excitement and intense pleasures of the African bush experience. I found myself looking forward to the next adventure, which was to be police driving school.

Ormonde Power had told me that I could expect to spend time behind the wheel at Support Unit. I would not, however, be driving police patrol vehicles. Support Unit was equipped with troop transport trucks, Land Rovers, and an assortment of mine-hardened tactical vehicles. It made little sense for me to come across until I was authorized to drive police vehicles, and that meant passing various training courses at the driving school in Cranborne, where I had recently been assigned riot standby duties.

On a Monday morning, I reported early to the school and checked in at the office. I had been expected. My instructor, I was told, would be Mr. Jamieson. I could wait in the classroom with the other personnel taking the course.

I made my way to one of the buildings that had housed Royal Air Force Bomber Command training during World War II. Rhodesia's superb high veld weather had been an attraction to the British airmen who trained bomber crews for the war against Germany in a climate where few days were lost to the poor weather that has always dogged the British Isles.

The old building had been well maintained, but little had changed during the previous three decades. The classroom had chalkboards along one wall, the ceilings were high, and small, steel casement windows opened to capture morning breezes. In one corner of the room were cutaway motors and transmissions, used as training aids for young people needing to learn the mysteries of modern motor vehicles in a hurry. There was an assortment of tables and chairs, and several other new students were milling around, some chatting among themselves. A majority were new women patrol officers, yet to be assigned to their first police station. I was, by far, the oldest student present.

Moments later, Bob Jamieson strode into the room, dressed in neat khaki shirt, trousers, and uniform sweater. The room quieted, and I shifted my attentions to the front podium from the window, where a young standard poodle gamboled outside the classroom and rolled in the red dust of his yard.

In front of the young charges seated at tables facing him, Bob Jamieson broke the ice by explaining to the students—all recently in training at Morris Depot—that he was to be addressed simply as Mr. Jamieson, not "sir." That, I mused, might be difficult for some used to calling virtually anything sir in the recruit environment. Then he asked how many of those present held a valid driver's license. Many, but not all, held Rhodesian licenses. I had four valid licenses at the time: Australia, New Guinea, Texas, and U.S. military heavy equipment.

Bob Jamieson was not a man meant for the classroom, and he wasted no time breaking the students into working groups and getting us into the field to drive. I soon learned that Jamieson, a former BSAP member, was a highly skilled driver and motorcyclist.

After undergoing classroom preliminaries that stressed traffic law and driving procedure, I found myself behind the wheel of a police Land Rover equipped with dual floor controls. Several colleagues sat on the rear side benches, while Bob Jamieson issued instructions from the front passenger seat. He had chosen open-road sections of Rhodesia's excellent highway system to evaluate each student's driving skills. I had driven police cars in the United States in emergency conditions, but that did very little to prepare me for the vagaries of what was basically a large, loaded four-wheel-drive truck at speed. The Land Rover had a tendency to drift and oversteer, although I did my best to power out of curves. I kept my thoughts to myself, quietly observing that I hoped never to have to reach a location in a hurry while driving this particular machine.

The BSAP had adopted the driving system that had been developed by the Metropolitan Police Driving School at Hendon, England. Responding to concerns about unacceptably high accident rates, the Met in the 1930s decided that every police driver needed to be trained in methods that would help ensure that police vehicles were operated safely and well. Drivers were initially taught the system's protocols and procedures for specific actions. These were recited in correct order by the instructor for the student to obey and assimilate while driving. We were taught how to stop a vehicle at a stop sign, according to the Hendon Method: brake, hand signal, bring the vehicle to a full stop, shift to neutral, engage hand brake. It seemed pedantic and unnecessary to some who had previous driving experience, but the effect was that drivers assimilated a method for essential maneuvers that had been developed over four decades. The method served as a foundation for further driver training courses where more advanced skills were taught.

Jamieson was a good instructor, and I enjoyed my time with him. I soon learned that the BSAP licensing program had distinct tiers according to the type of vehicle the candidate aspired to operate. Most policemen would not operate the few city patrol or traffic cars; thus, few were given the opportunity to take the course that stressed speed skills and defensive driving tactics. With a good driving record as a basic police driver and the recommendation of the appropriate officer, one might be given the opportunity to qualify for this second-tier police license. And, if particularly talented, one might ultimately aspire to a third-tier license for highway patrol duties. Few were recommended, and fewer still passed the rigorous cross-country driving course that might gain them entry to highway patrol duties.

In charge of highway patrol training was Section Officer Mike King, a former Kenya policeman. There were more than a few new patrol officers whose eyes became glassy when they saw one of the BSAP BMW highway patrol cars moving at speed. Section Officer King was fond of reminding them that there might be a place for them in the future—"if you're good enough." That was his way of encouraging the young charges to pay attention and assimilate the many skills that every instructor tried to impart.

I studied, passed my tests, and was qualified to drive Land Rovers, trucks, and other nonemergency vehicles. But it had all taken time, and Support Unit was apparently quietly asking the driving school if there was a way my instruction might be speeded along. The result was a pleasant one. Bob Jamieson agreed to take me on as a personal tutor for the final motorcycle phase. We had become friends, although that didn't change his penchant for driving learners hard to learn the skills.

One afternoon before my first lesson on two wheels, he summoned me to join him in a lesson for an aspiring city patrol car driver. I was attired in the summer police uniform of the BSAP, because it was desirable that the public was aware that the car being pursued by a police car was itself also manned by police, although I would certainly not be doing the driving!

Rhodesia's town police had driven full-sized British sedans—called B Cars—until recent years. When I visited in 1971, Austin Westminsters were used. By 1974 Peugeot 404 sedans patrolled the streets of Salisbury, and the

Patrol Officer Gerry De Bruin poses with an Austin Westminster B Car near Sinoia, Rhodesia. He was assigned to highway patrol duties at the time. (Courtesy Gerry De Bruin)

traffic branch was equipped with Alfa Romeo sedans, which had replaced the British Mini Cooper. Our candidate was to drive a Peugeot B Car in pursuit of a tiny gray 1200cc Daihatsu station wagon in the hands of the capable and elusive Bob Jamieson. I strapped myself into the passenger seat of the miniature station wagon and quietly wondered what I was in for. My law enforcement grounding had been in large American vehicles equipped with brute-force V8 engines. What kind of a contest would this be, pitting two four-cylinder cars against each other? I was soon to learn, as Bob bounced into the car with a wicked grin that told me he and the instructor in the B Car had some sort of a wager going.

The student driver was tasked with locating us, pursuing if necessary, and making a correct traffic stop. We drove quietly into one of Salisbury's quiet outer suburbs called Waterfalls and began traversing the streets. Bob clearly knew his way very well, and he intended to provide a vigorous test for the candidate and his mentor.

Waterfalls streets were quiet and largely empty. They were typically paved, with grass verges behind which gates, fences, and hedges marked front boundaries of the mostly modest homes. There were some curious stares, mostly from African domestics working in yards or walking along road verges, as they noticed a uniformed policeman in the car. But the curiosity factor increased exponentially when we were sighted by the B Car student as he passed on a right-angle street and caught a glimpse of us. The chase was on!

Knowing the student had taken the bait, Jamieson downshifted the Daihatsu two gears, accelerating away, with the tiny motor screaming for mercy. We ducked around the first corner, then quickly reversed into a partially hidden driveway, sitting with engine idling and the windows down to listen for our pursuers. The student took perhaps forty-five seconds to run a search grid. Catching a glimpse of the distinctive gray color of our vehicle, he braked quickly, passing on an adjoining street, intending to reverse and block us in. My instructor, anticipating this, again accelerated around a different corner, made two more turns, and reversed into a narrow road that skirted around a pile of boulders and balanced rocks towering thirty feet above us. With a grin and chuckle, he shut the motor off to listen for sounds of the pursuing Peugeot.

I relaxed, made myself comfortable, and enjoyed this little patch of unspoiled Africa. The balancing rocks had clearly been there for thousands of years in this setting of natural Africa. The only sounds were those of the breeze and a pair of birds in a nearby acacia tree. From time to time, we distantly heard the pursuing car, as the student carried out a further grid search.

On the driver side of the car was the rear property fence of an older home. In time, we caught the attention of the occupants of the domestic quarters. Two young Africans stood grinning at us from their side of the fence, and a few minutes later, they were joined by a giggling young African girl, a household nanny. We were becoming a center of attention. I wondered if the B Car driver would pass the other side of the property, notice curious people, and move to investigate. As it happened, that is exactly what he finally did. After a wait of nearly twenty minutes, the patrol car crept as quietly as possible up the laneway, blocking us in. There were broad smiles from the student and his mentor/instructor as we finally surrendered.

It was apparent from the outset that motorcycle instruction under the guiding hand of Bob Jamieson would be unforgettable. I had limited earlier motorcycling experience and took easily to balancing my machine, a battered two-stroke 350cc Yamaha police bike. My instructor rode a 360cc four-stroke single, a powerful machine with good handling characteristics on and off the road. We began by riding in tandem around the residential streets adjoining the school, then gradually progressed to the main thoroughfares. Here, the early lessons were very much about survival tactics, the process of learning to safely share streets and highways with larger vehicles. There would be an explanation of particular tactics followed by a demonstration. As I was his sole student, the lesson pace was very much about my apparent comfort learning the next set of skills. I learned defensive observation tricks to anticipate possible actions by other road users, I was shown how best to position my motorcycle on a two-lane road, and I practiced hand signals.

We were an odd pair. Jamieson dressed in his khaki shirt and trousers with a sweater and wearing a civilian crash helmet, being followed in every maneuver by me in my summer uniform, equipped with police helmet, shorts, and leather leggings.

With time, I graduated to the open highway, where I typically followed my mentor, practicing road positioning, watching how he coped with other road users and finally, learning how to set up the bike on corners. It was exhilarating, and we eventually began riding at speed through the road network around Salisbury.

To build confidence, strength, and balance, I was required to follow Bob on to dirt roads and trails that required a balance of power and balance to keep my machine upright. This, thankfully, was not done at great speed. "If you don't fall off at least once a day," he counseled me, "then you're not trying hard enough." And I did come off, usually while trying to balance the heavy street machine in an awkward climb or descent out in the dirt. It never hurt anything more than my pride, and when later I learned that my teacher had a steel plate in his skull, the legacy of a police motorcycle accident, I appreciated that he was attempting to equip me with skills that might spare me from a similar fate.

Jennifer had met Bob early in the driving course. When the time came for me to do a full-day ride in Domboshawa National Park, he invited her to join us as a pillion passenger on his bike. It would, he explained, be an opportunity to see some real Africa, just a short distance from Salisbury.

Somehow, Jennifer got a part-day off from her new job and met us at a parking lot in suburban Salisbury after I had attended morning parade at the driving school. Attired in white slacks and a heavy, warm parka, she climbed on to the back of Bob's bike and we headed north.

Domboshawa's exposed granite *kopjes* were less than twenty miles from town. At the end of a narrow road arose the granite massif that had attracted successions of Rhodesia's peoples to its heights and caves. Bushmen had left visual recordings of their hunts in the form of distinctive dark red paintings on cave walls and granite features. These ancient paintings depicted people and the animals they hunted and lived with.

More recently, the area had particular significance to the Shona people, who had long inhabited the northern reaches of Rhodesia.

It was an area of distinctively African beauty. Near to the road, a low shelf of exposed granite increased gradually in gradient to become a enormous granite dome. Later, from its top, we looked onward to successive *kopjes*, admiring massive, neatly stacked blocks of stone standing out from stands of waving golden grasses and flat-topped native trees—suggesting that a giant with a flair for bonsai had in some ancient time formed the geography with an eye for natural beauty. The three of us stood in quiet contemplation before Bob signaled that we would be following a descending, narrow trail into a *vlei.*

I started my bike and carefully followed Bob and Jennifer down the trail, avoiding holes and loose rocks, until finally the track opened out into what might in America be called a dry meadow area. This was the *vlei*; it was an area for a traditional African kraal and Jennifer's first glimpse of how the Shona people lived away from a city environment. A cluster of round, thatched huts stood just off the trail. There were fields of corn, called *mealies* in Rhodesia, drying after harvest. Children gathered as we approached to wave to the uniformed policeman on a motorcycle. Visits from *Mapolisa* were not that common, even in Domboshawa. Several young women in long, bright cotton dresses stood shyly, several with just-walking infants clutching their hands. We slowed, waved, and continued on. Minutes later, still basking in the glow of my very recent experience as a great *bwana*, I steered my machine over the edge of a dry gully, where my mentor waited on the opposite side. Reaching the dusty bottom without incident, I twisted the throttle sharply to power up the loose slope of the far side, but alas, it was not enough. My steed coughed and died just as the front wheel crested the far side. My long left leg was not long enough to keep us both upright and I gently toppled. Dusting myself off, I looked up the gulch to see two young herd boys smiling as if I had been the best entertainment they had enjoyed in a long time.

Bob Jamieson knew the tracks and trails of the area well. We stopped often to look at the wonders of the reserve. After the experience of steering a heavy street machine cross-country, we turned on to a series of graded dirt roads, where Bob turned up the speed dramatically. His motorcycle seemed particularly sure-footed. I pursued, grimly at first, until confidence in my own machine and my increasing riding skills gave me comfort to enjoy the ride and the scenery.

There were no further mishaps. Late in the afternoon, we stopped at the lot where Jennifer had parked the car. Thunderheads were gathering on the horizon. It seemed likely that rains would come before we could traverse Salisbury and return our motorcycles to the driving school. Saying a hasty good-bye to her, I followed my instructor out onto the main thoroughfare, pulling on my aviation-type goggles and gauntlets at the last moment. We drove hard and fast. There was little traffic, and as our speeds reached 160 kmh (100 mph), the lights of Jennifer in the VW fell far behind. Jamieson rode with real concentration; I did my best to emulate his example. It was the real test of the hard days he had spent teaching me the skills of a qualified BSAP motorcycle rider.

When the rains came several minutes later, we pulled to the side of the road long enough to don foul weather gear. In my instance, this was a gray greatcoat with button-down leg protectors. These felt comforting on my bare knees as we once again took up our high-speed run to the barn.

When at last we wheeled into covered parking at the school, I sensed that I had satisfied my instructor that I was now qualified to ride a police motorcycle. As he pulled off his helmet, Bob Jamieson turned to me and said, "We'll arrange for you to take the road test tomorrow with another instructor." That test was uneventful. I was, at last, authorized to drive vehicles in the BSAP.

CHAPTER 4

War Comes

THE NATION had long been on a path of disappointing, seemingly endless efforts to negotiate a peaceful political settlement and international recognition. Rhodesian media attention seemed always to be focused on meetings—planned or actual—aimed at achieving a diplomatic solution to the impasse between Britain, the Rhodesia Front government, and the black African nationalist movements, whose avowed aim was to assume control of the nation that some were already calling Zimbabwe. The Smith government's 1965 Unilateral Declaration of Independence (UDI) from Britain had been declared illegal, the United Nations responding by declaring sanctions as a means of forcing the minority white rebels to negotiate. The central stumbling block in those negotiations was always the question of universal, immediate suffrage. Britain and important members of the international community made it clear that there was an expectation that balloting would be on the basis of "one man, one vote." White Rhodesians, who had enjoyed self-government since 1923, knew that immediate implementation of that formula would spell the end of the country they had built.

They had recent illustrations of revolution, despotism, and tyranny on their doorstep; virtually every African nation to the north that had acquired independence in the decade previous had declined into near or complete chaos: Ghana, Tanzania, and Kenya had become one-party states, while the excesses of Milton Obote and Idi Amin in Uganda resulted in hundreds of thousands of deaths. The Rhodesians had welcomed survivors of the savagery associated with the Congo rebellions, and the memories of atrocities were fresh in people's minds. There was not a single example of a black nationalist democracy.

Though bellicose in the early days of their independence, by 1974 Rhodesia's leaders finally had publicly embraced the concept of power sharing with majority Africans—but they expected constitutional safeguards to protect their minority status and to ensure their representation in any future government. Prime Minister Ian Smith began negotiations with Bishop Abel Muzorewa, representing the African National Congress (ANC), to see whether agreement could be reached over critical issues that heretofore had stymied talks.

Two African nationalist organizations dominated the ANC: the Zimbabwe African National Union (ZANU) and the Zimbabwe African People's Union (ZAPU). These groups were divided not only by ethnicity but also by their overseas supporters. Joshua Nkomo, an Ndebele, headed ZAPU and its military wing, ZIPRA (Zimbabwe People's Republican Army); ZANU represented Mashona interests under the guiding hand of first Edson Sitole and then Robert Mugabe. ZANU and a number of incarcerated nationalists called for an end to talks between Prime Minister Ian Smith and Bishop Abel Muzorewa. The sides seemed to be polarizing, each determined to realize its own political objectives.

ZANU's military wing was known as ZANLA (Zimbabwe African National Liberation Army). Military training was provided to members both by attendance at courses in Communist China and by training cadre from the Chinese People's Army assigned to terrorist training bases in Tanzania and elsewhere. Training and logistic support for ZAPU's military organization, ZIPRA, was provided by the Soviet Union, while training expertise was supplemented by Eastern Bloc countries, including East Germany and Cuba. Relations between competing nationalists were frequently acrimonious, to the degree that host nation Zambia at one point expelled "freedom fighters" who had attacked opposing nationalist faction members—and even Zambians. This, once again, was illustrative of the tribal divisions that had been a feature of Rhodesia since before Europeans arrived. The Matabele, proud descendents of the Zulu nation of South Africa, had historically plundered at will the villages of their more numerous Mashona neighbors and even in the 1970s had a tendency to look down on them. During the 1960s, as nationalism grew, both groups developed rival political parties that fought open battles for control of the African townships. It was in this period of turmoil that the British South Africa Police (BSAP) recorded its first shooting since the days of the Pioneer Column, a sad milestone for a traditionally unarmed force.

Throughout the years of sometimes bitter negotiations between Rhodesia, Britain, and the nationalists, the process had been periodically interspersed with terrorist attacks and Rhodesian security force reactions. The first attack against whites had occurred in 1964, when a farmer and his family were ambushed on a remote road in the country's east. ZIPRA's disastrous attempt in 1967 to deploy a cadre of about 125 armed men from their Zambia base resulted in the virtual annihilation of the group by Rhodesian security forces. And because South African nationalists had participated in that incursion, Rhodesia's southern neighbor dispatched South African Police and supporting aircraft to assist Rhodesia in deterring future border incursions.

There had been a relative lull in terrorist activity in the years up to the Altena Farm attack at Centenary in December 1972 that Eric Kennelly had told me about during my depot training. I was certainly unaware of it at the time, but Rhodesian security authorities had been surprised and taken aback when attacks occurred in the country's northeast. ZANLA insurgents had covertly crossed Rhodesia's border from Mozambique.

In the years preceding 1972, BSAP Special Branch had methodically developed detailed intelligence about the location of ZAPU and ZANU facilities in Zambia. They also knew that insurgents were being trained in neighboring Tanzania. They suspected, but could not verify to the satisfaction of superiors, that ZANLA had moved into Mozambique, still a Portuguese colony as it had been for nearly four hundred years.

The Portuguese had been fighting their own counterinsurgency in Mozambique, where they were opposed by communist-backed nationalists called FRELIMO (Mozambique Liberation Front). As the war intensified and moved toward Rhodesia's border, security forces began joint external operations in Mozambique with the Portuguese. African tribal identities and interests extended across borders into both countries. Rhodesia considered that it was acting prudently through its covert operations in Mozambique by fighting the war away from the homeland.

BSAP Special Branch detective Winston Hart had monitored events and gathered intelligence about the northeast from his one-man post at Bindura throughout this early period, and he focused his attention on Mozambique as indicators of FRELIMO influence spread south of the Zambezi River to Rhodesia's border. As early as 1970, Hart received indications that ZANLA

Special Branch detective Winston Hart, lower right, and a detective colleague atop Mount Darwin after investigating a report of insurgent activity. They were accompanied by two dog handlers from the South African Police. (Courtesy Winston Hart)

was using the FRELIMO infrastructure to move people and materiel from Zambia south into the Rhodesian border area of Mozambique's Tete Province. But his reports failed to convince superiors of the increasing risk to the farmers and tribesmen of Rhodesia's northeast. In April 1970, a Rhodesian army vehicle detonated a land mine in Mozambique across the dry river that was the national border—opposite Mukumbura police post, which Hart and his colleague Peter Stanton used as a forward operating post. Three soldiers died in the explosion. Almost two years later, Winston Hart survived unscathed a land mine explosion.

Hart acquired his information through the careful cultivation of sources, but particularly through regular liaison with sympathetic Portuguese police, border control, and army personnel. Anecdotal information was accumulating through these many points of contact, all of which pointed to a growing Rhodesian terrorist presence in Mozambique. Anxious to finally verify this information and convince doubtful superiors, Hart let his sources know that he was anxious to actually interview a person with firsthand knowledge about terrorist movements. When finally a Portuguese army source in Tete informed him that a Rhodesian terrorist had been captured and was in their custody, he hurriedly communicated to his superiors and an aircraft flight was arranged through the Police Reserve Air Wing. With his boss and the pilot, they flew into the dusty airstrip in Tete.

Tete was certainly one of the farthest outposts of the crumbling Portuguese empire, a hot, dirty, one-horse town with only the army to keep it alive. Hart remembers long hours spent waiting for various authorities: "Nothing happened quickly in Tete. The trade store was probably the town's central attraction. Its owner was a fat, sweaty Portuguese, who was making a fortune selling beef to the army without asking too many questions about where the animals had come from. The Africans didn't like him much, and I understand that they later killed him at another, northern trading post."

In this environment, Hart expectantly hoped that his erstwhile colleagues would produce a talkative prisoner who would finally confirm or deny the scores of reports in his files. His hopes were dashed when a Portuguese official casually told him that the prisoner had been released. Soon after, he learned that there was uncertainty about the release story: perhaps the prisoner had merely been misplaced? Finally, with an increasingly dubious boss in tow, Hart was taken to a small room—already packed with expectant officials and one rattled African prisoner. He was told he might ask the man questions, but not in private.

It was a near-hopeless situation. A skilled interviewer with considerable experience and rapport with Africans, Hart knew very well that there was little likelihood the captive would confide in such public environs. And so it was: a clearly evasive man simply denied knowledge about any of the issues Hart so badly wanted resolved. He finally left Tete, with a still-dubious boss and a conviction that the prisoner knew much more.

Soon after, Hart was vindicated. Deep inside Mozambique, he received a call from Mukumbura police post advising that Chief Bushu had been murdered; there were political ramifications, because, although the murder scene was in Mozambique, Bushu was a regional chief who resided at various times on both sides of the river that separated the two countries. Hart rushed down the dusty track to the border accompanied by Portuguese army officers. At a traditional kraal, they found the victim—shot multiple times execution style. Empty AK-47 cartridges lying in the dust around the scene and the testimony of witnesses confirmed that the killers were a group of Rhodesian insurgents. They had killed the chief, who was sus-

Winston Hart is seen shortly after surviving the land mine blast that destroyed the vehicle he was driving. (Courtesy Winston Hart)

pected of being too friendly with Portuguese authorities, as an example to his people of what would happen to "sellouts."

Winston Hart's investigations confirmed that the group had been one of several that had been marching across Mozambique to the border and into Rhodesia, where the proselytizing process favored by Mao Zedong had begun. The killing had been an escalation of that process and was intended to rally the people to the cause by fear, intimidation, and naked force. The reports about Bushu's murder finally convinced police authorities that they had the beginnings of an active insurgency on their northern border.

Days later, Winston Hart was traveling in a police Land Rover with an African policeman on the narrow track on the north side of the Mukumbura River, a short distance from the police post, when one of the rear wheels detonated a Soviet antitank mine that had been buried during the night. A huge explosion virtually tore the vehicle in half, spinning it some distance down the road before it struck the ground on one side. His colleague was ejected from the passenger door. Though apparently unhurt, Hart had been momentarily deafened by the blast and was at first disoriented. Fearing that enemy forces were nearby and might assault, he managed to climb out of the cab's rear window and began a frantic search for the African constable, who was eventually found injured and unconscious some distance away. Scooping him up, Hart trotted up the road to Rhodesia, carrying the man over one shoulder, and eventually found help.

Headquarters transferred Hart back to Salisbury after the mining incident, but he remained deeply involved in intelligence matters relating to terrorist incursions. The attack on Altena Farm occurred soon after. Hart recalls that he was having dinner at the home of Major Dave Parker of the Rhodesian Light Infantry (RLI) when reports of the attack were publicly broadcast, accompanied by an interview with Prime Minister Ian Smith.

"Ian Smith made it clear that he had been taken by surprise when Altena Farm was attacked," Hart recalls. "It was clear that he had not been informed about the terrorist buildup on the border, and I expressed my dismay at this to my host. He told me that he had been reading my reports but couldn't explain why they hadn't found their way to the PM's desk. I can only guess that for some reason, they never got past Police General Headquarters."

There had been other incidents and indicators about ZANLA's buildup in Mozambique. In March of 1970, Rhodesian Special Air Service (SAS) had attacked Matimbe in Mozambique after receiving indications that Rhodesian insurgents were present. The dead were all attired in FRELIMO uniforms, but a document was captured that contained a secret message to an African stating that "the Zimbabwe boys have arrived" (in Mozambique). Still, the alarm was not sounded in the hallowed halls of police headquarters.

Finally, more than two years later, a captured terrorist took Special Branch detective Peter Stanton and a platoon of Rhodesian African Rifles (RAR) soldiers to an enormous ZANLA arms cache situated within Rhodesia in tribal trust lands near Mtoko. The prisoner indicated that the arms and material had been covertly carried by porters from Mozambique to the remote *kopje*, poised for use in the impending war against Europeans. A month later, the Centenary Farm attacks occurred and Operation Hurricane was launched in response by security forces. It was to continue unabated for several years.

By 1972 ZANLA had learned important lessons from the disastrous 1967 foray by ZIPRA; they had also listened to their Communist Chinese instructors, who praised the dictums of Mao's teachings. These stressed that the real target to ensure the success of a revolution was the people. Proselytizing had acquired for ZANLA the terrorist operatives and support it needed from tribesmen near Centenary, but realizing that these recruiting

Early insurgent attacks brought Rhodesia's leaders and defense chiefs out to the northeast border area. Here Special Branch detective Winston Hart, with his colleague Peter Begg behind him, briefs President Clifford Dupont (left of Hart in civilian clothes) and Commissioner of Police Sid Bristow. On far left and far right are Vice Marshal Archie Wilson and Major General Keith Coster, commanders of the air force and army, respectively. (Courtesy Winston Hart)

techniques were not enough to swell the ranks with the fighters, porters, and comfort women required to tip the scales in their favor, they soon resorted to the sort of brutality and intimidation of their countrymen that I'd learned to abhor from the Viet Cong. To subvert, intimidate, and control them, innocent Africans were subjected to mutilation and tortures so awful that survivors were sufficiently panicked into compliance. Thus, bands of insurgents entering the northeast could be assured of food, shelter, and the comforts of the young women of the kraal.

In the aftermath of the Centenary Farm attacks, it became apparent that attackers had been and were sheltering with tribesmen in adjoining trust lands. ZANU then upped the ante in the brutal struggle for control: mass abduction was a way to reap the youthful fighters they needed.

On the evening of 4 July 1973, a group of seventeen heavily armed insurgents attacked the northeastern St. Albert's Mission, herding 270 souls together and announcing that they were taking secondary students, staff members, and teachers away for military training outside the country. The abducted were forced to gather meager food and a minimum of clothing for a long march through Tete Province in Mozambique to Zambia, where it was expected they would be transported to ZANLA's Chinese-staffed military training bases in adjoining Tanzania. Then, an extremely difficult night march was begun that took the group struggling down a steep, narrow trail on the Zambezi escarpment.

In the predawn morning hours of the next day, the alarm was raised and Rhodesian security forces swung into action with an air search and deployment of army troops. Illumination flares dropped from search aircraft drove the enemy to ground for cover, uttering dire threats to the abductees to ensure that there was no movement to be seen from the skies.

Rhodesian air force activity had seriously delayed the planned forced march across the Zambezi Valley to Mozambique. The air search resumed at first light. The groups were split into two smaller bands, one made up of abducted adults, with the larger group of children in the other. A Rhodesian Light Infantry (RLI) patrol following their tracks eventually overran the group but came under fire by insurgents using the children as human shields. The troopers aimed their return fire high, allowing the children to run toward them to safety. These six insurgents made good their escape, but the children were rescued.

It was some time before the RLI could regroup and pursue the second group. Again, the air force was assisted by overflying the suspected trail to force the quarry and their captives into stationary status under cover. Ultimately, the troopers made contact, and this time killed three of the abductors—rescuing the remaining victims without injury.

This particular incident ended favorably. The aerial observation skills of Rhodesian pilots and a determined infantry force had been rapidly deployed in a determined follow-up. Unfortunately, the Rhodesian security forces were not often this successful. Abductions, intimidation, maiming, and murders continued to be favored tactics by ZANLA cells intent on following Mao's teachings.

My transfer to Support Unit coincided with several defense initiatives demonstrating that national leaders were focused on the northeastern operational area known as Operation Hurricane. In early 1974, the national call-up numbers were increased to put more men in uniform—and the army began raising a second battalion of the RAR.

National service was required of most young men of European extraction, followed by periodic call-ups. The BSAP began to accept national servicemen as national service patrol officers; they were trained alongside regular recruit squads in Morris Depot, although the training curriculum was not as full as that of the regular patrol officer recruits.

The use of African soldiers, traditionally called *askaris*, had a long and proud history in Rhodesia. During World War I, the 1st and 2nd Rhodesia Regiments were formed of African volunteers from the Fort Victoria region. Commanded by Europeans of Rhodesia's Native Affairs Department, the troops acquitted themselves very well in the East African campaigns against Germany. Thus, the BSAP began assimilating Africans into the force. By the 1970s, Rhodesia's police force had grown to about seven thousand, two-thirds of whom were African.

During World War II, the Rhodesian African Rifles fought with distinction in the Burma campaign, as did the regiments of the Kings African Rifles (KAR), the members of which were recruited mainly in Kenya and Nyasaland (today called Malawi). Although conscription had been introduced, Rhodesia's youthful European population volunteered in proportionately large numbers, and many were selected to become junior officers. Returning to their homeland after the cessation of hostilities, these veterans and others attracted to Rhodesia from other dominions would form the nucleus of the nation's leadership.

The BSAP Askari Platoon later became Support Unit. Many of its predominantly African members came to it after war service in the Kings African Rifles or RAR; these former soldiers were led by a conglomerate of white policemen with previous military service.

Rhodesians had always considered their police to be the nation's first line of defense. Indeed, the BSAP had protected the first column of settlers that settled and built Fort Salisbury in 1890. At formal occasions, they proudly took their position on the parade square at "the right of the line," just as Britain's senior service—the Royal Navy—does. Thus, it was widely held that the BSAP would defend Rhodesia against terrorist incursions; it was they who knew the people, were in touch with local problems, and it was police Special Branch that generated national intelligence. Support Unit was considered the point of the police spear in the fight against armed insurgents. Rhodesia's highly trained army and air force were, however, jointly involved in the war against terrorism from the outset and served with professionalism and distinction.

It may have seemed an odd decision for me, a law enforcement professional, to elect service in a paramilitary role. Rhodesia was facing an apparently escalating war against terror—one with disturbing similarities to the conflict in Vietnam I had left—and if my superiors felt I had skills that could help in the effort, I would gladly do my part. I chose to transfer to Support Unit because of an offer to assist in the training of the multitudes of new troops that were expected as the unit more than doubled in size. Force farrier Chief Inspector Bill Coetzer—the man who had carefully observed my progress in COIN (counterinsurgency) training—had asked me if I thought I could teach African recruits to fire the issue rifle. I was immediately attracted to the training role. I would be working closely with motivated young Africans, I would gain leadership experience in the unique environment of Africa, and I would be given more responsibility sooner.

Billy Coetzer, after expressing his desire to take an active role in the fight, had moved from his desk at Morris Depot's police stables to a roughly erected corrugated iron shed on the grounds of the African Training Depot at nearby Tomlinson Depot.

My initial introduction to Support Unit was a favorable one; I found the atmosphere to be very much like a large family. Superintendent Derek "Fats" Waller commanded, although it was then known that he would soon be replaced by a more senior officer to shepherd the unit through its rebirth and growth. On my first morning at the unit, Fats accepted my salute where he was standing outside the armory building soon after the troops had been dismissed from the parade square after morning physical training. Ormonde Power, turned out in the distinctive riot-blue trousers, starched gray shirt, and glistening black boots of the unit, stood with me.

"Welcome to Support Unit, P/O Hubbard," he said with a smile. A compact man, well liked in the force, Fats turned to Ormonde and asked him to show me around and get me settled.

Tomlinson Depot sprawled over several acres of prime real estate in the near suburbs of Salisbury. The office complex consisted of two wings of single-story brick construction, with lawns and garden in the center. An imposing brick and concrete armory, already bursting with new rifles and ordnance, stood immediately adjacent the small access road. Beyond that street was the parade square—the center of most activities at Tomlinson. Support Unit was really a long-term house guest of the African Training Depot, whose staff patiently shared their working spaces, tea pots, and even the parade square. On the square, different groups of young Africans in training were differentiated by the color of their boots—and by the fact that most new Support Unit constables wore camouflage denim battle dress as a standard working uniform.

BSAP pioneers had erected several rectangular timber-frame sheds in a row behind the original office complex. These corrugated iron buildings were to serve as offices and stores for the anticipated new Support Unit troops that I was there to help train. In one of them, I found Chief Inspector Coetzer, sitting behind a simple table, talking on the telephone. He motioned for me to sit in a folding chair, and I did so, as Ormonde took his leave. The phone call that was absorbing my new boss's attention was with the police quartermaster, and it concerned uniforms, boots, and other supplies for new African recruits. Clearly, the system was under pressure to provide what was needed, but there seemed to be a universal patience, an understanding that after all, this was Rhodesia. What I was quickly learning, however, was that supposedly punitive international sanctions had actually proven a catalyst for small local industry. Now, the Bata boot factory was manufacturing a well-designed combat boot at its national factory. Rhodesia's own distinctive camouflage denim shirts, trousers, jackets, and bush hats were locally produced, as was load-bearing gear—soldier's webbing—and the back packs. The war had set locally factories humming with activity.

The call finished, Bill greeted me and began explaining our immediate tasks. Police recruiters had experienced no difficulty finding healthy, fit, young African males who were ready to defend the nation as members of the soon-to-be raised new troops of Support Unit. Aspirants were brought to Tomlinson Depot, issued with basic requirements, fed, and quartered while they were carefully vetted by Special Branch. Many came from the traditional recruitment areas of Gutu and Buhera, near Fort Victoria. It could take some weeks for background checks to be completed, during which time the young men served in working parties or assisted in other ways around the depot. Under the watchful eye of an African noncommissioned officer (NCO), some learned the skills of spit-polishing boots and belts—and served as batmen. Now, enough of the recruits were cleared that they could be tentatively formed into troops and the training process begun.

Everybody was in a huge hurry to get extra "Black Boots" deployed into the operational area. Thus, an abbreviated initial training regime was to be introduced. One way or another, I learned, the first troop would be dispatched to the northeast in six weeks. That, I knew, was a tall order. Ormonde Power, with his extensive African training experience, had been using a thirteen-week training program for new and replacement recruits—

until the balloon went up. Ideally, there was a range of skills and knowledge that needed to be patiently imparted to new recruits, many of whom had come to us from traditional African communities. The African NCO drill instructors would bear much of the burden of preparing these young men for battle.

It was the NCOs who gathered up the disparate members of a squad and began creating a homogeneous unit, starting first with very basic lessons in personal hygiene and the proper care of the uniforms and boots that had been entrusted to them. Then would come the first lessons in parade square drill, which so effectively melds individuals into a unit. There would be hours of physical training and preparation before the all-important weapons-handling skills could be taught. I knew that Ormonde's training syllabus was without frills or extra time. We would need to prioritize every aspect of recruit training for getting these new men ready to serve in six weeks. Now it was especially apparent why Bill Coetzer was looking for a man who thought he could teach raw Africans to handle, maintain, and effectively fire a modern self-loading military rifle.

The transfer to Support Unit affected our lives immediately. Jennifer and I were arising in the cold, dark high veld morning at 5:00 AM and then driving together down near-empty streets to central Salisbury and through the gates of Tomlinson Depot. By 5:45 AM, the depot's narrow road was clogged with duty branch recruits on their way to the parade square for morning inspection. Attired in heavily starched khaki shorts and tunics, they waddled along the street straight-legged in polished boots and leggings, swinging their legs instead of flexing them to avoid cracking the razor-sharp creases they had labored to create in their brittle parade garments. Also at that time of day, all Support Unit men in training would be rushing to form up for morning physical training; they were distinctive in olive-drab shorts and combat boots. I would be joining the recruit troop for morning PT.

In the quiet postdawn moments, African troops formed in squads across the vast parade square. There was little conversation, just the sound of sleepy men shuffling into position, forming long ranks facing the road. I moved across the road, where duty branch instructors stood off the square, facing their men. As I did so, Ormonde Power, dressed in police greatcoat and helmet, rounded the corner on his Honda 55 commuter bike. Although never under any circumstances late, mornings were not Ormonde's best time. Moments later, he jogged up and stood next to me with a cursory "Morning, Doug." Seconds passed, then old Sergeant Major Tambo, with the two rows of ribbons that identified him as a Burma veteran of the Kings African Rifles, smartly marched onto his square, came to attention with the distinctive smack of a steel-shod heel into the tarmac, and screamed his command that simultaneously drew every man on the square to a similar posture. There was one distinctive crack and thump as starched uniforms fractured creases and boots were driven home.

After an about-turn, the sergeant major turned over the squads to awaiting instructors. Ormonde marched onto the square with the others, took command of his Support Unit squad, and marched them at the double toward the road that led from depot into the adjoining suburbs. I fell in behind him, working to take shorter, standard paces to stay in step. With typical African flair, the recruits quickly fell into perfect cadence running together, their boots smacking the road as one.

Never in my wildest dreams would I have thought that one day I would have responsibility to physically train young African men. But PT was an essential part of the training program. It has been said that fewer things are more useless than an unfit infantryman; it was essential that every man achieve a level of fitness that would permit him to operate and endure in the operational environment of patrol and skirmishing with the enemy. Ormonde was a patient, understanding instructor who shared his considerable knowledge with me. I learned that most fresh recruits living on the substantial rations served to them at the mess hall could manage a five-kilometer run in boots without too much difficulty. I would learn that the same could not be said for all of the Europeans who came to us for training. An apparently universal weakness of the young Africans was in abdominal strength. Ormonde's answer to this was to halt his runners at every bridge where the men would pair up. One man would hold the feet of his partner while the man sat with his back facing the water below. Then, to cadence, recruits would lean back over the edge and sit back up. Many struggled, but all completed the exercise. After an hour of running, interspersed with exercises, we ran back into the depot, where the squad was dismissed for ablution and breakfast.

I had a limited time in which to learn some of the techniques Ormonde used to teach his recruits about the issue rifle. African NCOs had begun the process with early lessons on how to disassemble and reassemble rifles. This was practiced frequently until some degree of speed and self-assurance could be seen. Rifle maintenance and cleanliness was stressed; bores were always inspected and were expected to reflect brightly back with a light coat of oil.

Soon, although Ormonde helped when possible, I was largely on my own—learning something every hour as I tried to teach the men.

Jennifer and I managed another weekend trip to Kariba. Our life was settling; we were comfortable in our home, despite a scarcity of furnishings, and although the Support Unit assignment was demanding, it was also challenging and satisfying. Confident I had found a mate at last, I asked for her hand and she accepted. We returned to Salisbury, talking already about our future life together. I was starting to think that perhaps I could manage the responsibility of one more person in my life.

International telephone communication always being difficult, Jennifer sat down and wrote a letter to her parents in Queensland, Australia, to tell them that we planned to marry in early July.

Support Unit's new officer commanding (OC), Assistant Commissioner G. M. Houghton, took charge as the buildup began. Guy Houghton came to us after a stint as staff officer planning at Police General Headquarters (PGHQ), where one of his most important duties was the daily preparation of briefings for the commissioner of police, Peter Sherren—a task that made him privy to policy at the most senior level of the Rhodesian defense establishment. He had served in the Royal Navy and in 1949 came out to Rhodesia to join the BSAP, supplied by his father with a grub stake of one hundred pounds Sterling, a tidy sum in those days.

Houghton recalls:

> Expansion of Support Unit was a reaction to the worsening situation with terrorist incursions throughout all operational areas. There was pressure building around Rhodesia on all its borders. Though there had been indications that the Portuguese were not managing well with their war in neighboring Mozambique, the north-eastern farm attacks emphasized the urgency of reinforcing the counter insurgency component of the Force. The Support Unit expansion was part of the response to national security problems posed by incursions and terrorist attacks.
>
> Support Unit had evolved from an Askari Platoon with guarding and public order responsibilities to a command of five operational troops that were rotated for counterinsurgency duties in the troubled North Eastern operational area. The police response to the requirement for more security was the expansion the Unit; ultimately it grew to twenty-five troops of about forty men each. Troops were normally composed of seven "sticks" of five men, plus a headquarters element; they were commanded by Section Officers and Inspectors. The concept was that each "stick" of five men would be led by a Patrol Officer. It was felt that the added leadership would create a more cohesive and capable unit.

Commissioner of Police Peter Sherren salutes Support Unit troops passing in review after the unit had reached full strength. Escorting the commissioner is Inspector Ormonde Power. (*Rhodesia Herald*)

Those of us charged with leading the expansion began to notice an increased drive as the tempo built up. Ormonde and I were both cheered to see the new OC moving boldly toward creating a truly effective counterinsurgency force. Guy Houghton clearly had his own vision as to how that should be accomplished: "My vision was always that the Unit should be trained and operated as a paramilitary unit. Others at headquarters were apprehensive of the potential effect of militarizing a unit of the police. They were conscious of the military effects and it was canvassed as a defensive measure. Commissioner Sherren may well have been concerned that he might be creating a monster with a newly-expanded Support Unit in a military role. Police were always the first line of defense in the early days of Rhodesia, but there was an apprehension about reverting to this status. It was not something that could be sold to Rhodesia's majority Africans."

Nevertheless, Support Unit's commander pressed ahead. He had been given a mandate to raise and train the new unit, accompanied by a large degree of self-determination. The accelerated expansion put enormous pressure on the African NCO ranks. There were simply not enough qualified men at the outset, and there would be a time lag before suitable men could be promoted upward. Equally serious were the challenges of equipping the force with military hardware: "There was reluctance at headquarters as more specifically-military equipment was requested. Support Unit sticks were going up against terrorists armed with light machine guns. I was able to acquire Bren guns that had been re-chambered at a South African armory, but their effectiveness was limited by a magazine capacity of only twenty rounds of 7.62 NATO ammunition."

More than a year would pass before the first belt-fed FN MAG light machine guns—identical to those in use by Rhodesia's army, could be acquired for Support Unit's troops.

The pressure was on at Support Unit. Bill Coetzer spent long hours at his desk attending to the myriad of details associated with recruitment and training. He was assisted by Inspector Sean Fischer, a friendly and normally quiet Irishman. Troops of about thirty-five African recruits were being raised continuously, sometimes within a week or two of each other. With them came transferred white patrol officers and support officers from duty branch who had been assigned as leaders. Most had been district policemen; few had military experience or expertise—and I soon discerned that not all were that excited about being transferred from the relative comfort of a police station to an operational role. Almost immediately, there were problems when I issued instructions from my seniors to men who wore a higher rank insignia than I. Inspector Fischer was quick to reinforce me when necessary, but it was a source of friction despite the fact that I was carrying out orders from our mutual superiors—not to mention the fact that I had knowledge and skills to impart that they did not possess.

Chief Inspector Coetzer called a favor at police headquarters soon after the influx of new troop leaders, and I was soon promoted to lance section officer (lance S/O). It was formalized soon after by publication in BSAP Force Orders. There was no pay increase, but it meant that I could wear the three epaulette bars of an S/O, a rank best equated to that of a sergeant.

Our brown-booted colleagues of the duty branch instructional staff had a highly refined training syllabus for their African trainees, much of it taught in Tomlinson Depot's classrooms. New constables were expected to absorb and understand lessons in the law and police procedures, in addition to practical, more physical lessons. We in Support Unit, however, had no classrooms to use in training our recruits. Classes were held under trees, in the open fields that surrounded the depot, and sometimes out in the commonage extending eastward to the edge of Highlands' suburbs.

The first of the short-course recruits seemed responsive to the extra pressure put on them by their African NCO drill instructors. Heads and

Sergeant Major Isaac, right, a respected Support Unit instructor, counsels a new recruit. (Author collection)

faces were shaven smooth, their new camouflage uniforms clean, and boots shined and maintained. I was more apprehensive about the cumulative ability to understand the workings of the new R1 South African rifles issued to each new recruit. These were built under license from the designers, Fabrique Nationale of Belgium. To us, they were simply FNs, a fine, robust, and accurate rifle—if properly maintained. Under a shade tree on a tarpaulin, students were tutored in safe handling procedures. They would chant together as they carried out each sequence of safely ensuring that their rifle was unloaded: "Magazine off!" There would follow the hollow clatter as the twenty-round magazines were released and removed. "Cock the rifle!"—"Look inside!"—the latter command prompting all to peer into the open breach to look for the distinctive, bright cartridge base that would indicate that a round was in the chamber and that the rifle might therefore be fired. In the early stages of instruction, no live ammunition was permitted anywhere near the classes, but that would soon change.

There was a whole awareness discipline about weapons safety that somehow had to be imparted in the few weeks we had with the men in the recruit stage of training. I would demonstrate how to walk with the rifle, ready for use but with the muzzle pointed outward and away from my patrol members; each man practiced how to safely climb into a truck without endangering others, and they were under constant scrutiny for carelessness.

Carelessness brought swift discipline, normally in the form of a sharply issued correction and an order to run to a distant tree and back. I soon learned that some men did not concentrate well, particularly after the noon meal. But a burst of unplanned physical activity was normally enough to refocus tired young minds.

It was satisfying to find most African recruits highly motivated to learn, and thus a pleasure to teach. Few had the manual skills associated with things mechanical, but they soon learned how to quickly fieldstrip their rifles—and to reassemble them also. I explained how gasses created by the discharging rifle cartridge pushed the bullet from the barrel under enormous energy and how some of those gasses escaped upward to the gas regulator and forced the gas piston rearward to extract the used cartridge and chamber a fresh one from the magazine below. And from this, I hoped that they would understand why gas regulator adjustment was important.

Holding, sighting, and firing were more mysterious subjects and thus more challenging to teach without actually doing it. We had teaching aids available that illustrated the correct way to peer through the adjustable rear site aperture, focus on the foresight post, and align it immediately under the target—normally a round, black bull's eye. These aids showed where shots might fall on the target if the foresight was out of alignment—over, above, right or left.

I demonstrated how the rifle might be held comfortably and firmly in the prone position. My row of recruits would do their best to mimic what they had seen me do as I scurried from one man to the next, making corrections, coaching, encouraging. When I told them that their first shots would be from the prone position, I stressed that each man needed to master the important elements: elbow placement, body alignment, cheek placed firmly against the rifle stock.

Imparting to my charges the all-important technique of trigger squeeze was far more challenging. Without yet having actually fired a live round, many trainees assumed that if they aligned rifle sites correctly on their target, pulling the trigger would certainly deliver a bullet to the point of aim. I racked my brain to think of ways to explain that achieving a good hit required concentration: holding the site picture while firmly squeezing the trigger.

"If you pull on the trigger, I will promise you that your bullet will pass to the right side of the target," I counseled. Gathering the squad in close, I would demonstrate, squeezing the trigger until my rifle hammer fell with a distinctive click. They were listening, watching how I placed my finger at right angles to the trigger surface and exerting steady pressure until the sear released and the rifle dry fired; the problem was probably that many did not think mastery of these esoteric details was really important in a bush firefight.

Finally, one serious young Ndebele, Constable Ncube, raised his hand and said, "But *Nkosi,* how can you hurry to shoot?" "Good question, Ncube," I responded. "The answer is that you squeeze much more quickly. You must practice and learn to do it." Again, I demonstrated a fast squeeze. There were some "aahs" uttered lowly and grins that indicated that I had done something that impressed at least some of the men. "But first you must learn to shoot slowly and carefully—until you are hitting the target well."

Finally, the day came when my first squad's theoretical lessons could actually be practiced. Whenever possible, Ormonde and I would team up for a recruit squad's first day of live firing at the rifle range. Support Unit did not have its own rifle range; thus, it was necessary to find one of the area's ranges not in use on a particular day. As I was to learn, the increased tempo of the war effort meant that more units were competing to use Salisbury's rifle ranges. Because the range at Chikarubi was in use almost every day, we began to use a range at Mount Hampden, a short distance to the north

In addition to just about every other commodity, Support Unit was growing faster than its transport assets. There were simply not enough trucks to transport new recruits, because the essential truck and trailer pool had to be maintained and reserved for the troops then deployed on operations. Bill Coetzer used his influence to borrow vehicles from the Public Works Department, an odd assortment of vintage British trucks—pre-UDI Thames Traders and Ford diesels—in a variety of nonregulation colors, including canary yellow, sky blue, and dark green. Sergeant Ringo Machanja formed the squad up on the small square in front of the armory and issued each man his rifle, while Ormonde and I opened our "inner sanctum," where ammunition and explosives were stored. Two recruits were instructed to haul one of the new pine boxes, which held a sealed metal container inside containing one thousand rounds of 7.62 NATO-caliber ammunition, recently arrived from a military arsenal in South Africa. Then, targets, patches, cleaning materials, and other necessary equipment were passed out of the armory under the watchful eye of Machanja. Ormonde had left the building ahead of me while I ensured everything was tidy and began to secure the steel entry door. In the distance, the bellow and clatter of a protesting, aged British diesel told me he had started one of the trucks and was bringing it across for loading. Minutes later, a smiling squad of recruits, proudly attired in new camouflage uniforms and each carefully cradling his rifle in the approved fashion, was packed into the open stake-side truck, and we began the drive to Mount Hampden rifle range.

Salisbury was by then awakening, and the first gentle flow of commuters was beginning. The Thames had a metal engine cover that filled part of the cab between driver and passenger seats. This was an inadequate insulator either for the noise or fumes that emanated from the old diesel, but with windows down and a fresh cool morning at hand, we ignored minor inconveniences and used the time to share stories of people and places we had known in New Guinea.

In the rear, our charges were happily chattering and occasionally waving to young female pedestrians on the roadside. It was their first outing since training had begun.

Mount Hampden was a name of historical significance in Rhodesia's brief but illustrious past. The distinctive *kopje* is said to have been the location the original British South Africa Company pioneer column used as its final marching plan way point. But history dictates otherwise—that a spot ten or so miles away was the location the column commander selected, near the *kopje* situated on the edge of what later became the city of Salisbury.

In 1974 Mount Hampden was rural grazing and small homestead country—still in many ways a part of the original bush that the pioneers settled in. The rifle range abutted a low hill, which served as a natural backstop for stray rounds. The grounds were lush and green—and recently mown.

Sergeant Machanja barked commands, and the recruits spilled from the rear of the truck and fell into formation. The atmosphere quickly became serious. Machanja called the men to attention as Ormonde walked around from the front of the truck. He thanked the sergeant, ordered the men at ease, and began to speak.

"Today is an important date; it is the day you will first fire your rifle," he began. "There are many things to remember from the subjects we have taught you, but the most important lessons you must think about are those which are about the safe handling of your rifle. You have never had live ammunition in your rifle before, but today you will. Remember that the rifle can kill you or your best friend if you are careless and forget. So, I want you all to THINK! Think every time you are given a command. Take your time—and shoot well!"

Support Unit Sergeants Machanja (left) and Leonard. (Author collection)

Next, the recruits formed a semicircle around us, removed their battle smocks, and laid them on the ground. Each rifle was quickly stripped, reassembled, then stripped again for inspection. Bores were clean and new, and they reflected back pleasingly with a light coating of oil.

I maintained careful control of the ammunition box. Sergeant Machanja marched half the men forward to the butts at the foot of the hill from where target frames would be installed. That detail would operate the targets from a protecting trench below the frames and then would change positions with the first group of trainees.

It was a cool, bright, extraordinarily beautiful African morning, the atmosphere palpably clear in the way of high veld country. Light reflected off the leaves of trees on the slope behind the targets. To my rear, the ground gently sloped away, a rich panoply of native grasslands and distant farms. It was perfectly quiet except for the low murmur of the Africans speaking quietly in their own dialect, every man anticipating his first experience with the rifle he had worked so hard to understand. This was the honeymoon night.

The first group was ordered up to the slightly elevated ground that marked the firing line, and each man lined up directly in front of a numbered position. The pit crew had by then raised targets on frames.

"That is your target," I told each man as I walked along behind where they stood at ease, looking downrange. "Memorize where it is. I don't want to see anybody firing on the wrong target." There were nods from the men. "Now, get down in the prone position—just as we taught you, and make yourself comfortable—and watch where you point those fucking rifle muzzles!" There was still no ammunition on the line, but every man was encouraged to act as though his rifle was loaded and could fire.

Suddenly, off to the north end of the firing line, three men stood and bolted to the rear, babbling in fear as they went. Concerned, I turned to Ormonde, who, with his linguistic skills, had a fair idea of what the ruckus was. Others were moving too, wide-eyed. Ormonde grinned and walked to the end of the line, stooped, and picked up a long, large, dry snake skin, which he identified as that of a cobra. The snake had shed its skin several days before; to the young Africans, this meant that the reptile could not be far away—and that perhaps they were encroaching on its territory. To a man, all were deeply fearful of any snake.

Ormonde turned and roared at them: "You lot are like a bunch of old women, not bloody great warriors. No snake is going to linger around rifle fire! Get your arses back to those firing points!" The men moved sheepishly back as Ormonde disposed of the skin in the unmowed verge of the range and began to take up their positions, lying prone and facing the targets.

I had always been firmly convinced that the best way to create a competent rifleman was with a carefully regimented routine that let the students understand and become competent in the critical skills of marksmanship: sighting, trigger operation, and weapon handling. In this first lesson, we wanted to create an opportunity for the new riflemen to think their way through the lessons we had given them, fire the rifle from a stable position, and begin to gain confidence in their ability to strike where they aimed.

"Right!" Ormonde barked. "In the prone position, practice aiming your rifle at your target." We walked along the firing line behind the now-prone rifleman, speaking to each man, correcting body positioning, reminding men to make elbows comfortable, watching especially to ensure that rifle butts were firmly planted in shoulders and that there was an ease to the sighting we could observe.

Finally, he announced, "Ground your rifles, muzzles forward. Remove one empty magazine from your webbing." From the ammunition box I took a box of twenty rounds and distributed one round for each man. "Load one round in the magazine!" There followed a clatter as nervous fingers forced bright, shiny new 7.62 rounds into magazines. Then, "Load!"

Every man responded to the command he had practiced for days before, attaching the magazine to the rifle, drawing the cocking lever fully to the rear and releasing it. Almost as one, the bolts slammed home.

This time I spoke. "I want you now to think and remember what you have learned about your rifle: how to put your sights on the target, how to hold the rifle firmly, and how to squeeze the trigger firmly and smoothly so the sights don't move. When you receive the command, I want you to move the change lever to the firing position, take some deep breaths, start sighting your rifle, then take a final breath and hold it as you carefully keep your foresight at the six o'clock position on the target and squeeze the trigger. Your rifle will fire when it is ready. You must not jump or move when the rifle fires, and you MUST NOT close your eyes, ever!"

It was dead quiet. The men were tense and nervous, but they were as ready as ever we could make them. Beads of sweat stood out on shaved heads. Finally, the command came. "In your own time, fire one round." I watched to see which new riflemen were practicing breathing control and holding rifles firmly. Then the first few rounds crashed out. Some men jumped or winced at the harsh crack of the discharges. We urged them to settle, take their time and concentrate on making the shot count. When the last man had fired, Ormonde issued the command, "Unload!" Magazines were removed, rifles cocked and cleared, change levers placed in the "safe" position. Downrange, the men working in the pit behind earthen abutments were using long-handled pointers to indicate bullet strikes on the targets overhead. There were murmurs as the new riflemen saw first results, which ranged from strikes in the black bull's eye to clean misses, indicated by waving a red flag.

A clean miss was often symptomatic of a tense shooter reacting to recoil and noise by closing his eyes—flinching, we called it—or jerking the weapon instead of allowing a natural recoil and follow-through. Ormonde and I congratulated those with strikes recorded in the black and noted those appearing to have problems. Recruits were this time ordered to insert three rounds in their magazines, and as they again settled in and began aiming and firing we were watching more closely those with first-shot misses. These were again the men with problems, those fearfully reacting to noise and recoil, forgetting most of what we had tried to teach them in their panic. Sergeant Machanja came in close with us as we urged them to stop, breathe deeply, try to relax—and begin again with the process of aiming and squeezing the trigger. Machanja spoke intensely to the recruits in a burst of Mashona, interjecting the command "Think!" to emphasize and remind his charges of the hours of tuition they had experienced before the day.

Some of the men settled, regrouped, and gradually began to improve their groupings. When a shooter's pattern of hits on the target became grouped, we helped adjust sights for elevation and windage to move the shots to the aiming point. For those whose shots were in no discernable pattern, there would be another day at the rifle range soon. Ormonde and I noted those who might need particular attention, though we need not have: Machanja knew exactly who his problem children were.

When at last the range session was over, all empty brass cartridges had been carefully picked up and rifles and magazines closely inspected to ensure that no live ammunition was unaccounted for, the men were ordered to fieldstrip and clean their rifles for inspection. Most remained excited about their first shoot. There were grins, gentle banter, and an enthusiasm about preparing their rifles for our careful inspection. Toothbrushes were produced to scrub powder residue from gas regulators and bolt faces. As each man raised his hand and indicated his readiness to stand inspection, Ormonde or I would take the rifle, open it, and inspect bolt, bolt face, receiver, and bore for cleanliness and the obligatory light coat of oil.

I discerned a growing pride in this group of young men we had been pushing very hard—and most of whom had made remarkable transitions from rural herd boys and laborers toward the goal of being trained Support Unit constables. We drove our ancient trucks back to depot that afternoon with a seemingly changed squad riding proudly in the rear.

I reflected on the circumstances and good fortune that had thrown Ormonde Power and me together as the front line of Support Unit training. We complemented each other in many ways—me with my Vietnam experience and Ormonde with British army and Africa knowledge. He had at his disposal a range of skills that could help me do my job better—and was very good about sharing and assisting.

Although Ormonde had aspired to an army career when he and Tanya emigrated to Rhodesia, his previous commissioned British army experience did not put him in line for similar status in the Rhodesian army. He had instead accepted an offer from the BSAP: complete a four-week indoctrination at training depot, then transfer to Support Unit as a section officer. All of this had occurred in late 1973. Well-trained in ceremonial drill by British guardsmen, Ormonde was immediately given command of Support Unit's ceremonial guard, known as G Troop. With a complement of forty-one Africans under the command of gentle Malawian KAR veteran Sergeant Major Tambo, G Troop stood guard at Government House whenever Rhodesia's president was in residence. Coincidentally, Tanya Power secured employment on President Clifford Dupont's Government House staff.

Under Ormonde and Sergeant Major Tambo, G Troop ran very smoothly. Guards, dressed in ceremonial fez and long-sleeved tunics, stood inspection every shift before an old truck carried them (all standing so as to avoid wrinkling the uniform and scuffing spit-shined leatherwork) the short distance to the Avenues. There the new guard was mounted and the relieved troops returned. Sentry boxes at the entrance to Government House sheltered the sentries from the elements.

G Troop's men were predominantly long-term veterans. Although all were expected to serve in an operational role from time to time, an assignment to G Troop was normally an assurance of living in depot with family and town amenities. Their standard of drill was high, as was their turnout.

Before Support Unit's expansion, there were four operational troops in addition to G Troop. A, B, C, and D Troops had regularly been rotating into the operational area doing patrols and laying ambushes for insurgents. Ormonde, in addition to his G Troop responsibilities, always had a squad of recruits in training at the depot. The curriculum then called for every Support Unit recruit to satisfactorily complete a twelve- or thirteen-week initial training period, much of which was patterned after British army basic training.

Despite my limited skills in ceremonial drill, I was appointed second in command of G Troop. As Ormonde intended it to, this would be my first experience in a leadership role where he and senior troop NCOs could teach me the job and all that it entailed.

I was most concerned about commanding the troop on the parade square. My recruit drill course had been cursory: I now had to face the prospect of standing before a disciplined body of smartly turned-out men on a parade square for all to see the most minor mistake or infraction of the drill manual. There was no answer to my quandary except to practice, then do it. Ormonde patiently drilled me in Support Unit's parking area when time permitted, and I began practicing giving commands to a recruit squad under training.

Chief Superintendent Ron Dick was a colorful character with a bushy moustache in the pattern of an RAF group captain. As one of three senior

Support Unit officers in the new command structure, his recent tenure in the northeastern operational area instilled a distinct drive in all that Ron Dick did. His focus was on the Support Unit "family," just as a senior officer in the British army would regard his regiment.

Ron's interests extended to all levels of the organization, particularly to morale. "Fit body, fit mind" was a dictum he subscribed to, and soon there was an afternoon devoted to sport. African police embraced intratroop soccer matches. A devoted fan of cricket, Ron Dick was determined that this Yankee should learn the sport from whence American baseball had originated. Dreading the process of learning a sport from scratch that all of my peers had played since childhood, I became adept at scheduling activities away from depot on Wednesday afternoons.

There were no club or recreational facilities available for the young patrol officers and others assigned to Support Unit. In the spirit of fostering a regimental family, a timber-framed metal shed was hastily erected on the north side of the parade square to serve as an impromptu mess for patrol officers and above. Old refrigerators were found and stocked with pint bottles of the excellent local beer—and a bar quickly fabricated. Thus began the regular Friday afternoon Support Unit Prayer Meeting. Just as in many regiments of the British Commonwealth, Friday Prayers was an opportunity for every tier of Support Unit's management to gather in an informal setting, where the usual rules governing interaction between ranks were set aside and straight talk was the rule. Officer Commanding Guy Houghton almost always attended—and was the first to leave. He rubbed shoulders with young section commanders just in from the bush, asked them questions that told him how well his support infrastructure was working, or was not—and he heard gripes in an informal setting. This was the stuff that cemented the organization together and ensured that our commander got what he wanted.

Ron Dick played a key role in the creation of Support Unit's informal mess, having had experience with similar projects in the operational area. He was invariably present at depot on Saturday morning, traditionally the day various elements of Support Unit paraded for inspection. It was Ron who inspected G Troop, my first such parade on a Saturday morning after a particularly big night at the mess the evening previous. In anticipation, I went to his office and was invited in. Ron sat behind his desk, which was decorated with an assortment of memorabilia, perhaps the most fascinating of which was a Fairburn fighting knife of the variety favored by SOE

(Special Operations Executive) and OSS (Office of Strategic Services) during World War II. An SAS plaque emblazoned with the motto "Who Dares Wins" was affixed to the wall over his head.

"I'll be ready to inspect at 11:30, S/O Hubbard. Will that be satisfactory?"

"Of course, Sir," I responded—taking my leave. I had fifteen minutes to ensure that my first inspection would be a success. Ron Dick was a very perceptive man who was aware of my shortcomings as a drill instructor. He would be watching to see how well I commanded the president's ceremonial guard.

I need not have worried about the G Troop detail that Saturday. Sergeant Major Tambo was moving about the men where they gathered in shade off the parade square. I announced to him the inspection plan, then hurried off anxiously to dress.

Four recruit candidates awaiting their clearances to begin training were acting as batmen for me that Saturday. They had spent several hours seated under a nearby fruit tree, patiently polishing my leatherwork to a blinding, black sheen. As I approached where they were working under the guidance of a G Troop constable, one man had completed a final buff on the leather leggings; another grasped a wad of cotton and was gently spitting on the toe cap of my steel-shod boots to achieve a full reflection. Two others, who had worked on my belt, brace, and swagger stick, stood proudly to show me their work.

Calling them to follow, I moved hurriedly to a nearby office, shed my combat boots and camouflage utilities, and pulled on just-ironed shorts. My summer parade uniform had not been tailored for comfort. The fit was impeccable, but there was absolutely no extra room either in the shorts or tunic. Finding a chair, I stood, propped one foot up, and carefully pulled on my right boot. Ensuring that each lace was flat and even, I tied and hid the knot, slipping the right legging on over the boot top and drawing up the leather top strap. I repeated the procedure with the left boot and legging, then quickly ran a soft cloth over them to remove smudges or fingerprints. Then came the tunic: metal buttons emblazoned with the BSAP lion fastened, epaulette insignia aligned, then slipped carefully over one arm so as not to cause wrinkles or creases.

With three minutes to spare, the belt *batman* stood behind me and carefully passed the ends of the belt and brace for me to fasten. I did so as quickly as I could and—already bursting out in a healthy flood of perspiration; carefully aligned my uniform cap; picked up my black, brass-tipped swagger stick; and after a quick personal inspection in front of a full-length mirror, marched quickly to the parade square.

Sergeant Major Tambo had assembled the men in ranks on the square. As I approached, he drew to attention and marched toward me, halting and reporting that the parade was ready for inspection. I thanked him, and as I did an about-turn, he returned to the front rank. Perhaps twenty seconds later, Chief Superintendent Dick marched purposefully onto the square, moustache bristling, swagger stick in hand.

"Parade . . . Parade SHUN!" I screamed out—and the seasoned men of G Troop obeyed smartly and simultaneously, much to my relief. Ron Dick drew up in front of me; I snapped my best salute and reported that G Troop was ready for inspection.

"Let's get on with it," he responded.

Sergeant Major Tambo joined us with his clipboard in hand as we began the process. There was very little in the troop that was less than perfect: each fez was aligned with gold tassel in place on the right side, belt buckles cast with the BSAP's charging lion were brightly polished and centrally positioned, boots and leather burnished to reflective brilliance.

Ron Dick clearly knew what to look for. His criticisms were invariably about a worn piece of equipment that, although carefully looked after, was due for replacement. In minutes, my parade and inspection had ended, apparently successfully. With rivulets of perspiration running down my back, I marched off the square, already thinking about the first pint of cold Lion lager that awaited at the nearby Copper Pot.

The routine at depot grew more frenetic as the challenges of growth increased. In particular, we concentrated on the physical fitness of new recruits. Squad exercises were introduced using logs. These were carried and passed overhead; men clutched them to their chests and did sit-ups—and sometimes carried a squad member on them. Recruits practiced lifting and running with a peer slung over one shoulder, and forced marches with water, rifles, and ammunition became commonplace.

Throughout all of Support Unit's growing pains, our duty branch colleagues on Tomlinson Depot's instructional staff carried on with patience and good humor. Ormonde and I regularly retreated to their tea room between instructional periods to share news and laughs, while slaking huge thirsts developed by yelling commands on the parade square or the nearby commonage. Our tea was delivered steaming hot from the recruit's kitchen

Chief Superintendent Ron Dick inspects G Troop, escorted by the author. (Author collection)

in a large metal pot. The "tea boy" was actually a police recruit awaiting training. It was his job to ensure that his tray was delivered on time and in sufficient quantity for the assembled thirsts. We all acknowledged that hot tea had particularly strong qualities as a thirst quencher, and we drank it with equal fervor on the hottest summer days.

The tea room was the seat of a good deal of banter and storytelling: one young, naïve, recently married instructor was cruelly convinced by an older peer that the tea boy's cold sores were actually symptoms of syphilis, and that thus he might have an urgent problem to discuss with his new wife. There were tales about certain district policemen who were adept at climbing gutter downspouts at the hospital nurse's quarters—and there were African stories that had been passed along by the men who had served in all the best—and worst—locales.

African female constables were also trained at Tomlinson Depot. One morning, an instructor who had been on duty the night previously related a story that halted all the usual banter: "I had to charge my sergeant last night," he began. "Jah. I was walking around on a night inspection, and when I got to the female's compound, I thought I heard something at the fence. I pointed my torch at the sound, and there he was." There was a pause for effect as the tea drinkers focused their attention. "The sergeant was poking one of his recruits through the chain link fence. She was backed up to it, hanging on for dear life, and he was giving her a good one! He didn't even miss a stroke when I put the light on him, just grinned."

There were chuckles around the room. A wag commented, "He'd better hope her knees don't fold!" The sergeant, despite his infractions, was probably thereafter guaranteed a degree of notoriety and fame at the depot.

Pressure intensified to find rifle ranges for recruit and continuation training. Troops returning from deployment to the operational area underwent further training, much of which was still concentrated on instilling basic weapon-handling skills. We knew that most of our new Support Unit constables could not obtain real proficiency during initial training; they would be given every opportunity to shoot and improve. We began to train at rural rifle ranges, some of them some distance away.

We were thus spending less time in Salisbury and at the depot, typically packing up camping gear and our trainees for a few days of training. Chief Inspector Coetzer arranged for Training Wing to use the rifle range at Marandellas, a drive of two hours or so. With our convoys of borrowed trucks and perhaps one Land Rover, we would set off in the morning and normally have a camp set up at the range by noon.

Marandellas was a pleasant farm community in the eastern sector of Rhodesia. The drive from Salisbury took us through pine plantations, past mushroom farms and fields of maize. The range itself was located away from the township on high ground in a setting of rural Africa. The range backstop was a small *kopje*, and there were native trees under which to camp and hold classes. Although there was a dearth of grass, it was a pleasant spot. We noticed both small and large game in the area, even a family of hyrax—also called *dassies*, or rock rabbits—inhabited the boulders and rocks around us. Their habits were reminiscent of the pikas I saw during my childhood treks in the high country of Yosemite.

Instructors traveled with tents and cooking equipment stowed in one of the trucks—and several orderlies whose job it would be to set up the camp, find firewood, and tend the camp. Recruits bedded down with their NCOs nearby, learning the skills they would need to live operationally under field conditions. There were long days spent on the firing points, working individually with the men, always trying to help them past fears and bad habits that stood in the way of good marksmanship. I found that I was having a fair degree of success with my students, despite language and cultural differences.

After the evening meal, always cooked over a fire, there was little that needed to be done by the instructors, and always the temptation of the comforts in nearby Marandellas, where there was a hotel called The Three Monkeys. It was Inspector Sean Fischer who introduced me to this friendly country pub, with its high ceilings and thatched roofs. Cozy in the winter chill, the bar and cozy fireplace were welcome after long days in the field.

Sean was normally a quiet man with a keen sense of humor. Married to an Afrikaner, he had truly made Rhodesia his home. What I didn't know was that he had a streak of fervent Irish republicanism in him. Encouraged by several pints of local ale, this conviction suddenly came to the fore in the form of republican songs bellowed out to The Three Monkeys bar patrons—and its British owners.

I immediately sensed that my Irish boss's serenade was less than welcome. The publican knew who we were. He, like most Rhodesian civilians, would normally bend over backward to make members of the security forces comfortable and welcome—but he was not happy about what he was hearing. The outrages of the Irish Republican Army's (IRA's) bombing depredations in the United Kingdom were fresh in every memory, and there was almost universal condemnation of any terrorism in Rhodesia; it was one of the few common experiences shared both by Rhodesians and Britons. I urged Sean to cool it. We weren't ready to leave yet. A cold winter wind whined through the trees outside reminding me of a long, cold night ahead.

I provided momentary distraction by ordering another two pints and again appealed for quiet, but to no avail.

"Up the Republic!" Sean bellowed—just as the publican's wife approached from behind the bar.

"We lost family to the IRA," she said menacingly, "and your songs and sentiments are not welcome here."

Turning to me, she said, "Take your friend and go."

We had been politely ejected. I pulled Sean behind me out the door and over to our Land Rover. He was still singing as we drove out the dusty track to our camp site at the range.

* * *

Bill Coetzer had been a man of action all his life. When I came to work for him at Support Unit in 1974, he was nationally known as a rugby player of some prominence, having played many years for the BSAP team. Then in his early forties, Bill had recently retired from rugby. He was doing well at his new job as the unit expanded, but it was plain to me that the attendant drudgery of administrative duties was taking its toll. I was always pleased when the boss agreed to join us on training trips away. He enjoyed them, as did we.

During a cold week in 1974, Bill was in charge of a training contingent set to train at the Marandellas rifle range. This was a fairly large party made up of a newly assembled troop, including its new commander, Inspector Tony Grice, and patrol officer section commanders. There were also elements of other recruit squads in the final stages of training. The group loaded into a collection of aging military trucks and a Land Rover, setting off for Marandellas early one morning.

The range was bleak and blustery as we arrived and began to set up camp. I had a small tent and a spartan metal-frame camp cot known as a Hounsfield camp bed, which when assembled, kept one off the cold ground. I was grateful for the summer-weight down sleeping bag I'd brought with me and intended to sleep on a warm wool blanket that night. I had my tent up in minutes, partially sheltered behind a large tree, laid out my bedding, and went out to see about getting the first lesson started.

Two pretraining recruits had accompanied us in the old Bedford RL truck, to manage camp duties. I had driven the truck, sometimes reaching forty-five miles per hour on the straight stretches. The 1950s vintage British army four-wheel drive truck was not known for comfort, and despite the chill, I was glad to move around after the long drive. Our orderlies set about off-loading the metal equipment boxes containing our cooking gear; then folding tables and chairs were set up and firewood hastily gathered. Soon, an old metal teapot, nestled into the flames of a newly started cooking fire, was spouting steam. We gathered together with Tony Grice and his men to share a welcome cup of steaming, sweet tea—backs turned to the wind and battle smock collars turned up to shield necks. With hands wrapped around metal cups, we reviewed our range training plan for the day with Chief Inspector Coetzer.

A short distance away, troop NCOs assembled their men into small working groups to clean weapons. They chatted contentedly, fieldstripping rifles and neatly laying out the components on groundsheets in anticipation of inspection.

By late morning, as the first group of recruits moved out to the firing points, the wind had abated almost entirely. It became a typical Rhodesian winter day: clear and very bright. The rock rabbits on the *kopje* came out to sun themselves as instructors concentrated on last-minute coaching.

Because the troop was deployment ready and had its complement of leaders, we encouraged patrol officers and NCOs to listen and participate in our preevent briefing as well as the actual shoot itself. They needed to know and understand the strengths and weaknesses of each man—and understand our suggested remedies for shortcomings.

The qualification shoot was over in two hours. The new constables had become more familiar with their rifles, and most showed improvement in their scores. For those who had not, I checked their rifles for mechanical soundness, and in some instances, personally zeroed them in.

Late in the afternoon, I erected a series of man-sized silhouette targets on one side of the range. As an introduction to tactical shooting, I demonstrated reaction shooting at close range, firing in very close succession the two-round "double tap"—six shots into three targets in three or four seconds. This was, I explained, the sort of close-range shooting that could save their life during a surprise contact in heavy bush. With each man's patrol officer leader standing close by, the men practiced pointing and shooting, slowly at first. There would be many more such lessons in the future, all designed to sharpen fighting skills.

Support Unit personnel deployed to the field were expected to provide their own rations and feed themselves. An allowance was paid to each man for this purpose. African police had their ration preferences, as did we. Rural Rhodesian towns always seemed to have at least one quality butcher—and this was certainly so in Marandellas. Troop leaders and instructors had all pitched in to a common kitty overseen by Bill Coetzer, and he had done his usual excellent job of buying fresh meat and some vegetables. That night, over coals created by burning native hardwood, he cooked *boerewors*, steaks and chops with potatoes, an enormous feast of the sort one might expect from a very large, strong Afrikaner with an appetite to match.

We ate well, clustered around the fire, as sparks steamed upward into the heavens, even then dotted with a myriad of stars. There was friendly talk, an enjoyment of the quiet evening—a certain amount of relaxation. Then one of the men said, "Perhaps we could go in for a quiet drink at the police canteen?"

All eyes turned to the senior man. Bill cracked a very small smile, then nodded his head. Twenty minutes later, we were all clustered around the bar at the police station canteen, our camouflage battle dress and unshowered bodies in sharp contrast to our off-duty colleagues in duty branch still in their district police uniforms. It was a small, cozy setting in which most conversation centered on news of colleagues in the force. Although I was a newcomer, Tony Grice had served in a variety of stations around Rhodesia—and Bill Coetzer was known to all.

At 9:00 PM or so, we drove back to our camp pleasantly fatigued and full of good spirit. There I said good night and gladly crawled into the comfort of my sleeping bag—as the wind began to kick up.

I never slept very soundly while away in the bush, listening for the unusual. The war had not yet come to Marandellas, but I always kept my rifle close by. At about 5:30 AM, I roused myself, pulled on my boots, and walked to the fireside, where some thoughtful soul had already fueled the flames. I tapped on the side of the old Bedford truck to awaken the orderlies, then walked out on to the clearing of the range. There was a sliver of orange on the horizon, an announcement of the dawn to come. The stacked boulders on the *kopje* were silhouetted, and a few stars still danced in the heavens. A cold wind blew periodically. It was an idyllic moment to savor, and I did so.

The camp came to life, men arising in the cold under duress and instinctively clustering around small cook fires awaiting the first cup of sweet tea. And the sun rose quickly, although it did not bring warmth with it.

Bill Coetzer sat in a camp chair near the fire, nursing a cup of tea. As I greeted him, I sensed that he was not feeling well—and this was confirmed when he refused a hot breakfast. After the day's activities had been planned, he quietly told me that he was feeling not at his best.

"Sir, we are organized here," I responded. "Why not take a run into town and get fixed up with something to make you feel better?"

He declined. I continued with what I had been doing, but watched him.

A few minutes passed. He suddenly told me that he was not feeling any better. I turned to one of the patrol officers and ordered him to take the boss to Marandellas Hospital, handing him keys to the Land Rover. I would have preferred to do this myself, but I was expected to oversee the training program, then starting. Moments later, they were gone.

Less than an hour later, an ashen-faced patrol officer trotted up to me and announced that Bill was dead; he had suffered a massive heart attack moments after arrival at the hospital, and all efforts to save him had been unsuccessful.

We were stunned. Our leader, whom we had grown to love as well as obey, had been struck down. He had been a man of enormous strength who could fell a recalcitrant mule with his fist, and his death was at first incomprehensible. Tony Grice and his men were stunned. Few of us had appetite for another day of training, but after consulting with Support Unit headquarters in Salisbury, we rallied to complete all assigned tasks on that sad day.

It was a long, silent drive back to Salisbury.

CHAPTER 5

The Other War

WHILE SUPPORT UNIT was gearing up for counterinsurgency operations, there was another secret, far more unconventional war under way in Rhodesia.

There had been rumors that the army was raising a special tracker unit that would have a high percentage of African members—and when eventually I heard that its European members would grow beards and blacken their faces, it became more obvious to me that what was being planned was something more than a tracking operation.

The Selous Scouts, as the regiment came to be known, was in its infancy during 1974—its new commanding officer reaching everywhere to find the uniquely qualified men that he needed. I first saw Major Ron Reid-Daly one day at Tomlinson Depot when he pulled up in a battered camouflage Land Rover, parking it next to the office wing that housed our commander, Assistant Commissioner Guy Houghton. A man of medium height with the erect carriage of a career soldier, Reid-Daly's rows of decorations on his army camouflage denim order battle dress were illustrative of extended service. He was, I later came to learn, one of the Rhodesian Special Air Service (SAS) contingent that served in the Malaya Emergency as a noncommissioned officer (NCO). Now, he was looking at what Guy Houghton might provide for his emerging regiment. I was curious that first day, but not curious enough to ask many questions. The world of special operations, after three years in Vietnam, was not a new concept, and I was not anxious to learn things that I didn't need to know to do my job.

There would be more such visits, and over time selected African volunteers transferred from Support Unit to the Scouts. There were also a very few patrol officers who likewise moved across from the British South Africa Police (BSAP), passed a rigorous selection program, and put on the unique brown beret of the Selous Scouts.

I was also unaware that my friend Winston Hart was by that time an integral member of the Scouts in his Special Branch role. His early involvement in gathering intelligence about enemy activities both within Rhodesia and externally, made him a logical choice—but the organization had not gotten off to an easy start.

When the Altena Farm attacks had firmly focused attention on the emerging war in the northeast, a joint group of senior officers met at Mount Darwin to consider options for countering the threat of marauding terrorist gangs. During that meeting, it was pointed out that the British forces during the Kenya Mau Mau insurrection had successfully countered terrorist gangs by fielding "pseudos"—friendlies dressed and trained to act as though they were also insurgents. In Malaya, the British had again employed the technique against groups of Chinese terrorists operating in the jungle. Tactics called for the pseudo gang to find, befriend, then attack the enemy once they were able to do so.

The officers who met at the Joint Operations Center (JOC) Mount Darwin that day decided that the pseudo concept had merit, deserved further investigation and testing—and should be managed by Special Branch (SB). Because SB was always represented in the JOC command structure, they decided that responsibility for the pseudo program would pass to the SB officers who moved through Mount Darwin JOC on regular rotation.

The first pseudo team was assembled using two African detective constables, who were placed in charge of four captured insurgents, believed to have been reindoctrinated.

As Special Branch detectives were assembling and testing the all-African pseudo team, the Rhodesian army decided to field their own teams. Two Special Air Service NCOs then attached to the Tracking Wing at Kariba were selected to lead: Sergeant Andre Rabie, an accomplished African linguist with a comprehensive knowledge of native customs and lore—and skilled tracker Sergeant Alan "Stretch" Franklin. With beards—and blackened faces and hands—they would lead pseudo African insurgents recruited from the Rhodesian African Rifles.

The absence of continuity and commitment did not auger well for the SB program in its earliest stages. There were mixed results as different tactics were tried under various Special Branch officers. The team, when infiltrated into a suspect tribal trust land area dressed as insurgents, proved adept at testing SB ground coverage and information sources as a means of determining whether subversion had taken place. And when commanders assessed the results, there was encouragement about the volume of raw data that was being generated, but disappointment at the absence of tangible results—dead insurgents.

Winston and his colleagues operated under a cloak of extreme secrecy as they began to pull the Special Branch program together. Senior officers were never made fully aware of the mission. A cover story was drawn forth when required to answer awkward questions from superiors in duty branch. In the very earliest days, genuine terrorist clothing, equipment, and arms were secretly stored at a suburban Salisbury police station. The officer in charge knew better than to ask what the gear was for.

Ultimately, three pseudo teams were operating under Special Branch control in the Operation Hurricane area of northeastern Rhodesia, two from the army and the SB African group. Senior SB personnel came to realize that for the program to reach full potential, it would require a firm hand from an assigned coordinator. Winston Hart was selected to provide much-needed overall backup and operational guidance. A strong spirit of comradeship had already developed between Hart and the two army NCOs.

Initially, the teams operated mainly as observers by manning key high points in the bush and watching for terrorist movements and activities. It was then decided to send Franklin and Rabie's teams deep into Mozambique, where they would turn around and follow the Ruya River back into northeastern Rhodesia. This was a known terrorist incursion route, and the plan was for the pseudo gang to pose as a Zimbabwe African National Liberation Army (ZANLA) group marching across from a Mozambique base camp. Once in the field, Franklin and Rabie soon succeeded in capturing a terrorist who was armed with a Soviet Tokarev pistol. Hart headed for the site immediately and interrogated the man to try to gather current information that might lead to attacks against other enemy groups. In the back of his mind, he knew that he would very shortly be expected to turn their prisoner over to police authorities; the BSAP had a firm policy about captured insurgents, requiring an investigation and formal charges to be laid. Stiff sentences were prescribed under the relevant antiterrorism acts, including death by hanging.

The captured man provided good information. Realizing this, Franklin and Rabie approached Hart and begged him to allow their capture to join them as a member of the pseudoterrorist team. Moreover, they wanted the man's Tokarev pistol returned to him. Winston realized that there was considerable logic to the argument, despite potentially draconian reaction from senior police at his unilateral and highly irregular decision. The prisoner was fully aware that he faced a hangman's noose and he had cooperated during interrogation. However, he was dumbstruck when Hart returned his pistol to him, instructing that he carefully obey the instruction of the group leaders. He did not know, however, that the powder charge had been removed from the pistol's cartridges.

Hart and SB colleague Peter Stanton did not report this capture. On the few days between operations, the former terrorist was kept quite happily locked in a shed at Stanton's suburban Salisbury home, clearly a violation of multitudes of police regulations and procedures. In point of fact, all of the pioneers of pseudo operations were then making courageous decisions as means were sought to make the program effective. Franklin, Rabie, and their team were trusting their cumulative judgment that the benefits of having a recent enemy on the team outweighed the obvious danger that he might decide to turn on them at some unknown future date.

The United States and South Vietnam operated a successful *chieu hoi* (open arms) program designed to rally Viet Cong and North Vietnamese army personnel to the allied ranks. I had seen these former enemies used effectively as scouts for U.S. Marines operating in I Corps. So, the concept of using rallied enemy combatants was not new in the annals of recent military history. However, in the years that followed, the Selous Scouts—as the pseudoterrorists were soon to be known—recruited scores of insurgents and actively assimilated them into their ranks as equals. By so doing, they gained a huge repository of current information, men who personally knew the enemy, and men who knew how to win the confidence of their former colleagues-in-arms.

The "turned terrorist" (TT) did not have long to spend sleeping in Peter Stanton's garden shed. He was soon returned to field operations with Rabie and Franklin.

When Section Officer Dave Ward's wife was killed in the land mine explosion near Centenary, Andre Rabie and his team were called into the area to help locate those responsible. Rabie, an exceptionally skilled tracker, knew the area and its people well. In the meantime, Stretch Franklin's group operated on the fringe of Chesa Tribal Trust Land, not far from the mine where Len Koenig had been abducted and murdered. Posing as ZANLA freedom fighters, the group used their newly acquired turned terrorist to arrange a meeting. Then they retreated to a safe location, where Stretch awaited in cover. At a bush meeting soon after with Winston Hart,

Franklin expressed confidence that the meeting would occur—and that his group would scratch more ZANLA insurgents from the enemy roles.

Franklin's pseudo team turned up at the meeting place, surprising a gang led by a man carrying an RPD Soviet-pattern light machine gun. Seizing the moment, Franklin's group shook out into a skirmish line and attacked the group with AK-47s and a grenade, first killing its leader.

Kennedy Zwavamutsana, his RPD lying in the dust, was dead; other insurgents had scattered, leaving behind heavy blood *spoor*. Follow-ups later verified that two more had died from wounds, and a third man was later captured.

Chief Inspector Dave Perkins at the police armory in Salisbury tested the captured RPD, confirming it was the weapon used to fire dozens of rounds into the abducted Len Koenig's head and torso. Stretch and his team felt considerable satisfaction from settling that score.

In the meantime, Andre Rabie's team had not been successful in their efforts to locate the killers of Mrs. Ward. Determined to emulate the successes of the Franklin team, Andre was keen to return to the field, telling Hart he wished to remain until he too had kills to report.

The team was sent into an area near Shamva. To protect pseudo groups, who certainly looked and acted like insurgents, the JOC carefully created no-go areas for all other security force elements. "Frozen" zones were carefully annotated on maps and were respected by other security force elements, though they were unaware of their true purpose.

Winston Hart and his SB colleagues briefed the team carefully before the operation began. ZANLA groups were believed to be transiting and operating in the area.

Soon after entering their operating area, locals provided Rabie's pseudo gang with information about a local arms cache, which the team recovered for its own use. Then all became quiet. Except for regular radio checks and constant observation, nothing was happening. Andre kept the team near the water, checking water holes and local tracks. With him was the TT he and Stretch captured and rearmed with Winston Hart's concurrence; the balance were soldier volunteers from the Rhodesian African Rifles, dressed and equipped as insurgents.

In the interim, Special Branch sources reported the presence of an enemy group in the area. Winston Hart, concerned that the sighting might be Andre Rabie's group, immediately contacted the JOC in Mount Darwin, requesting that they confirm the team's location. In a radio transmission, Sergeant Rabie replied to the JOC query, encoding the team grid reference position in shackle code. That position was plotted on a map, indicating that the pseudo team was about ten kilometers from the terrorist sighting reported to Special Branch.

A decision was made to mount a follow-up by a locally based element of the Rhodesian Light Infantry (RLI). Rabie was so advised by radio. He later commented that he was hoping the RLI would chase the enemy downstream toward his group.

Later in the day, several of Rabie's African soldiers approached him, asking for permission to go down to a nearby water hole. There were fish there, they said; the intention was to try to net them using their camouflage face veils. Rabie agreed and, following them down the bank, placed his RPD machine gun on its bipod at a convenient location.

"Andre was a keen photographer," Winston Hart recalls. "He had a small camera and was moving to the water hole to photograph the fish netting."

What nobody realized was that Andre Rabie had made an error transposing his locating grid reference into shackle code. The RLI group was nearly upon them—and when the troopers heard African voices emanating from the riverbed, the lead scout and SB Inspector Vic Opperman went to full alert and began a quiet approach.

They saw Andre's distinctive Soviet RPD on the riverbank and almost simultaneously saw movement behind river reeds. There was a rapid fusillade of fire, and Andre Rabie was killed instantly.

Concerning the incident, Winston Hart has said, "It was an enormous tragedy, one that affected us all in some way. The African soldiers *bombshelled*—scattered—when the shooting started, but not the TT Andre and Stretch had captured. He stayed with his sergeant, despite the obvious danger and was utterly inconsolable at his death. He was still in tears when I saw him."

The body was secretly transported to a discreet mortuary in Salisbury, where trusted Criminal Investigation Division (CID) detective Bob Wishart removed the terrorist clothing and began scrubbing blackening from Andre's hands and face. His death was explained as accidental, as indeed it was; but the nature of the mission remained a closely guarded secret. Wishart later joined the Selous Scouts, ultimately losing a leg in a land mine incident near Mangula.

The turned terrorist who cried at Andre Rabie's death went on to serve with distinction in the soon-to-be created Selous Scouts.

It was the direct intervention of Prime Minister Ian Smith that caused the unit to be raised, and with a degree or urgency. Briefed about initial

Winston Hart as a Selous Scout. The photo was taken as the Scouts were launching an assault on the ZANLA training camp at Massangena, Mozambique. Hart recovered considerable material of intelligence value following the attack. (Courtesy Winston Hart)

experiments with pseudo operations, Smith ordered that a unit dedicated specifically to that role was to be created. It fell to the commander of the Rhodesian army, Lieutenant General Peter Walls, to locate the right man to command the new regiment. Walls knew that he wanted Ron Reid-Daly for the job; they had served together in Malaya and later then-Sergeant Major Reid-Daly had been regimental sergeant major (RSM) of the Rhodesian Light Infantry when Walls commanded the RLI. Reid-Daly was in the final stages of permanently retiring from the army, but Walls prevailed upon his former RSM to accept command of the fledgling unit.

The new regiment was named for Frederick Courtney Selous, a renowned English hunter and adventurer who came to Africa in the 1870s as a nineteen-year-old and assisted Rhodes with the early establishment of the country that came to be called Rhodesia. His qualities as a bushman were such that he was serving in the British army during the East African campaigns of World War I, and it was in Tanganyika that he was struck down by German fire at the age of sixty-two. An avenue in Salisbury bore his name; it was an appropriate name choice for a Rhodesian scouting unit.

Significantly, leadership of the Selous Scouts was effectively shared by the army and Special Branch. Winston Hart came across in a seamless move, to serve under SB superintendent Mac McGuiness. Commanding

Captain Rob Warracker (far left) led the Selous Scouts raid on Massangena, Mozambique, from this armored Mercedes Benz Unimog, affectionately known as a Pig. (Courtesy Winston Hart)

officer Major Reid-Daly would go on to recruit, select, and train about two hundred men, most of whom were then serving in the Rhodesian defense force. Special Branch would covertly pay several hundred "tamed" insurgents that were assimilated into the Scout's operational organization.

A critical element of the Selous Scout mission was generation of timely intelligence that could be effectively acted on. Intelligence was its lifeblood and the composite teams very soon adapted themselves to a role of aggressive information gatherers by posing as enemy insurgents. African soldiers posing as insurgents—together with "tame terrorists" who were former insurgents themselves—became adroit at the game of soliciting information without suspicion from local tribesmen about the whereabouts and activities of their erstwhile comrades.

Army leadership was painfully aware that their operational shortcomings in the war heretofore were almost entirely the result of an inability of more conventional units to find, fix, and destroy the enemy. It was hoped that the pseudo concept would remedy this shortcoming by providing immediate, useful intelligence that could facilitate effective attacks against the enemy.

Major Reid-Daly and his Special Branch counterparts came to realize that some of the tactics employed by the British in Kenya and Malaya were inappropriate to the insurgency in Rhodesia. In particular, there was an awareness that if pseudo gangs continued to launch attacks on terrorist groups it could easily compromise their ability to remain under cover. The news of "terrorist-on-terrorist" attacks had a tendency to spread like wildfire through the tribal trust lands. Instead, other security forces units came to be tasked with actual attacks, under the careful direction of a Joint Operation Center. The army's Fire Force became particularly adept at inserting ambush and stop groups around terrorist elements. Using a combination of Rhodesian air force troop-carrying helicopters and a rotary-wing command ship often armed with a 20-mm cannon, the fire force reacted on very short notice to enemy sightings and contacts from forward air fields. As the war progressed, C-47 Dakota transports were also used to deploy paratroopers operating in a Fire Force roll.

The Selous Scouts grew rapidly under the careful, methodical leadership of Major Reid-Daly, who was later promoted to lieutenant colonel. Using a comprehensive in-house communication system and a series of rear area forts to maintain operative cover, they operated pseudoterrorist teams throughout Rhodesia's border areas and even launched a number of highly effective cross-border raids into Mozambique by traversing bush tracks in fast truck convoys. The Scouts targeted terrorist training and logistics bases in these attacks, killing literally thousands of would-be insurgents almost entirely by skillful use of small arms.

* * *

As if the challenge of training young Africans to master modern, sophisticated military weapons wasn't enough, Ormonde and I both had real concerns about the abilities of some of the long-serving members of Support Unit. Senior members had been trained by a succession of well-meaning policemen, but there had been no formalized training doctrine. The result was that a critical stratum of the unit did not, for instance, necessarily use the same words to describe weapon components. Of more concern were the drills they had learned for safe and effective weapon handling. There had been some near accidents involving Support Unit NCOs during live-firing exercises. We concluded that a uniform instructional doctrine for all weapons should be adopted by Support Unit, and we thought that the Rhodesian army's many decades of development and experience made it a logical source of learning.

Together, we marched into Assistant Commissioner Guy Houghton's office one morning and explained our concerns. As was his habit, the officer commanding listened attentively, then asked simply, "What do you suggest?"

Our response was to volunteer to attend the School of Infantry, Gwelo, where the army trained its trainers. There we would undergo training with potential army instructors both on small arms then in universal use in the BSAP, but we also would learn about some that we hoped would eventually be incorporated into Support Unit's armory. The MAG light machine gun was one such weapon.

Guy Houghton's focus was on creating an effective paramilitary force. He also realized the benefits of having his troops trained in the universal small-arms doctrine used by the national army. He agreed to put our request forward with his endorsement.

Less than a week later, a grinning Ormonde approached me after a class and said, "Doug, we are going to Gwelo!" The army had agreed to place us both in a class then under way in its initial phase. I expressed my concern at the possibility that I might have a difficult time in an ongoing class for drill instructors but was told that we would join the class after that phase, in time to learn army tactics and weapons.

There was much to be done in a short while. We set about arranging rifle range practice sessions for troops scheduled to rotate through the depot for continuation training during our absence. On this occasion, our continuation training regime would be carried out under the auspices of troop commandeers. There were also some seemingly thorny questions about what equipment to take for the course. Police uniforms were many, varied, and unfamiliar to the eyes of army drill instructors. They were also difficult to keep in a state of perfection such that we would not find ourselves performing punishment fatigues for infractions of the very high standards. The typical army trainee had only two pairs of boots and two nonleather belts to worry about. He had no cap strap to polish, nor did he have leather leggings in his kit. Ormonde and I decided that our best course of action would be to take only battle dress, the Rhodesian pattern camouflage denim order. And, we would share a *batman* between us.

We both knew very well that at the School of Infantry, we would once again be reduced to the status of soldiers in training. I was anxious to learn new skills but also apprehensive about the process. Ormonde had far more experience in the army school environment but was as keyed up as I. We would certainly be the oldest men on the course—and there was an expectation that we were to come away with top marks. We were, after all, representing Support Unit, and the Rhodesian army would be watching our performance carefully.

At last the day came. The last of a myriad of details had been finalized for Support Unit training, our gear was carefully packed, and our rifles had been stowed in the trunk. With words of encouragement, we headed southwest down the highway driving toward Bulawayo. Gwelo, in the Midlands, was several hours away, particularly at the reduced speeds attendant with fuel rationing. It was my first trip to the central region of the country, passing through the towns of Hartley, Gatooma, and Que Que. These were tidy small towns that provided amenities to farming, mining, and the growing manufacturing sector.

On a bright, warm afternoon, we drove down the main street of Gwelo, a bustling commercial center with broad streets bordered by the neat facades of business houses that appeared to have been long established. In the town center was a clock tower and the Midlands Hotel, one of those imposing three-story edifices built to accommodate weary travelers in the days when the train was a preferred means of travel. We noted a bustling bar doing a brisk afternoon trade and wondered whether we'd be able to escape the confines of the school sometime soon.

The School of Infantry was carefully signposted in typical army fashion. Quite close to the city proper, it nestled in behind two *kopjes* in a wooded preserve. At the end of the access road was a guardhouse, situated in the road median. A carefully maintained but now inoperable Vickers machine gun sat next to the guardhouse, pointing menacingly down the road. Behind it was the sign announcing that within was the School of Infantry.

The beret-clad sentry, armed with pistol and clipboard, approached the car, asking what our business was as he glanced at our carefully packed kit bags and our Support Unit uniforms. He smiled when we announced that we were reporting for training, noted our names and the vehicle registration, and waved us through.

My attention was almost immediately directed to a large paved parade square off to the right. A series of full-length mirrors had been erected along one edge. These, Ormonde advised, were there for trainees to practice drill routines. I felt quietly pleased that we had somehow managed to avoid that aspect of the training course.

We parked the car, carefully locked it, and with our rifles, walked a short distance further to where a small, neat office perched on a slope. A sign announced that the school training officer was within. Approaching

The staff of Training Wing at the School of Infantry, Gwelo, are well represented in this parade of successful course graduates, most wearing the distinctive fawn beret of the SAS. Sitting in the front row, from left, are Colour Sergeant Piet Farndell, Military Police, WO2 J. Pretorius, Captain Peter Cooper, Maj. "Bullet" Stansfield (OC Wing), RSM Don Collyer, Sgt. (later WO2) Tom Van Rensberg, and Sgt. "Punchy" Pretorius, Military Police. (Courtesy Peter Cooper)

the door, Ormonde and I knocked, then marched in, came to attention, executed a right turn, and saluted by bringing our right hands smartly across to slap our rifle forestocks. Captain Peter Cooper stood and acknowledged us, bidding us to stand at ease. He said that he had been expecting us and directed that we should report to his sergeant major, Warrant Officer Second-Class (WO2) Tom Van Rensberg.

Peter Cooper, of whom I would be seeing more, was an impressive figure. Formerly a sergeant in the Grenadier Guards, he had risen through the ranks to become the regimental sergeant major of the School of Infantry, Gwelo, before accepting a commission in the Rhodesian army. He was known to run a tight ship, as in my experience many former enlisted officers did; they knew the tricks, ruses, and ways of the other ranks from personal experience. I sensed a small amount of deference as he quickly briefed us, no doubt acknowledging our maturity and experience. But there would be no special treatment for us, nor did we expect it. We would be considered of similar rank to an army sergeant.

Dismissed, we walked down the walkway and steps, taking in the place that we would be calling home in the weeks ahead. It was clear that the school had not been built at once, according to a master plan. Rather, it had expanded as funds and necessity dictated. Thus, there was a collage of different structures representing different periods in history. The commanding officer's premises, on one hand, was a substantial white-plastered brick structure built in a colonial pattern for comfort in the summer heat. The CO and his regimental sergeant major occupied two offices connected by a breezeway. Nearby was the officer's mess, a large rambling white building where itinerant officers were housed. Ormonde and I would use the facilities of the sergeant's mess, rather less imposing but central to the pavilions used for instruction.

Before checking in with the sergeant major, we walked across the road to the armory. Here we were greeted by a lance corporal who, noting our BSAP rank epaulettes, asked why we were at the school. He smiled when we said we were "on course" and accepted our rifles.

We had heard the rumors and stories about the school's sergeant major, WO2 Tom Van Rensberg. Some of these had been perpetuated by police instructors who had attended classes in drill at the school; others we had heard through the army grapevine. He was known to be a perfectionist and a ruthless—but almost always correct—judge of his charges, all aspiring instructors. It was he who would begin the dreaded RTU process, army-speak for "returned to unit" when a soldier failed to measure up. Ormonde and I were determined to hit the ground running, and to excel.

Sergeant Major Van Rensberg greeted us in his office, where he was finishing the day's work. He looked us over quickly and said, "The course troops are together in the first barracks," glancing over his shoulder at a long, rectangular metal-clad building perched above the sergeant's mess. "Find yourself a bunk and locker and store your gear. I'll see you at the mess."

Our new home was one of several very basic barracks buildings clustered together. All bore names of legendary British commanders from World War II: Alexander, Slim, Wavell. Our barracks was empty except for two rows of basic steel-frame cots lined up along the long axis of the building—and a collection of lockers. The mattresses of two of the cots had been folded back, the previous users apparently having been RTU'd, and these we laid claim to. The walls were a single sheet of roofing iron secured to exposed studs. There was no heat source, nor were there fans. Plainly, we would be having an experience not unlike recruits trained in World War II, at least with billeting. I would have about thirty young men to share that experience with.

Most of our classmates were not sergeants; they were corporals and lance corporals who had been selected for potential leadership and instructional capabilities. The successful junior NCOs would go back to their regiments and there assume training assignments. They would train recruits and take an active role in the ongoing program that the army called continuation training.

At the appointed hour for the Sunday evening meal, Ormonde and I made our way down the pathway from the barracks to the rear entrance of the school sergeant's mess—a single-story plastered brick building that had the look of a structure added on to meet the exigencies of growing staff. The dining room itself was functional, the central furniture being a series of dining tables situated in the pattern of a U. Several African mess men were in attendance, setting places and bringing food to a growing number of diners. All were sergeants, colour sergeants, and staff sergeants, still attired in Rhodesian army camouflage short-sleeved shirts, wearing the distinctive stable belt that identified their parent regiment. Most wore the green of the Rhodesian Light Infantry, although several were territorial soldiers completing national service.

We introduced ourselves to the NCOs who would be our instructors for the course. Though not overtly friendly, most were curious about both of us. We took our seats at the table and chatted while the meal was served by stewards. It was not, by any means, the fare and service of an officer's mess in the British army, but the food was plentiful and substantial.

Sergeant Major Van Rensberg made an appearance, explaining that classes would begin in the morning after breakfast. After a desert of a typical English pudding, we adjourned to the mess bar for a beer—then returned to the barracks.

Bare bulbs cast raw beams through the several old windows of our new home, and muffled laughter told us that our new classmates were back, most from a weekend away on a two-day pass. Walking down the aisle between bunks, we were casually inspected as we made our way to our bunks. Some of the men were already stretched out and some were asleep, but others patiently checked and rechecked their personal equipment in readiness for the morning's first lesson. An RLI corporal sat next to me patiently spitting on the cap of his parade stick boots while gently burnishing the black leather with a ball of cotton.

"You Ous came at the right time," he observed. "The drill and all the other bullshit finished last week." He made a few more statements about long hours spent on the square, then suddenly asked, "Met the RSM yet?"

"No." What about him?"

"His name is Collyer. Came from the Brit Paras. Takes no shit."

"Umm," I acknowledged as I began to roll out my parachute silk sleeping bag onto the old, dusty mattress I'd been given. "I guess I'll be finding out tomorrow, huh?"

"Jah. And the rest of us will be reminded."

Opposite us were two sergeants of the Rhodesian SAS, just returned from the weekend in Salisbury. They were young, but there was a distinct air of maturity about both, one of whom looked to be of Mediterranean descent. As I would have expected also, they were cautiously curious about the two older men from the BSAP who would be their classmates.

Eyeing my lightweight sleeping bag that had been painstakingly crafted by a police tailor from a discarded cargo parachute, one said with a smile, "Nice sleeping bags, the police issue." I felt obliged to explain my good fortune of being in the right place at the right time.

For the final time, I rechecked my battle dress uniform and webbing in anticipation of the morning, then carefully locked all in the old green metal wall locker. Seeing what I had done, a soldier sitting on his bunk and reading a dog-eared paperback book said, "Good idea. Some jackal scaled my webbing last week, and I had to buy a new set."

The corporal polishing his boots spoke up before I could reply: "You are a fucking waste of rations, man. Didn't you learn anything about caring for your kit in training? Lock it or loose it!"

"Jah, Corp. Jah."

It was 9:30 on a Sunday evening, and I crawled into my sleeping bag. The lights would soon be switched off. I was tired. In the distance, steam locomotives in Gwelo's railway yards whistled plaintively. I found my spirits at a low ebb, aggravated by concerns about the unknown demands that would begin in the morning. I thought, "You've done it again, Hubbard: found another really great opportunity for an experience that maybe you don't want or need. You've got a comfortable home in Salisbury, and here you are in a drafty cold barracks in Gwelo with thirty hairy asses. That's smart, right?" I drifted off to sleep, still bathed in the light from the bare overhead bulb dangling from a wire over the aisle.

I slept lightly, not yet used to the sounds of other men in close proximity. And I dreamed. Back in Vietnam again, my slumber was troubled by the imagined trials of life in that war zone, situations and sadness that could never be remedied in the world of my subconscious. At about 4:30 AM, my eyes fluttered open. It was cold and I pulled a woolen blanket tighter around my light sleeping bag. In the adjoining barracks, where young officer candidates were billeted, I could hear sounds of men hurrying in anticipation of their initial morning parade. Their day began a full hour before ours in the coldest, darkest time of the morning.

I was glad for extra minutes before 5:00 AM reveille but arose early to beat the rush at the ablution block. Grabbing my shaving gear, I padded down the aisle, out the door, and into the toilet block. I was starting to lather my face when Ormonde arrived, eyes still showing the effects of deep sleep.

"Morning Doug," he grunted. "Didn't feel like getting up, but there will be a huge rush here momentarily." And he was right. We got out early, dressed, and were early at the mess for breakfast.

There was an animated air at the communal table as instructional staff discussed lesson plans and exchanged information. We ate and listened carefully, learning that our first course lesson would be offered by Sergeant Major Van Rensberg in the classroom.

We were to quickly learn that classroom instruction would be a rare event at the School of Infantry. On this occasion, Van Rensberg employed his considerable communication skills to explain what the course was about: what would happen, what the objectives were, and how we would be evaluated. As instructors, we would be expected to learn a considerable amount of factual data about the weapons we would be teaching. This was important information, necessary to impart to our students to ensure competency and understanding. Beyond the information, we would be expected to learn the fundamentals of instructional techniques, the army way. These followed a formula devised in the British army and constantly revised for relevance and effectiveness.

"You will introduce the lesson first to explain the subject matter relevance to your soldier trainees," he began. "For instance, the FN is the issue rifle of the Rhodesian army, and all soldiers must know how to care for and fire it accurately."

"Next, you will explain the aim of the lesson. Continuing on with the FN class, you might say, 'The aim of this lesson is to teach you the fundamental use and operation of the FN rifle.'"

I carefully took notes. It was not complex material, but it was becoming apparent that the school expected us to know a vast amount of material, even before we began learning how to impart it to others.

My classmates, most of whom were intently concentrating on the lesson in the certain knowledge that they would soon be tested on the knowledge imparted, were a diaspora representing several generations of European migrants to Africa. There were the ginger-haired Irish; working-class English; Portuguese, whose families had fled from nearby Mozambique; even one or two "toffy" Englishmen, whose accents identified their pedigree as originating in the upper strata of British society. And there were Afrikaners, white South Africans whose people had migrated northward seeking land and enhanced economic status, often as farmers and skilled tradesmen. Afrikaners, a unique group of white Africans, had evolved from European settlers who began migrating to South Africa during the seventeenth century, developing their own curious Dutch-based language, culture, and religion. It was apparent that the Afrikaans language and culture permeated some regiments of the Rhodesian army, where a curious English-based lingua franca had developed in which Afrikaans nouns and even Shona words had been integrated. I was hearing words from RLI troopers that were absolutely alien to me.

Rhodesia's defense forces in 1974 represented in some ways where the political evolution of the country had by then progressed. In the army, the Rhodesian Light Infantry, Special Air Service, and artillery were made up exclusively of soldiers of European descent. The Rhodesian African Rifles, becoming two battalions strong, were all African, except for officers. The Selous Scouts was a conglomerate of African and whites, while the mixed-race soldiers of Rhodesia (traditionally called coloureds) were subject to conscription and served in a variety of military support functions. The British South Africa Police had many more African members than whites and the Rhodesian air force was also a mixed organization. African NCOs were trained at the School of Infantry in courses designed for them, in which English was not the exclusive language.

Sergeant Major Van Rensberg concluded his lesson suddenly by announcing that the class was to be divided up into squads for the first practical lesson. Ormonde and I, seated next to each other, were with several others from the table assigned to a young sergeant we knew as Teach. He wasted no time, barking orders that reminded us that every student was in trainee status and could be expected to be treated as a recruit. We grabbed our notebooks and spilled out the door behind our fresh, youthful leader.

Teach, we learned, had been selected by Van Rensberg from a pool of dozens of soldier trainees because of a demonstrated acumen for training. He was a territorial soldier, a Rhodesian school teacher doing his national service.

Teach looked like he had just begun to shave. With a short shock of blond hair and boyish exuberance, he had learned to drive and train troops through a mixture of enthusiasm and unyielding discipline. Minutes later, we were gathered under an overhead shelter in the nearby wooded training area. A tarpaulin was spread on the ground next to the shelter with an array of training materials. Our sergeant instructor had evidently prepared well for our introductory lesson.

"Listen up!" he barked, sweeping his eyes to those of each trainee. One or two of the younger men squirmed on the hard wooden bench, but the murmuring stopped, and Teach began FN Lesson One by explaining how the issue rifle fit into the armory of weapons available to the Rhodesian army, how it was employed, and something about its characteristics. His manner was no-nonsense, his voice clear and penetrating—and he constantly revised points of importance, then selected a trainee to answer a question about what had just been covered.

"Corporal Wilson, what is the muzzle velocity of the 7.62 bullet when it exits the barrel of the FN?" he queried.

"3,400 feet per second, Sergeant."

"Is that right, Trooper Suarez?"

Suarez, a slightly built nineteen-year-old of Portuguese decent, had been struggling to appear alert. Teach, in one of his visual sweeps of squad eyes, had noticed the fluttering eyelids of Suarez, who had clearly been surprised by the question. Now he hesitated before answering, "Um jah, that's right, Sergeant."

Teach didn't pause an instant: "Right! All of you! I want to see the last man back from that tree," he said pointing to a distant mopani. The squad thundered off in full sprint mode almost instantly, each man determined not to be last back and thus eligible to run the course again. Boots pounded in the dry dust. I heard a deep, accented voice behind me say to Suarez, who was struggling near the rear of the pack, "Listen up, you fucking wanker." Nobody liked being sent off on a chase to nowhere.

Teach knew that the trainees themselves were often the best means of ensuring that classes were effective. When we returned, the last man was not required to repeat the run. As we gathered, all of us breathing heavily from exertion, he reminded us of a point we had just heard from the sergeant major: "Fault correction is a vital part of effective instruction."

The class quickly returned to an atmosphere of charged tension as our sergeant instructor worked surely and methodically through a carefully planned lesson that he had presented many times before. Ormonde and I listened closely, trying to assimilate as much of the instruction as possible. Tomorrow, we would be presenting the lesson to others as instructors—and we would be assessed on how well we did it.

Though instruction was always delivered under pressure, there were welcome breaks for tea and meals, normally in the sergeant's mess. The NCOs of the School of Infantry were drawn together—inclusive of visiting sergeants and warrant officers—into a loose military family under the aegis of the mess. The father of the family was the regimental sergeant major, WO1 Collyer, who presided over much of the day-to-day events in the lives of Gwelo's sergeants.

Collyer, formerly of Britain's Parachute Regiment, was an imposing figure in his early forties, a man who prided himself in knowing as much as possible about anything that concerned the soldiers of the school. He was the commandant's right-hand man, the NCO Lieutenant Colonel Tom Davidson turned to when he needed to know what was really going on. The RSM was a hard, old soldier who quickly mastered the names of every "guest" at the mess, made it his business to learn something about them, and could always be counted on for some not-so-gentle chiding if things were not going as well as they might.

Ormonde was the first to notice the person of the RSM, marching alone on the access road up from the office he shared with the school commandant. Ramrod straight, he carried a brightly polished pace stick under his left arm, swung his right arm in a brisk cadence with his hobnail-clad boots, and peered out from under the brim of a fiercely setup barracks cap. Soon after, at morning tea, we together approached the RSM at the mess and introduced ourselves as a matter of courtesy. Collyer obviously appreciated our adherence to military protocol and gruffly welcomed us to the school and his mess. He would, we knew, be watching to see how police were performing in and out of the classroom.

That night, we escaped from the barracks environment to find a quiet corner in the mess where we could study the next day's lessons and begin to plan how we would teach them if called upon. Every trainee was expected to prepare a lesson plan for every topic included in the next day's schedule. These were called "mutuals." With large file cards to use as aids memoire, we committed topics and their critical elements into a logical sequence, then reviewed the cards many times to commit as much as possible to memory. A smooth performance without a lot of recourse to the reminder cards, as our well-practiced instructors routinely did, was bound to make a better impression, we reasoned.

I was first called on to deliver a lesson about the workings of the FN submachine gun, a Belgian copy of the robust Israeli 9-mm Uzi. I was reasonably well prepared, having studied the night before, and it all went quite well. My main hurdle was remembering and correctly pronouncing the names of my classmates, whom I was expected to call on for responses. As most of them had prepared the same lesson, my questions were normally answered forthrightly.

Long days of teaching and practicing every aspect of weapon handling were demanding, and there was never enough sleep, nor was it often uninterrupted. High-spirited troopers lucky enough to get away from the school for an evening were often noisy when they returned. On one night, a motorcycle was ridden through the barracks. Ormonde and I were always glad to pack up on Friday evening for the drive back to Salisbury. There, at our respective homes, we studied more—but in far more salubrious environs. Sunday afternoon, and the drive back always came too soon.

After several days of lessons and a shoot at the miniature range, we completed final lessons on the MAG light machine gun—and there were days spent afterward at the nearby school rifle range, where each student qualified on various weapons in much the same way their future students would. I set no records with the issue rifle this time but did manage to qualify well with submachine gun, beaten only by one of the SAS troopers who bettered me by two points.

It had been a cool, clear high veld winter morning begun in buttoned battle smocks, but soon shed as the sun began to climb. For the submachine gun shoot, large Figure Eleven silhouette targets were placed at ground level in front of the backstop. We began at about seventy-five meters, firing single shots and advancing under command to nearer firing points where change levers were switched to full automatic. I had no problem keeping the foresight post in the target center by firing two- and three-round bursts. The trick, I had learned, was not to be distracted by the open bolt slamming home as the trigger was squeezed and the first round fired.

Promptly at 10:00 AM, an old camouflaged army Land Rover banged out onto the mowed firing range, a large metal canister of sweetened, strong tea adjacent the tailgate. This was part of a ritual I had learned to enjoy, the "brew up" that had kept soldiers of the British army marching for years. Here, it was soldiers of that strange, unique amalgam of Rhodesia, drinking tea cultivated in their own Eastern Highlands, sweetened with sugar raised in the Hippo Valley with milk from a nearby local dairy. Soldiers lined up behind the old truck carrying metal canteen liners hastily proffered from the webbing that we all wore. As soldiers do, the men quickly found a place to sit, loosened equipment—and many smoked.

There was desultory talk about the shoot, the predictions about the next class, and the usual chuckling about recent misadventures while on leave.

I learned that another American was then at the School of Infantry, enrolled in a Potential Officer Course. Bob McKenzie was a sergeant in the Rhodesian SAS. Normally stationed in Salisbury, he was looking for weekend transportation home to his wife and family. Ormonde and I called on him at the officer's mess to make the arrangements.

We walked down toward the mess together, looking up his room number—one of several with doors leading off a wide veranda. I knocked on the door and a distinctively American voice called back, "Come in." We walked in as Bob was dressing in his uniform shirt. I noticed immediately massive scarring on his chest and left arm, where part of the triceps was missing. We chatted briefly as Bob finished dressing, arranging a departure time after classes on Friday. I asked him if he had been in Vietnam.

"I was in the 101st Airborne," he said. "I got unlucky in an ambush out of Duc Pho. One of the VC was armed with a captured M-16 and he nailed me."

I had been to Duc Pho and told him so. "You were lucky to survive a chest wound like that," I offered—and indeed that was so: McKenzie had spent a full year in a U.S. Army hospital in the United States before being discharged on medical grounds.

Later, I learned more about Bob McKenzie as we drove northward to Salisbury. He was from Maryland. After his hospitalization and discharge, he had enrolled in university courses under the G.I. Bill. But, although his grades were satisfactory, the collegiate atmosphere was uncomfortable—even overtly hostile. Students and professors alike were quick to understand that there was something different about this man, who still wore some of the pinched facial hardness of a soldier who had suffered greatly. When he refused to speak out against the war in Vietnam, he was ostracized.

"One day I just had enough. I fucked a couple of them up and was asked to leave. I was ready."

Feeling there was very little in his country of birth to hold him there, McKenzie traveled to Rhodesia and enlisted in the army. Moreover, he passed the incredibly grueling SAS selection course, where his navigation and field skills were noted. After an initial stint as a trooper in the SAS, he had gone AWOL, returned briefly to the United States, but decided to return and face punishment. Starting from scratch, McKenzie rose from trooper to sergeant, then was selected for commission. He had married a Rhodesian girl and had a daughter to whom he was devoted.

We were never close friends, simply because we lived in very different spheres; but Bob McKenzie and I had a common kinship based on similar experiences and convictions. He was soon after commissioned a lieutenant in the Special Air Service regiment, where he began a distinguished combat career that extended throughout the entire duration of the Rhodesian War.

As the course at the School of Infantry drew to a close, the training began to focus on field training and the lessons of basic counterinsurgency field tactics. We lived in the same barracks, but instead of the more formal environment of the school, we ventured out into some of the pristine native woodland that surrounded us.

One of the first tactical lessons was to be about countering a vehicle ambush. Sergeant Major Van Rensberg, in conspiratorial tone, called me aside to tell me he wanted me to ambush the students.

"They're going to come up that track in the truck. I want you to find a vantage point and give them a fucking big rev." With that, he handed me a Thunderflash explosive device and told me to draw an MAG machine gun with a blank firing device and a belt of ammo.

I grinned back, acknowledged the order, and walked to the armory. Minutes later, I was walking quickly and quietly through the bush alongside the truck track, scouting a suitable ambush site.

I found something that was virtually made to order: two old adjoining anthills, partially covered in trees and low vegetation. From the rear side, the hill provided a slightly elevated position for my machine gun with clear fields of fire. Scraping away sticks and vegetation, I folded down the gun bipod, concealed it behind a low bush, and lay down, pulling the gunstock up to my cheek to check the kill zone.

It was a warm afternoon. I lay comfortably on my belly, smelling the fresh earth and the heady odors of the forest and watched a weaver bird build his distinctive hanging nest. As I thought about it, this had been probably the first moment I had had to experience and enjoy the bush since arriving at Gwelo, such was the nature and pace of school life.

Perhaps twenty minutes passed before my reverie was broken by the distant grumble of the old army Bedford RL truck, grinding up the track in first gear. The driver was taking no chances with tree roots, large rocks, and ditches as he navigated, mindful of complaints from the rear, where the class sat back to back on two hard center benches facing outward, rifles ready. I lay motionless in the cover of the anthill and its vegetation, clutching the Thunderflash that was intended to simulate a grenade. As my quarry neared, I primed the long paper cylinder and lobbed it in a high arc, where it hit immediately in front of the truck front bumper and rolled under the engine before detonating with a huge bang. The driver lurched the truck to a stop, the cab enveloped in smoke, just as I fired a long burst at my intended targets, who were by then clambering rapidly over the steel sides of the truck. Knowing they would waste no time assaulting my position, I grabbed the gun's carry handle and bolted to another prepared position some distance rearward. I dove over the brow, rolled over, and got the gun up and ready to fire at the assault party as it encircled my first firing point.

The soldiers had moved very quickly, spread out and covering each other, and I again took them under fire just as Sergeant Major Van Rensberg jogged up and called the exercise to a halt. As he gathered participants together for a critique and the smell of cordite and hot gun oil cleared from my nostrils, I noticed another far more unpleasant odor. Apparently, a passing individual had also been attracted to the position for another reason: I had rolled over an enormous pile of fresh excrement. Shaking my head, angry, I stood up, cleared the gun, and walked toward my peers, who were quick to smell my misfortune. I was allocated a position on the tailgate for the ride back, downwind from complaining passengers.

A series of field problems were planned for the final phase of the tactics course. Captain Cooper deployed instructors and trainees en masse to the Rhodesian air force gunnery range at Kutanga, a short distance from Que Que. Students packed their field equipment and assembled to join an assortment of vehicles for the trip north; two hours later we had passed through the town and were in the midst of nearly seven thousand acres of pristine bush.

Although the reserve was surrounded by farms, the air force had carefully preserved it, even employing a ranger to care for the area and its wildlife. Other than a central section that had been cleared for aircraft gunnery and bombing training, Kutanga was untouched. One of the first things I saw when we entered on the dirt access road was a massive kudu bull standing slightly back in dense bush, displaying long, imposing spiral horns and pink ears.

I had been spared from riding on the hard benches of a troop-carrying truck because of a recurrent shoulder injury that had been aggravated by the training regime. A kindly air force doctor at Thornhill base injected me with cortisone, insisting that I wear the arm in a sling for the final training period. I had managed to stay on full duty, missing no classes and mastering my graded mutuals with the assistance of volunteers, who carried out class demonstrations under my instruction.

As one of the wags in the convoy was quick to point out as we pulled in to the small cluster of buildings and living quarters erected to service the range, the air force had typically considered the comfort and convenience of its people. Though not luxurious by any means, the facility lacked the austere, bare-bones atmosphere that seem almost universal to army depots.

"Leave it to the Blue Jobs," he quipped. "I wonder where the club and pool are?"

Of course there was no pool or pub dispensing cold beer. But we at least had sheltered areas in which to sleep, and there were limited messing facilities.

After weeks of technical instruction about modern weaponry, even in the open-air environment of much of the School of Infantry, the final field exercises were designed to teach lessons that related directly to how best to fight a counterinsurgency war in the wilds of Africa. Some of the sternness left Captain Cooper, and his lessons were tempered with the advice that one might expect from a seasoned warrant officer.

The next morning, in a section of dense, untouched high veld forest, he assembled us on the dirt road.

"Look into the forest," he ordered. "Do you see any enemy, or anything that might suggest the enemy is present?" Most of the men were seasoned soldiers with attendant bush skills. None answered Captain Cooper.

"Very well. If enemy were concealed, where would they be? Behind the trees, perhaps?" With that, he ordered a group of men forward and ordered them to load their rifles.

"This is a practical exercise in reconnaissance by fire. Fire a double-tap [two rounds fired in rapid succession] at every point where you think an enemy might conceal himself." The men, standing in line, quickly poured fire from their FN rifles into the base of trees and low-lying shrubs, then cleared their weapons.

"Now go forward and look," he ordered, stepping off with the men who moved into the trees, looking behind trees that had been fired on. There they discovered previously placed Figure Twelve silhouette targets depicting the head and shoulders of an enemy. Most had been struck by tumbling bullets that had previously penetrated the tree that had concealed them.

"Listen up! The lesson here is clear. The 7.62 NATO round will penetrate many trees, even large ones. Remember that when you choose cover for yourselves and your troops. Remember it also if you can preempt a surprise attack by fire."

Captain Cooper's reconnaissance-by-fire class set the tone for the final lessons, each of which was designed to be assimilated and used by instructors charged with training new soldiers in the skills they would need to survive and prosecute Rhodesia's war.

Following on from lessons learned in brief, savage firefights typical of the bush war, the army devoted considerable training time to teaching the skills associated with instinctive snap-shooting. A soldier's ability to react and fire very quickly while maintaining accuracy was a critical skill for men whose contact with the enemy was often at close range and almost always unexpected.

At Support Unit, we had begun to teach new recruits the skills of instinctive pointing and rapid fire, the double-tap. We had learned that this type of instruction could not be rushed with young African trainees; the discipline of safe weapon handling was not yet firmly bedded in many, with the result that we were always vigilant about where rifle muzzles were being pointed. We had not, yet, had a range fatality.

Thus, when Captain Cooper announced that we would learn the construction and use of a jungle lane to train men in fast, instinctive shooting, Ormonde and I focused our attention to see what new techniques we might learn; it was a certainty that Support Unit troops would need to master this type of training if they were to reach full potential.

With the practiced eye of true infantrymen, instructors had selected a near-ideal location for the demonstration jungle-lane firing course. Deep in the forest, a small heavily wooded wash rose gently to a low hill. The test had been set out along what must have been a seasonal streambed.

As I could not fire a rifle while wearing a sling, I would follow close behind to assist the instructor who shadowed each shooter through the course. I felt unsettled, uncomfortable as I first stood under the overhead canopy of trees. The topography of the forested ground had triggered my survival instincts. On both sides and to the front the ground sloped upward. I could imagine even a modest enemy force on either side, holding the high ground and pouring deadly fire downward into the hapless souls who had chosen to advance through such a natural trap. Soon, the first shooter, Corporal Gallagher from the RLI, walked up the trail from below to our position, eyes sweeping ahead and to the side. Targets remained hidden, but Gallagher's body language told me that he too was thinking that we were in bad ground.

Gallagher moved ahead of us, received the order to load a magazine and began to advance very slowly, as any good point man would, up the trace. The instructor remained far enough back that he could pull hidden cords that were attached to concealed Figure Twelve targets.

The first target, backed by plywood, had been hinged with a piece of a truck inner tube to the back of a large tree. When the instructor pulled on a concealed rope, it snapped smartly into position facing Gallagher, displaying a grimacing black and white face with poised rifle. Already tense, the shooter swung right in one fluid motion and in less than three seconds loosed off a double-tap. I noted with satisfaction that both rounds struck the target in the head. It was obvious that while Corporal Gallagher may not have taken high honors in distance shooting, he was an adroit survivor, schooled in the realities of bush warfare.

The following two targets popped up at a distance of no more than seven meters. Gallagher, staring over rifle sights with both eyes open, poured fire into both—again scoring well. He finished the course with strikes on every target. We patched targets and then brought the next shooter forward to repeat the process.

I had the advantage of seeing every man shoot, to observe both the skilled riflemen and those needing to improve their skills. However well the trainees shot, the aim of the exercise had been clearly illustrated: instinctive shooting was an acquired skill that every rifleman needed to master.

With the completion of the field training component, the course drew rapidly to completion with final written and practical examinations. These would form the majority of the scores used to provide each student with a final mark. In those final days, also, Sergeant Major Van Rensberg drew closer to Ormonde and me. Though we both thought it would have been far more prudent to study for exams in a quiet corner somewhere, Van Rensberg enjoyed our company, as we did his. It was with some trepidation, however, that we retired to the bar for the sergeant major's favorite drink—the Afrikaner favorite—brandy and coke. With heads thumping early the next morning as we sat down to the final written exam, we speculated that we were deserving of some sort of service medal for survival.

Finally, it was all over. Students would be advised of final grades by means of reports written to our commanding officers. As we gathered our gear and began packing up the VW sedan for the drive back to Salisbury,

Tom Van Rensberg called me over to where he was speaking with several senior NCOs.

"Tell me, S/O Hubbard, how did you come to join the police?" he said.

My inquisitor was by then aware of my Vietnam service in an intelligence role. I assumed that he saw little logic in my service in Rhodesia's national police force, even if I was a competent trainer of men.

I told him quite honestly that when I initially made the decision to come to Rhodesia, it was to become a district policeman—a low-key posting to a bush environment had seemed attractive after the Vietnam experience. I had later agreed to a Support Unit posting because I felt that I could best serve there.

My new friend clearly thought that my talents were not being used to full potential.

"You should consider an army career," he said with a smile.

This was a sergeant major's way of telling me that he thought I would fit in the large family that was the Rhodesian army. It was a kindly complement, one to which I would give consideration in the weeks ahead. But now, my attentions were firmly focused on the enormous task of training Support Unit to the standard of a battle-ready group.

As Ormonde and I drove out of the gate of the School of Infantry and turned onto the highway to Salisbury, we were already considering where to begin.

CHAPTER 6

Mozambique Falls: Border Tensions Rise

THERE WAS IN LATE 1974 an air of unsettled concern pervading the Rhodesian defense establishment. It had been noticeable among the troopers with whom we shared Slim Barracks at Gwelo and was discussed after hours in various watering holes across the country. Portugal had suddenly lost its war to retain Mozambique, their colony for more than four hundred years. Mozambique shared a vast border with Rhodesia's eastern provinces. Nobody was certain what having an independent Mozambique as a neighbor would mean, but the concern about it was credible.

Although Portugal had referred to its African colonies—oil-rich Cabineta, Mozambique, Guinea-Bissau, and Angola—as overseas provinces, by the 1970s, all had active internal insurgencies. These were a consequence both of the genuine political aspirations of the African citizenry and the persistent meddling of the Soviet Union and China, which supported various armed freedom movements as a Cold War strategy for expanding their influence and power base. Portugal's army, made up to a large extent by draftees, had engaged in a prolonged struggle against armed nationalists and certainly in the earlier stages of the conflict was reasonably successful.

Rhodesia's Special Air Service, air force, and the British South Africa Police (BSAP) Special Branch all had actively cooperated with Mozambique's Portuguese administrators and soldiers, much of it covertly. Rhodesia was not shy about the principle of preemptive attack; it made good sense to prosecute the war against insurgents, sponsored by the Eastern Bloc, on somebody else's territory, particularly as there was a credible danger that Rhodesian insurgents were an element of the enemy force.

It had been a successful alliance, although Rhodesians noted vast cultural differences in the ways the Portuguese prosecuted their war. By 1974, however, it was becoming increasingly obvious that Portugal's army was in trouble. Some units were simply unwilling to leave safe compounds to engage Mozambique Liberation Front (FRELIMO) guerillas in what many considered a futile war.

The catalyst of what became a Portuguese army coup was a leftist rebel general named Antonio Spinola, who authored a highly critical book attacking colonial wars and the rationale that supported them. The army subsequently collapsed into a morass of self-criticism and discussion, becoming an ineffectual force both in Portugal and its African colonies and creating a power vacuum that ushered FRELIMO forces into power in Mozambique. The Soviet-backed Popular Movement for the Liberation of Angola (MPLA) followed into office in Angola. The entire process was to take slightly over a year. After four centuries of rule, Portugal's two most-important colonies became independent and slipped quickly under the influence of the Soviet Union.

* * *

The transition in the east was worry enough for Rhodesia's government and soldiers, but the changes in Africa's political map also drew the attention of major power brokers, in particular South African prime minister John Vorster. Vorster's reactions triggered a range of signals and actions directed at Rhodesia, which, at the time, seemed utterly confusing—at least to me and to much of the common citizenry. In hindsight, it now seems quite apparent that the reality of suddenly having hostile black nationalist governments on South Africa's Natal border and the entire north border of the nominal South African colony (then called Southwest Africa—later Namibia) panicked the prime minister. To buy time, he rushed to engage independent African states in a strategy of détente, requesting assistance from neighboring countries and even pledging to change South Africa's racial segregation policies that were considered anathema in most of Africa.

South Africa, whose industrial base supplied much critical material required for Rhodesia to prosecute the war, was to play its northern neighbor as a pawn in a game of self-preservation.

Vorster was a powerful personality, an Afrikaner nationalist with very little sympathy for things British. While in World War II South African troops joined the British army to fight Field Marshal Erwin Rommel's

Afrika Corps, Vorster was interned for alleged involvement with a radical movement with reported links to Nazi Germany.

Many thinking Rhodesians must have believed that South Africa's efforts to force the leaders of the Zimbabwean African People's Union (ZAPU) and the Zimbabwean African National Union (ZANU) to the conference table could do no harm. Even normally bellicose President Kenneth Kaunda of Zambia, who hosted both the training camps and leadership structure for these organizations, publicly hailed Vorster as a voice of reason—and he pressed ZAPU and ZANU into attending talks with Rhodesians.

On the military-logistic front, there were mysterious delays in filling Rhodesian orders for ammunition and ordnance—crude reminders that Rhodesia was economically tied to its southern neighbor, like it or not. Conversely, there were splendid displays of support from common South African citizens sympathetic to the plight of Rhodesian farmers and others caught up in the war. Civic organizations banded together to purchase vehicles and equipment to make the lives of soldiers and Rhodesian citizen reservists serving in the field more tolerable.

By far the most visible sign of changes in the relationship between South Africa and Rhodesia was the withdrawal in February 1975 of South African Police (SAP) units, which had been engaged on the borders in the fight against armed insurgency since 1967.

I had learned early that the SAP contingent was considered by Rhodesians to be something of a mixed bag. Their Special Branch elements proved adept at gathering useful local intelligence. The uniformed policemen themselves, frequently drawn from the ranks of town police stations, were issued arms, personal gear, and communication equipment that was the envy of Rhodesian soldiers. Moreover, the SAP element in Rhodesia was supported by aircraft and pilots seconded from the highly capable South African air force. But to a large extent, despite the counterinsurgency training provided in Rhodesia by the BSAP, SAP field units were not a highly efficient counterinsurgency force; most were simply policemen who changed into their own unique camouflage uniforms for the assignment. What was important to Rhodesians about the SAP presence was the overt gesture of support. As the SAP said good-byes and departed, Rhodesians did not expect change in the tactical situation of the war, but there was wonderment and confusion about the political factors that had prompted the move.

"What are they thinking of?" I heard more than once. "South Africa is the big prize—they will be next!"

* * *

Confusing signals were not emanating exclusively from South Africa. Despite UN trade sanctions, Rhodesia was overtly supported by a number of pro-Western governments. France sold automobiles in kit form; Japan did a flourishing trade in trucks, cars, and motorcycles. The heavy vehicles used throughout the security forces were British, the venerable Bedford RL and RM military truck. And there was steady regional trade between Zambia, Mozambique, and Rhodesia.

I was first and foremost an American. I found myself focusing more on trying to understand how the United States was viewing the changing situation in Southern Africa. The Soviet Union actively supported and trained the FRELIMO in Mozambique, and a new government headed by Samora Machel would likely look favorably on future defense ties with the USSR and her allies—a circumstance that could imperil the all-important Cape sea route if the Soviet navy established bases. In the event of another Suez Canal closure, the Cape of Good Hope was the only available route to the Indian Ocean from the eastern United States. By a stroke of good luck and persistence in their Cold War strategy, the Soviets might gain naval bases in Mozambique and Angola with the potential to choke ocean commerce around South Africa.

After all, I reasoned, Rhodesia—while not by any means perfect in the eyes of the world—was certainly pro-Western, and it was actively engaged in a war against America's avowed communist enemies. Southern Africa seemed to me yet another front in the Cold War, a fact later reinforced when the United States mounted a covert war against the Soviet-sponsored MPLA government in Angola.

In 1971 the U.S. Congress had passed the Byrd Amendment; this legalized purchases from Rhodesia—despite UN sanctions—of strategically critical mineral products (chromium in particular). Senator Harry F. Byrd (Virginia) and his colleagues reasoned that it made better sense to pay less for Rhodesian chrome than to purchase it from the other major supplier, the Soviet Union. Could it be, I speculated, that this was a clever ruse for supporting Rhodesia against its foes without overtly offending their British allies, who were trying to bring their errant kith and kin back into the fold?

In Britain, public opinion about Rhodesia seemed neatly divided, with conservative forces apparently more sympathetic to the colonial rebels who had said no to a Labour government's attempt to force political parity on them.

In the final analysis, I was disinclined to read very much into any of the multitude of ideas and issues then rattling around in my mind. All presumed that world leaders were applying critical thought processes to important issues, and I was no longer confident that happened often. The recent capitulation of the Republic of Vietnam to the North Vietnamese army had left a bitter aftertaste, prompting me to feel far less confident about my nation of birth. The American people had walked away from a trusted ally—and I felt not only a strong sense of shame but growing uncertainty about just what the United States might do as it tried to gather up the remnants of its foreign policy and began to cope with a severely damaged international reputation. Worries and bad dreams about the unknown destinies of Vietnamese I had left behind were driving me toward bitter self-examination.

Restive, I dove into the challenges of training Support Unit, armed with new skills learned at the School of Infantry. Ormonde, still retaining command of G Troop, became training officer and I his second in command. Our most immediate task was to find and train people to teach with us.

One afternoon as we sat considering whom we might use and how they might be trained to be trainers, Ormonde received a telephone call from Inspector Fred Mason at nearby police general headquarters. Fred asked Ormonde to sit on a screening board set to convene shortly to consider an application to join the force. The candidate, he said, was an Englishman who seemed to have military qualifications of potential interest to Support Unit.

When he returned, Ormonde announced that he thought we had another instructor. Colin Shaw, recently of the elite British Parachute Regiment, had stated his willingness in the interview to attest in the BSAP, with the understanding that his duties would be of a paramilitary nature. The BSAP was so happy to have Colin Shaw in its ranks that they waived the requirement for an induction stint at training depot. This was unusual. When he reported aboard at Tomlinson Depot one morning, one of the first things he had to learn was how to wear and maintain the myriad uniforms.

Colin was not a parade-square soldier. Far more comfortable in camouflage battle dress and his own configuration webbing that sported a *kukri* fighting knife presented by a Gurkha regiment with whom he had served, he quickly fit into the training staff family. Of immediate benefit was the fact that he was a fully trained British army company medic, capable of performing basic surgical procedures. Before his arrival, Support Unit personnel had only primary first aid training. No morphine ampoules had been issued, nor were intravenous drip kits taken to the field for medical emergencies. Colin took on a training plan to teach more relevant battlefield first aid to men both under training and operationally deployed—and he made recommendations that select Africans be sent to the army medical training facility to learn the skills of battlefield medics.

Colin and his wife, Margaret, had arrived in Rhodesia with little other than the family cats and several suitcases. Jennifer and I grew to know this couple from the English Midlands as they set about moving into a home, and Margaret located a receptionist position at a doctor's surgery. After several weeks, their automobile and personal effects arrived by rail. A party was held to celebrate, and Colin returned the steel cots and camp stove they had been using as a courtesy of the Support Unit quartermaster.

Then-Corporal Shaw had seen a good deal of operational experience: two tours in Northern Ireland and also in troubled Aden. He showed an immediate comfort in the environment of the African bush and had excellent weapon-handling skills. In his early days with us, I noticed Ormonde watching carefully as Colin issued orders and instructions during the daily training routine. In many respects, Colin remained a junior NCO at heart, and it was some time before he became comfortable in his somewhat elevated status as a section officer in the British South Africa Police Support Unit.

Soon after Colin came to us, a fully trained instructor arrived after his enlistment in the Rhodesian Light Infantry (RLI) was complete. Colour Sergeant Mike Davis had been assigned to Training Wing, RLI, as a drill and weapons instructor. He had ushered many young civilian trainees into the ranks of the Rhodesian army.

Mike Davis was everything that Colin Shaw was not, the quintessential drill pig who instantly made the transition to a new uniform. Gone were the painstakingly wrapped and folded puttees and RLI green beret. All that he brought with him to his new post was a pair of well-worn stick boots, with their extra layers of leather sole, full set of hobnails, and lace-up extensions. Scores of layers of black parade gloss had been painstakingly applied over the years and carefully buffed to a deep, glowing sheen. Tall, wiry, and slender, red-headed Mike Davis had a face that reflected a decade of unshielded African sun, the reddened nose and cracked lips of a Celt in the tropics. In drill instructor mode, his carriage was erect, movements quick

Sergeant Major Isaac. (Author collection)

and sure—all accompanied by a pitched voice and word of command that rose to a near scream. He won the immediate attention of every squad member before whom he paraded.

To our relief, both Shaw and Davis adapted quickly and well to the uniform lesson plans we instituted upon our return from the School of Infantry. Having extra instructional staff meant that far more attention could be given not just to recruits in training, but in particular to recently established Support Unit troops returning from deployment. There was a constant, ongoing requirement for lesson revision and practice of newly acquired military skills.

Our African NCOs, in particular the sergeants major, continued to play a critical role. Sergeant Major Isaac had graduated from an advanced drill course at the School of Infantry and now proudly sported the red sash of rank. He and other NCOs began assisting with some of the weapon

Support Unit troops skirmish through an explosion toward an imaginary enemy in this exercise. (Courtesy Colin Shaw)

training classes in addition to their usual responsibilities for constant leadership of the junior members.

Adjacent to Tomlinson Depot were several acres of commonage—open *vlei*, where certain types of training could be carried out without bothering surrounding neighborhoods. A majority of the training was directed toward allowing the men to learn and practice field skills. Troops were broken up into sticks of five to seven men to learn patrol formation and skills of field observation. Most rural Africans had well-developed visual acuity; we had only to demonstrate what to look for in the bush, including tracking skills. Insurgents often used footwear with distinctive sole patterns that left signs behind as they traversed the bush, all of which were collectively called *spoor*.

Colin Shaw introduced a class in booby traps. Although a huge concern in both Aden and Vietnam, improvised explosive devices (IEDs) had not been a major problem in Rhodesia's bush war. We assumed that eventually insurgents would begin to defend their camping places with trip wires and fragmentation devices, so we included indoctrination in the training.

Always a man who liked to be assured that he had the full attention of all his students, Colin might set a trap in the classroom for an unwary student to detonate. A favorite was to use a pressure device under a wooden bench, set to detonate when an unwary man sat down. These were not tiny charges; typically there was a very loud explosion, flash, and smoke. Colin, after gathering scattered trainees, might begin his lesson with a statement like, "Constable Moyo, you should be more careful. If that was the real thing, your balls would be small pieces sticking to the ceiling."

The troops listened to the lessons and came to pay careful attention once in the field. Dark, slender trip wires were notoriously difficult to see in the long grass. Here it was that Colin would deploy one of his more diabolical training aids, a plastic fertilizer sack full of manure and water—suspended from a tree limb and armed with a small explosive charge activated by an unwary trainee brushing against a trip wire. The resulting explosion was scary as well as malodorous. We hoped our troops would remember the lesson and develop careful habits while in the operational area.

The instructors shared the training program for new recruit training. Ormonde's weekly training roster gave each of us ample time to prepare. Early one morning I noticed that Colin Shaw was intently studying a British army manual—the chapter that dealt with bayonet fighting. Here were black and white illustrations of Tommys striking fearsome poses with aggressive grimaces and brandishing Enfield Number Four rifles with fixed bayonets.

"My last recruit class on bayonet fighting seemed flat," Colin commented to me. "They never quite got into the spirit of it."

Certainly at the School of Infantry, the bayonet instruction had stressed the significance of aggressive spirit—the importance of letting the enemy clearly know that the intent was to impale them. There was ample rhetoric about "fear of cold steel" and the effectiveness of the bayonet in close quarters. I had adapted my lesson plan slightly to suit the rather more shy personality of the young, rural African male but learned that it was important to keep the adrenalin flowing while actually teaching techniques for attack and defense with bayonets. My charges were always encouraged to produce blood-curdling screams when attacking straw-filled dummies. Always desultory at first, yelling and grimacing could be encouraged with sarcastic observations:

"You lot sound like a bunch of fucking nannies playing in the park! Show me that you really want to kill that man before he kills you!" we remonstrated.

These thoughts and personal experiences I shared with Colin, and I promised that I would come to his class and offer assistance if required. He left the office, walking briskly over to the armory, where the trainee squad awaited him. I heard the sergeant call them to attention, after which Colin told him to issue each man with a bayonet-equipped Number Four rifle. I returned to my modest pile of paperwork, conscious as the minutes ticked of the distant yells and commands of classes under way. After perhaps twenty minutes, I whiffed the odor of burning grass. My curiosity piqued, I picked up my hat and left the office to see what sort of results Colin was getting with his bayonet-fighting lesson.

Rounding the corner of the armory, I looked eastward toward the commonage and observed that an area of tall, dry grass was burning vigorously. Through the smoke were running trainee Africans attired in battle dress camouflage and carrying rifles with bayonets fixed. In the midst of the flames was Colin Shaw, swinging his kukri, chasing the slow ones and encouraging all to attack him if they could. I smirked inwardly, confident these young men had by now decided that the *ishe* had completely lost any trace of sanity. They wouldn't consider bayoneting or butt-stroking the instructor; however, with that flailing fighting knife in his hand, one had better make a good show of pressing home an aggressive attack. There was spirited yelling, though the smoke made some hoarse—and every man was sweating. Straw-filled sandbags on the ground were attacked with increasing vigor, and I found myself musing, "These guys are really starting to get into it."

As I got up abreast with the class, Colin emerged from the smoke and now-dying flames to collectively address the squad. "What's the bayonet for?" he yelled at them. "It's for *killing*, Sah!" they shouted back. "So," he continued, "do you think the enemy would believe you now?" "Yes, Sah!"

Colin then turned to the south and pointed to the small guard kiosk at the rear entrance of Tomlinson Depot, where a sleepy duty branch African recruit was standing guard in the afternoon warmth, armed only with a rubber truncheon.

"Right. Do you think that fucking brown boot wanker down there is frightened of you lot?" I saw some grins emerging on sweaty faces. "Well, is he?" "Show me!"

In an instant, they were a thundering herd running en masse with rifles at high port and bayonets affixed, every man with his eye on the hapless guard. They were yelling and one of the words to emerge was "Kill!" The intended victim stared for a brief moment, then dropped his club and scurried up onto the roof of his shelter. Colin pursued his class, as did I, both of us yelling "Stop!" The mob was gathered around the kiosk, brandishing rifles, clearly enjoying the intimidation of the sentry.

Regrouping, Colin said "Very well men. Well done. You've learned a valuable lesson today: few things frighten a man more than cold steel." He turned the class over to a grinning sergeant, who had clearly enjoyed the spectacle. There was one injury, a man possibly cut by the kukri? I didn't ask. Colin told the man to come to the office for treatment, and the two of us began walking together up the laneway. "I'll bet you thought they were thinking about skewering that Brown Boot," I offered. Colin just nodded his head.

Back at the office there was some good-natured banter with the cut recruit as Colin sutured his hand—and an acknowledgment of his bravery during the close-quarter skirmish with his instructor. The young man left soon after, sporting his bandage like a campaign ribbon.

Throughout our efforts to get Support Unit up to battlefield standard through training, there were other responsibilities and duties also. Ormonde managed the daily affairs of G Troop, with some assistance from me, as the presidential guard force. It was, however, on the rolls as an operational Support Unit troop and was expected to do its share of patrols and counterinsurgency operations in the operational area. We worked hard to get weapon-handling skills and field craft up to standard in G Troop, where there were a number of senior men who needed retraining. On the whole, G Troop had done very well in its operational role, achieving the unit's first kill in an ambush near Mount Darwin the year previous.

Ormonde and I were keenly aware of the changing circumstances in the northeastern bush war: changes to deployment areas, of operational hot spots, in command structure. All were developments that we struggled to keep up with, both to keep our training relevant and to ensure that we and the men of G Troop were ready to go to war.

* * *

We were not permitted to deploy operationally as often as we would have wished. Command, rightly, reckoned that it was far more important that Support Unit operational standards be brought to a high standard of military readiness. I managed, however, to travel regularly with senior officers to the forward operating areas of the unit.

In many ways, the time-tried logistic support system of the British South Africa Police was particularly well suited to the exigencies of low-intensity counterinsurgency operations. Individual Support Unit troops operated independently of field resupply; they could do this because everything from portable gas-operated deep freezes to transport, tents, and radios was issued to them and carefully inspected after each operational deployment. The men were paid a daily subsistence allowance, meaning there was no central messing in the field. They cooked for themselves. When a troop drove out of the gates of Tomlinson Depot in a collection of trucks, trailers, and mine-protected Land Rovers, they had virtually everything they would need while away. The occasional bush store would provide the rest. The convoys drove directly to their area of operation and reported to the relevant Joint Operation Center and normally set up camp where directed. That might be nearby, or some distance away, depending on the operational tasking.

Support Unit senior officers were deeply involved with ensuring that troop movements were smooth operations. In early days, deployments were so labor intensive that there was not a great deal of time for field inspections. But as procedures were streamlined, trips to the field became more frequent. I seized every opportunity to join them. Visits were an opportunity to see how a troop functioned on its own out of the atmosphere of depot, to observe strengths and weaknesses that might be addressed in later training sessions.

My first trip to Mukumbura, the border post Winston Hart had used in his early forays into Mozambique, was in the company of Superintendent Mick York. Michael David York was an Englishman, long established in Rhodesia, well liked and respected in the unit.

A decision had been made to transport most of the members of a troop by air. Mukumbura was situated on a dry river bed on the low veld, with road access only via a difficult dirt road around the Mavuradonna Mountains and down the steep escarpment to the Zambezi Valley. This seemed a sensible plan, although it would be the first time many young Africans had ever been aboard aircraft of any sort.

We assembled early one morning and were driven in open trucks to New Sarum Air Force Base, situated on the eastern side of Salisbury's very long main airstrip. After saluting Mr. York, a smartly turned-out air force sentry waved the convoy through the gate to the air movements area. There, sitting on the tarmac, stood an immaculate C-47 Dakota in white livery—bearing the air force insignia, the gold Rhodesia lion clasping an elephant tusk, encircled by a roundel of green. Crew and maintenance personnel were carrying out last-minute checks of the old transport, which I knew to be a veteran of World War II.

Support Unit troops were ordered off the trucks, then began loading personal gear onto a packing pallet. I looked around at the neat, well-maintained facilities of New Sarum, much of which had been constructed at least twenty years earlier. To my eye, much of the base could easily have been transplanted from Britain. It was both attractive and functional, the home of Rhodesia's Canberra bomber squadron as well as the transport elements we were there to use, yet another example of how very good the Rhodesians were at making best use of what was available.

A last-minute weapons check was carried out to ensure all rifles were clear and unloaded. I boarded the aircraft with the first group, climbing up a short ladder into the open cargo doors on the rear side and escorting the men to the sling seats mounted along each side of the open interior and showing them the lap seat belts that each was to use. There was an element of hesitant anticipation in these young Africans as they buckled up for the first time, each carefully balancing his rifle between his legs, muzzles pointing upward.

As I was about to take my seat, far forward near the bulkhead, the pilot boarded and made his way directly to the cockpit, carrying a large, well-worn aviation briefcase packed full of maps and manuals. I noticed a proliferation of the distinctive stickers used by Australian Customs on the bag, and when finally he spoke to his copilot, I realized that we would be flying with an Aussie not long from home. Just another surprise that I shouldn't be surprised about, I quietly mused.

I listened as the pilots went through their checklist. My young African charges were mostly silent, uncertain as to what to expect. Momentarily, our waiting was rewarded with the distinctive whine of the starter motor on one of the two big radial engines, which quickly burst to life with a hollow roar and a cloud of blue smoke. The second motor soon followed, filling the open fuselage with the distinctive noise of the multiple cylinder sound of Pratt and Whitney 1820 aircraft engines. I had not heard that sound since Vietnam—and there were a lot of memories accompanying it.

The air force crew chief worked his way up the center past the men, who were seated facing each other, checking that each was buckled in securely with rifle held firmly. Then the chocks were pulled and we began the taxi to the end of New Sarum's main 15,000-foot main runway. After both engines had been carefully run up and checked, we rolled out on to the runway and, as the engines roared to near-full power, began the run to takeoff. The tail lifted first, then the noise of tires on the tarmac stopped, and we gently gathered elevation. Most of the men stared intently out of the windows as the ground and metropolitan Salisbury became smaller below. Several gripped their rifles and stared straight ahead, coping with the apprehension of first flight.

We climbed gently to an elevation several thousand feet higher than Salisbury's five thousand feet and settled into a northeasterly course over the broad expanse of rural Rhodesia. Below was the panoply of established pastures of maize on the larger farms, citrus orchards, and always the distinctive *kopjes* and granite formations that made the view unmistakably African. Interspersed with the regulated activity of the white farmers were the traditionally farmed lands of the Shona people, most within the borders of various tribal trust lands. Periodically, we would fly over the small cluster of round native huts that made up the typical African kraal.

With cruising altitude achieved, our pilot throttled back the engines, and the men began to relax a little more. There was more conversation, though opportunities were limited in the noise of the unpressurized cabin. The crew chief, dressed in khaki shorts and an olive-drab T-shirt, approached me, saying that I was welcome to go forward to the cockpit if I wished. I thanked him and made my way through the narrow passage and stood immediately behind the pilot and copilot, who nodded while continuing a conversation through headsets. The flight deck was as well maintained as I had expected, perhaps even better than the Navy aircraft I had flown so many miles in over Vietnam. There was one noticeable difference: on both sides of the cockpit, flare pistols had been mounted to the aircraft's outer skin ready to fire downward in the event a heat-seeking missile was fired at us from the ground. There were shoulder-fired missiles in the theater, and Rhodesia's tiny air force was taking no chances.

As a reminder of our potential vulnerability, the aircraft suddenly descended after we had passed a majority of the developed, farming country. The ride became much less steady. I braced myself, expecting to be told to strap in at any moment, and savored the view as we began flying at tree-top level, the prop blast blowing leaves from the crowns of the green umbrella-shaped trees. On the horizon, I could see a geological formation not unlike a large ledge, beyond which was the blue haze I knew must be the vast, scorching Zambezi Valley. This was the edge of the Zambezi escarpment, the point where the high veld abruptly dropped into a vast valley that was the personification of rural Africa. Our Aussie pilot, mindful

Mukumbura police post featured blast walls and defenses against hostile fire from across the nearby border. (Courtesy Dave Parry)

of what a large target the old aircraft would make as it flew suddenly out over the precipice, shoved the nose down as we cleared the edge and followed the cliff contour down to the valley floor in a rapid descent not unlike a roller coaster. In the distance, through a haze of dust and shimmering heat waves, was Mukumbura's modest airstrip.

With our descent, the trees, grass, and even the smell changed. The air I breathed was tainted with the faint grit of the ochre dust that was all pervasive, coating even the leaves. Interspersed across the vast plain stood baobab trees, with their huge trunks, reminiscent of the swollen limbs of an elephantiasis victim. It was as if the world was standing still in the growing midday heat. Animals were sheltering and resting, as were smart humans.

We made one fast pass over the landing strip to assure our pilots that no large game was either in the way or lying nearby in the bush where it might be frightened onto the landing area. There was none. In the near distance on the dirt road from the police post, a truck and Land Rover could be seen en route. Wasting no further time, the pilot came around, banked, and planted the wheels firmly on the grass airstrip, braking hard and drawing up not far from where the police vehicles had arrived. I thanked the pilots and crew chief; the Australian obviously not wishing to engage in conversation. He was, I felt certain, a fairly recent arrival who wished for the time to remain anonymous.

The cargo doors were flung open and ladder installed. The men were on their feet, lining up to exit. All was quiet. There were cheerful grins and a few obvious sighs of relief as they filed off and began loading themselves and their kit into the waiting truck. Mick York was already greeting and speaking with the troop commander.

I had heard much about this outpost of the force, perched at a dry riverbed overlooking Mozambique. The original founders had recognized their unique posting and the vagaries of duty there by creating the Mukumbura Surf Club. This exclusive group of hearty souls who perhaps dreamed of water in the dry riverbed posted appropriate signs in the canteen and had specially inscribed beer tankards made in recognition of their membership. Now, well after the days when Winston Hart and Pete Stanton had worked in a near vacuum out of sight and mind of headquarters, Mukumbura had taken on more strategic importance. No longer were friendly Portuguese colonists on the other side; now FRELIMO troops wandered around largely with impunity and shots were often fired at the police flag that flew over the heavily sandbagged bulwarks.

The BSAP duty branch continued to man the post. There remained the usual cases of stock theft and occasional homicide requiring investigation as well as the important business of running Ground Coverage, the grassroots intelligence-gathering operation that relied on local African cooperation. Sadly, the border between Rhodesia and Mozambique sliced through the territories of native groups that had traditionally migrated back and forth both because of whimsy and weather conditions. As tensions grew, a barrier of wire and mines designed to prevent enemy incursions—or at least impede them—had been erected by army engineers. Ramparted Mukumbura maintained much of its beau geste mystique, but there was now more of the urgency of war about the place.

From its modest origins, the post began to sprawl as the exigencies of war brought more people and materiel to defend the border. I noted with interest now-abandoned traditional pole and *dagga* outbuildings that had once been part of the police presence.

A short distance away in a slight draw that must once have been a river overflow stood the cluster of dark green tents that marked the headquarters of the Support Unit troop then deployed. An effort had been made to use as much cover as possible from the few trees present to escape a blistering

The Hyena, built on a Ford F-250 chassis, provided good protection from anti-tank mines. (Author collection)

sun. A mask of tan dust covered every canvas surface, and a powdery talc rose from each of my boot steps into the camp.

The nucleus of the camp was an improvised command center, where radios were monitored and section movements noted. A young patrol officer sat at an improvised desk with his radios, perspiration soaking through his olive-drab T-shirt. Nearby, under a canvas overhang, stood two large gas-operated chest deep freezers enclosed by a protective timber framework. Folding tables were set up under the tent fly for dining and clerical tasks. Other than the distant crackle of the radio, all was quiet except for an occasional insect.

The men's camp sites were clustered nearby. Though the depression afforded some protection from distant small-arms fire, I was concerned that little appeared to have been done about preparing earthworks against potential mortar or rocket attacks. So far, these had been rare, at least in the Support Unit context, but my instincts told me that this so-far relatively low-key bush war could suddenly get much worse. I made my suggestions about camp defense works, then gathered with a pair of patrol officers to discuss training matters. "How well," I wanted to know, "were our lessons being understood and used by the recent trainees?"

We would not be staying overnight at Mukumbura. Superintendent York elected to return to Salisbury by road. This involved a drive across a corner of the Zambezi Valley followed by a steep ascent up the brow of the escarpment. The road was primitive and rough—and had been mined by the enemy on a number of occasions. Thus, we would drive a Hyena, one of Support Unit's purpose-built mine-protected vehicles.

Antitank mines of the Soviet TM46 configuration had proven a serious threat to road users in the operational areas of Rhodesia. Packed with an explosive charge of about five kilograms of TNT, they had been designed to disable a battle tank. Against unprotected civilian vehicles, these devices typically blew entire sections of the vehicle apart, while shredding occupants with shrapnel created by the disintegrating automobile. With hundreds of miles of rural, unpaved roads, Rhodesia had quickly realized its vulnerability to land mines—and research was hastily begun to devise mine-protected vehicles.

The South African Hyena was a second-generation vehicle—the product of a cross-service Rhodesian military working committee in close conjunction with South African scientist Dr. Vernon Joynt. The vehicle made use of a Ford F-250 four wheel drive truck chassis, engine, and running gear—to which was fastened a monocoque metal shell shaped in the manner of a boat hull to deflect upward forces away. The driver had for his use a large pane of bulletproof glass facing forward; there were several smaller visibility ports on the side for passengers and roll bars and canvas for overhead protection. Because mined light vehicles very often were tossed over by blast forces, despite ballast water in their tires, passengers were strapped in on hard metal bench seats by means of full aviation-type seat belts.

The first version of the purpose-built mine-protected vehicle was the Rhino, a lighter and smaller version of the Hyena that was built on a Land Rover chassis. Other local techniques were employed to enhance the protection characteristics of Rhodesian government vehicles already in service. The ubiquitous Land Rover pickup was "mine proofed" by installing deflector plates of 10-mm steel between the cab and all four wheels. Conveyor belting was affixed to the rear of the cab, a roll-bar system installed and doors removed. The driver and passenger were also to wear aviation-type seat belts with straps across both shoulders.

All of these methods proved remarkably effective, though a land mine detonation typically damaged vehicles beyond repair. The protection of troop-carrying trucks was far more problematic—and was not fully addressed until later in the war. Support Unit trucks had some protection by using conveyor belting and plates as well as sandbags on some occasions. It was an amazing testimony to the determination of Rhodesia's engineers;

Strapped into a passenger seat in a mine-proofed Hyena, Superintendent M. D. York prepares to move off. (Author collection)

by the end of the war, dozens had walked away from land mine explosions with nothing worse than a splitting headache and a few bruises.

Most fortunately, Rhodesian insurgents had not mastered the technique of combining vehicle land mine explosions with an ambush, a technique that had been masterfully deployed by the Viet Minh in their war against France.

That afternoon in Mukumbura I was glad that we had a near-new Hyena available for our trip across those expanses of dirt road, scant miles from hostile Mozambique. Our driver first swung open the armored rear door and made his way forward. We followed, carefully strapped ourselves in and made ready our rifles. Seating on felt-covered steel benches was far from luxurious, and in many ways, I wished it might have been possible to see over the steel sides at the bush beyond. I settled back, while Superintendent York conversed with the driver, and we began our drive across the flatlands toward the rising escarpment. The narrow dirt track filed through the relatively open country, punctuated by msasa and baobab trees, each different in some way from the others. We watched always for signs of activity: tracks in the dust—anything that might indicate the passage of humans or large animals. There was none.

At the base of the escarpment, with the Hyena transfer case in low-range, four-wheel drive, we began a careful ascent of the rutted, narrow road past dozens of locations that would have been ideal, well-concealed sites for an ambush by the enemy. Hunkered down behind the reassuring armored sides, we did no talking as every eye swept the bush for telltale signs. Slowly, we ground our way up the track as the Zambezi Valley fell sharply away below. I was disappointed that it had been such a short trip and hoped for others. I had not seen nearly enough of the Zambezi Valley from up close, but that was soon to change. That evening as we drove into the relative civilization of Tomlinson Depot in Salisbury, I was prompted to muse at how very much this country could change in a matter of several hours of road travel.

Soon after, I made another inspection road trip with Assistant Commissioner Guy Houghton to the northeastern operational area. This time, the officer commanding would visit troops deployed to provide security for road-building projects in the vicinity of Nyamapanda border post. There was a heightened security awareness along the frontier, where incursions and attacks had been aimed to halt Rhodesian government attempts to improve communication and regional control. The trip was largely uneventful—not unlike many others I had made. What made it unique was that one of the Support Unit troops reported a deserter, presumably a defector. One of the young African constables we had carefully trained at Tomlinson Depot had rallied to insurgents operating in the area: He had taken his rifle and equipment with him.

This was a sobering event, the first that I had experienced. I had never encountered disloyalty in the Rhodesian Africans with whom I served, and it was most unexpected. Many questions came to mind: how had the enemy contacted and proselytized him? Why were there not indications of disaffection? What had his peers seen immediately before the defection, and why was it that our NCOs had not discerned the problem? Those questions remained unresolved, although undoubtedly Special Branch would conduct a careful investigation. Back in Salisbury, I shared my concerns with my peers about what might be done to ensure that no further defections occurred. I was concerned that for reasons I did not know or understand, others might desert. Fortunately, it did not occur again while I served at Support Unit.

* * *

After out initial schooling at the School of Infantry, Ormonde had been accepted into an advanced instructor's course. Soon after his return to Salisbury with the best mark in his class, we were both invited to attend a Saturday afternoon social function at the Rhodesia Light Infantry officers club. We said nothing about the invitation, but at the appointed time arrived at the mess and joined in a pleasant afternoon of socializing with the family that was the RLI officer corps. Our invitation had come from the commanding officer, Lieutenant Colonel David Parker. Young and highly respected throughout Rhodesia's service establishment in the days before Unilateral Declaration of Independence (UDI), David Parker had been awarded the Sword of Honour at Sandhurst by placing first in his class of new subalterns.

We were made to feel at home by Colonel Parker in the warm and casual atmosphere of an afternoon affair, perhaps convened after a morning sporting event. I noticed immediately both that he enjoyed enormous respect from his officers—and that he led them very naturally and with little actual direction by letting people know his wishes. Ormonde and I were attracted both by the army professionalism and close-knit nature of the officer corps. Probably our reexposure to the army way at Gwelo had refocused us on the things we liked about army life, particularly if it came with a commission. Ten years my senior, Ormonde, I was certain, would surely go immediately to the army if there was an opportunity. I was less certain. So much had changed since I had arrived in Rhodesia, planning a low-key district policeman's life for a couple of years. I had made the transition to become a police training officer and accepted that the training was to be largely focused on military training. Was I ready to accept a commission into the Rhodesian army? I had wanted to lead men, do the things that I had seen good platoon commanders do in Vietnam, but I was not certain that I was ready for this quantum leap. I remained a loyal American: I was uncertain that my country would necessarily understand that serving under a foreign commission—even in a war against its enemies—was an honorable and good thing to do.

Our Saturday afternoon at the mess was a success. We made useful friends, enjoying both the camaraderie and ample supplies of cold Rhodesian ale. Behind the bar an instruction was inscribed: "Thou shalt not fade away."

On Monday morning, soon after Officer Commanding Support Unit Guy Houghton arrived, we were summoned to his office. "What," he demanded, "were you doing at the RLI officers mess on Saturday?"

We told him briefly and quite honestly that we had responded to an invitation to attend. I was amazed that word had traveled so quickly to our boss, and that the information obviously had originated from an outside source.

"There is an informal agreement between the services," he continued. "Piracy of personnel is not encouraged; you would need to serve out your time in the BSAP before considering the army option."

We were dismissed. There was no animosity. Ormonde and I walked back to the office to resume our training day. I remained quietly incredulous at the day's events, although I was certain that Ormonde felt some disappointment.

In the days ahead, I saw Lieutenant Bob McKenzie at the wheel of an SAS Sabre taking the back road through Tomlinson Depot to army headquarters. He recognized me and stopped to ask how things were with me. Bob had done very well in his officer selection course and had moved directly into a command position at SAS regiment. I knew not to ask what his professional life was like—other than to inquire how he was fitting into his new life as an officer—but was confident it had been eventful. Bob had by then flirted with death so many times in Vietnam and Rhodesia that I wondered whether he could ever live without the air of danger and uncertainty. Rhodesia had been very lucky to acquire his services.

Almost coincidentally, I was unexpectedly contacted by an SAS corporal who brought with him greetings from my former agent roommate in Da Nang, a U.S. Navy Reserve intelligence officer. More than a little curious, I asked where it was that he had met Commander Carl Sundstrom. "Oh, we met at Coronado in San Diego while I was training with the SEALs." Thus, I met Clive Mason, an Englishman who had seen service with the Australian SAS regiment, and it was through this affiliation that he had trained with the Coronado SEAL Team. I was taken aback by this introduction from afar but ultimately very glad to hear that my old Vietnam bunky was well—and pleased to make the acquaintance of Clive.

As is often the case with special forces soldiers, Clive Mason was of a compact, wiry build. Almost nondescript, he would fit well into most crowds. He was a weapons expert and skilled demolition man who delighted in experimenting and creating new unconventional weapons. It was he who methodically explained to me how to manufacture a miniature claymore mine from a soap dish, C4 explosive, and finishing nails. I had received basic explosives training and was discovering in my role at Support Unit that I needed skills with explosive ordnance. I had set about learning as much as I could from various experts and practitioners of the art of demolitions simply because it was necessary for me to destroy grenades and other ordnance in the field. Clive was gracious about imparting his considerable skills and even began working to have me included in an SAS course that would finish with an operation to drop an old railway bridge.

In the Australian SAS, Mason was known as a shottist of uncanny skill. He was later in the war to employ these talents as a sniper defending a post on the southeast border.

Winston Hart recalls: "Clive was a perfectionist. His rifle of choice was a British No. 4 rifle configured for sniping. I helped him cut holes in the border fence to ensure nothing went wrong that might divert his carefully aimed shots—and I acted as his spotter. Mason dispatched a number of FRELIMO soldiers; by that time in the war, there was open hostility between Mozambique's new rulers and Rhodesia. That was particularly true because Rhodesian special forces were then launching forays into Mozambique to destroy rear area enemy bases."

* * *

In 1975 Support Unit contacts with insurgent groups were not a regular occurrence, as they were to become in the years ahead. Perhaps monthly, a patrol would bump into a small group and shots would be exchanged. And there were more incidents of violence and intimidation against African rural citizens: land mines, hut burnings, mutilations, and executions all took their toll of the rural African population. Support Unit seemed to be learning its role in the war, adapting and acquitting itself fairly well.

The more seasoned, senior unit troops normally were dispatched to known areas of increased enemy activity, the idea being to best use their better-developed military skills. They moved into an area, set ambushes by night, and observed kraals and the people.

To bring the entire force to a state of operational readiness, field training took on a particular air of urgency. Support Unit's instructors spent more time away from Tomlinson Depot on exercises that might last several days.

Goromonzi remained a favored venue for the battle camps. Here we introduced men to small-unit assault tactics, in particular fire-with-movement—and rehearsed them when they returned for more training following deployment to the bush. There were demonstrations with grenades, trip flares, and illumination and even basic demolition. Always, however, there were problems with standardization and supply.

Rhodesia was at war. Support Unit was well down the supply ladder. OC Guy Houghton worked hard to acquire light machine guns for his troops—but all that could be acquired were magazine-fed Bren guns of World War II vintage that had been converted from .303- to 7.62-mm NATO caliber. A wonderfully accurate weapon, the Bren's usefulness was greatly limited by the fact that the magazine capacity was a mere twenty rounds. Nevertheless, instructors worked hard to identify young Africans with apparent talent for firing and maintaining the gun so that a Bren could be sent out with every section patrol.

Grenades were in short supply; neither could a dependable source of supply be identified. Individual men were not issued grenades, though section leaders might carry one or two optionally. Support Unit's armory received limited stocks of Portuguese grenades patterned on the U.S. World War II "pineapple" type. Then, a number of boxes of British 36 "Mills" grenades were supplied. These had been manufactured in South Africa during World War II. Importantly, the 36 grenade could be fieldstripped and cleaned; the detonator device and delay fuse were supplied in a separate air-tight container, to be installed only to ready the device for use.

Finally, there was the option of using captured Eastern Bloc grenades. We never resorted to using Chinese stick grenades, even for demonstration, but on occasion fell back on stocks of East German or Soviet fragmentation grenades when little else was available. I was always very nervous about handling captured grenades, fearing premature detonation.

We heard rumors that claymore antipersonnel command-detonated mines were being manufactured in South Africa—and thus might be somewhere in the supply pipeline to Rhodesia. Claymores are a particularly effective weapon for use in ambushes, where their shrapnel pattern can be directed down a trail and can be more effective than small-arms fire from a small party of ambushers, particularly at night. Although we hoped they would become available to our operational troops who were trying to staunch the flow of insurgents into Rhodesia, none had by then appeared.

At Goromonzi, we had several fighting holes dug for explosives training, behind which there was a natural fold in the ground that afforded cover for those not actually undergoing one-on-one training. Several yards downrange, a silhouette target was erected on plywood backing. Classes began with an explanation of when and how the weapon should be used, then proceeded to actual handling of an inert training grenade. The 36 grenade was particularly useful for demonstrations, because the detonator assembly could readily be removed through a threaded base plate. There were always grimaces as men watched the striker lever fly off an inert grenade after the safety pin was removed, par-

The author training at Goromonzi. G Troop's Bedford RL truck is in the background. (Author collection)

ticularly after a demonstration when the old British grenades actually detonated, loudly casting large chunks of cast iron overhead.

Finally, the time would come when students were allowed to throw the real thing. I would crouch in the hole with each man, first asking if they were ready and then handing them a live grenade. We would review the procedures to be followed and then, as calmly as possible, I would order the student to grip the grenade with his fingers over the striker lever and remove the safety pin. With the pin out, the grenade was ready to fire within three to five seconds of the moment the spring-loaded striker lever was allowed to fly off. Then, I would order the grenade thrown: the student yelled "Grenade!" as a warning to his squad member and gently lobbed the bomb downrange to the standing target. We watched to see where it landed before ducking below the parapet.

Normally, but not always, the grenade exploded seconds later. Then the trainees would gather around the target, always curious to count new holes in the silhouette target and to see where it had been hit. I took time to satisfy myself that trainees—whether constables or potential leaders—had a good understanding of how best to use the weapon. On some occasions, intending to spark interest in good tactical planning, I would string several 36 grenades together with a length of detonator cord so that they could be fired simultaneously. Grenades concealed in overhead foliage and fired at an ambush site as enemy passed might be an effective way to initiate the attack, I proffered. The results of these demonstrations never failed to impress.

The disadvantage of using this mélange of ordnance—beyond the immediate safety issue—was that it didn't always detonate when it was supposed to. A grenade "blind" was always a concern. It was possible that the delay fuse might actually function late. Or, the old explosives might be rendered so unstable that even jarring the device might initiate an explosion. Thus, when explosives failed to detonate as planned, all concerned remained under cover and waited to see if the hang-fire might eventually go off anyway. Then it became my job to ensure that the offending device was destroyed, because no explosive ordnance disposal (EOD) team was available.

I would send my students to the rear, get out the red explosive storage box, and make up a charge suitable for destroying the grenade by sympathetic detonation. What we had available for this task was captured Soviet TNT. Sometimes the detonators and fuse were obtained commercially; sometimes not. Always there was first a fuse test burn to satisfy oneself that the burn rate was as stated. Then the charge was assembled, carefully placed close to the item to be destroyed, and several minutes of fuse lit. I would walk back to my hole, carefully monitoring the fuse burn time with my watch, and I always felt a sense of relief from my sheltered position as finally it all went up with a big bang.

At Goromonzi, basic small-unit tactics were practiced with live ammunition. The instructor would usually begin by explaining the importance of well-directed, heavy fire when assaulting an enemy position. Pointing up the slope where the heads of Figure Twelve silhouette targets could be seen, the proposition was posed: "These men want to kill you. If you turn around, they will shoot you. So your best chance is always a good attack—an attack that will force your enemy to keep his head down until you can close on him and kill him."

The greatest concern in these exercises was simply that of careless weapon handling, a man surrounded by the din of firing weapons who permits the muzzle of his rifle to stray from the forward position enough to accidentally shoot one of his assault party. Our African NCOs approached the problem by using discipline generated by hours on the parade square: Lining up the group abreast, the men would be told to march toward the targets counting out cadence. All in step, they would call out "Bullet!" each time their right boot struck the ground. This would instill fire discipline as well as focus. After several dry runs, perhaps five rounds would be issued to the squad, and they would step off toward the imaginary enemy position, rifle butts clutched under arm, calling out "Bullet," and firing their rifles simultaneously. A sergeant moved in very close behind to ensure that nobody drifted back in the rank to become a danger to his squad members.

Initially, the men focused more on staying in step and together, rather than on achieving hits on the target and earthen parapet before them. But by the time each was allowed ten rounds and permitted to actually overrun the targets, shooting improved noticeably. Then, the lesson changed slightly. If the unit had Bren guns, the gunner and his support would crawl to a flanking position from where they could pour fire on the enemy while the other half of the group made an in-line assault. The trick was to impart fire discipline in the support group. I always made a point of standing immediately behind them, ready to call "Stop!" if the attack party got too close to friendly fire.

Finally, we taught men how to pair up, one buddy providing cover fire as the other dashed and crawled forward to seek a new position, leapfrogging ever closer to the enemy.

In retrospect, this training might seem almost infantile in its simplicity, but it seemed to work. Our objective was not just to build skills; we wanted all the men to gain confidence through practice with weapons—and most of all, we wanted them to start thinking tactically about good reactions under fire. Rhodesia's bush war remained a conflict of sudden small-unit clashes, where the victors were most often those who could fire best, quickest.

* * *

I had become convinced soon after arriving for duty at Support Unit that the greatest task we faced was that of finding and training good leaders for the scores of young African recruits. Previous to the buildup, the BSAP had always managed to find within its ranks those unique individuals with both the background and the inclination to take on operational leadership duties—with the attendant challenges, discomforts, and deployments. The decision to expand the unit so quickly taxed police headquarters in many ways; finding suitable troop and section commanders was one of the most significant.

I never fully understood what the internal recruiting processes were, but, at least in the earliest stages of the expansion, members were arriving who were not happy about the posting. Some of this could be attributed to the shock of military discipline, something they may not have experienced since recruit training at Morris Depot. For some, the relative freedom and independence associated with a previous rural police posting made the immersion into a troop that could not function without military training and discipline not an easy thing to stomach. Suddenly, they were looked up to by a body of new, young African constables and expected to know the answers and lead by example. Most made the transition—some better than others.

Physical training is always a critical element of any effective military body, and it was no different at Support Unit. Africans and their leaders, to be effective, had to have a high level of fitness to permit them to carry critical war fighting equipment in the field—and to have the reserves of energy required to pursue and dispatch the enemy. Support Unit's leaders led by example to instill the ethos of fitness throughout. Chief Inspector Pat Deasy—as close to a regimental sergeant major as Support Unit ever got—was at every morning parade, monitoring troops then in depot from the field to ensure that a rigorous physical training program was performed by all. In those early days, there were troop commanders incapable of keeping up with their troop during morning five-kilometer road runs. Ormonde and I both despaired at the impression this made on the body of young men we had so recently trained and who expected much from their leaders; but we also recognized it as a symptom of accelerated growth in the climate of a growing war. The unknown in the equation was how well the troop would actually perform under the stress of combat. I hoped that there would be time to season both leaders and their men before the worst happened.

It had been Guy Houghton's vision that BSAP patrol officers would be used to lead at the section level, the lowest organizational tier of a Support Unit troop. He reasoned that a junior leader with five or six African constables could provide the necessary cohesiveness with relatively unseasoned personnel. In many ways, this important decision provided an important element of effective discipline and direction in operational Support Unit troops as they began deployments.

The preexpansion Support Unit patrol officers assigned to the original four operational troops were predominantly volunteers, individuals—some

Newly operational Support Unit troops were often used to provide security for road-building projects in Rhodesia's northeast. (Author collection)

with a penchant for things military—who had gravitated to the unit and stayed because of its unique esprit and way of life. There were a few mainstay Brits in this group, adventurers of the variety who had made Rhodesia and the BSAP what it was in years past. They were quite content to have a room or share a police house in Salisbury for periodic refreshment and debauchery following bush deployments, but the domesticated existence of a city policeman was not in their makeup.

The problem, it seemed to me, was that there probably were no longer enough men of this ilk in the BSAP. The demographics of Rhodesia had changed and so too had the police job. This was at the core of personnel problems associated with young policemen who were not really ready to give up the amenities associated with life at a police station, whether city, suburban, or district.

Training Wing began to accept several different types of leaders for indoctrination. Every duty branch man assigned to Support Unit for command of a troop or section of men required instruction and training in military topics. Some received more than others, a reflection of the tempo of the push to get men quickly into the field.

In those first months, training squads for new assignees from the force varied considerably in their degree of motivation and interest. All young men of European extraction, the best of them approached training with verve and the curiosity to learn as much as possible in the shortest period of time. Those with less enthusiasm for the tasks ahead encountered the best of their instructor's imaginative solutions: When a group spent lunch break at the police hostel canteen having a few beers, I simply changed the curriculum. My charges discovered, soon after I became aware of their laconic state at a lecture held in the shade of one of Tomlinson Depot's larger trees, that relatively sedentary classroom environment could suddenly change. I didn't appreciate that my instruction was considered of such little consequence that students might drink during a break and thus be less than attentive. I displayed my displeasure:

"Right. Change of plans," I barked at my seated pupils, redolent after a lunch of curry and beer. "Fall in at the armory. Check out your issue rifle, fill two water bottles and at least five magazines with ammunition. We'll be leaving on an endurance march in fifteen minutes."

There was some muttering, but the squad followed instructions. Fifteen minutes later we were marching together out the depot gate at a near trot, the afternoon sun beating down on sweaty backs and brows. Webbing, heavy with magazine pouches and water bottles, slapped and chafed. I led from alongside the column, as we marched over a hill and through the suburbs. We were not far along when the first man broke ranks to vomit in the ditch. "Mark time!" I commanded to the remainder who kept up the pace while stationary.

An hour later, we were back at depot. My shirt was soaked and my feet hurt, but I survived better than my pupils had. I had said nothing to them about my low opinion of lunchtime drinkers, but that proved unnecessary. The lesson had been learned.

Rhodesia had practiced conscription of its white and mixed race men for a number of years. National servicemen made up an important element of the army's regular regiments, and they formed the important citizen militia regiments, called the Territorial Army. In an important development for the BSAP, national servicemen were accepted into the police to serve a two-year stint as national service patrol officers. Some of those men were transferred to Support Unit for duty as section leaders after initial training at nearby Morris Depot.

Ormonde and I noticed almost immediately a variance in the quality of the national service intakes. There were always one or two who were not that enthusiastic about wearing black boots at Support Unit, but these initial reservations often evaporated once the man was assigned to a troop and came under the wing of a mature leader. On a positive note, we became aware that the real stars of the national service intake often had been students at Gwebe Agricultural College. These were farmers' sons, men who had lived closely with Africans their entire lives and who enjoyed language skills and an intimate knowledge of African customs.

Almost simultaneously, Morris Depot further refined their induction training program by selecting out national servicemen who were destined for Support Unit service. Candidates were formed into a separate squad with a curriculum that stressed physical fitness and the field skills that junior leaders would require.

When the national service squads passed out of recruit training and were assigned to Support Unit, we were not receiving a candidate who required less training; rather, we faced a more receptive trainee who better profited from the lessons we had ready for them. There was a pleasing cohesiveness in these recruit squads, in particular among the Gwebe country boys—some of whom had known each other for years.

I was cheered at the interest, enthusiasm, and motivation in the leadership squads as the new training regime took hold. There was, I believed, good reason to believe that the new blood from the national service program could provide quality leadership at the base level. If anything could raise the quality of new troops quickly, it was the constant, unremitting attentions of junior leaders striving to ensure that every man under their control was learning and improving.

CHAPTER 7

In the Field

THE 1975 RAINY SEASON swept over northeastern Rhodesia, bringing with it a fresh batch of insurgents from Mozambique. Rains induced fresh growth in the forests, providing overhead concealment for the enemy as well as more sources of potential drinking water. The bad weather associated with seasonal precipitation may also have reduced the flying hours of Rhodesia's aggressive airborne forces, though not by much.

Mount Darwin's Joint Operations Center (JOC) was handling more intelligence indicating enemy activity in neighboring tribal trust lands—and thus it was that G Troop was selected for a short-notice deployment, a journey into the bush that is representative of the operations the troop participated in that year.

Turbulence and war were not new to the Mount Darwin district, though some long-term residents could look back over several decades of peace since World War I.

It had likely been the lure of gold that first attracted traders from the coastal region of Mozambique to venture inland to the ancient kingdom of Monomatapa for trade. These were initially Muslim Arabs who for centuries successfully plied the Indian Ocean coastal regions in their dhows in search of trade goods: gold, ivory, and slaves.

In ancient times, the trickle of gold from Africa's hinterland inspired the sorts of legends that led to great tales of the ilk of King Solomon's mines. There were gold reefs in the Mount Darwin region and alluvial gold to be found in some of the waterways. Centuries earlier, the native civilizations had learned to exploit the gold-producing terrain, smelted the ore, and traded with mariners plying the waters of the Indian Ocean—some from as far away as China.

Portugal's grip on Mozambique, while tenuous in the early sixteenth century, became more robust as it began competing with Arabs for regional trade to the rich interior region of Africa. A Jesuit missionary named Father da Silveria in 1561 entered the fray, competing for African souls as well as treasure. He was so successful in his efforts in baptizing converts to the Catholic faith that it inspired Muslim retribution. A rumor was circulated in the royal court that da Silveria was actually bewitching people; the emperor at the court of Mutapa ordered the missionary killed. He was strangled and tossed into the Musengezi River as an offering to the crocodiles. The chief's court was situated in the vicinity of what was later to become the Mount Darwin administrative center.

Although Portuguese from Mozambique enjoyed some successes in establishing trade links in what was to become northeastern Rhodesia, these were largely confined to large market events where gold and ivory were exchanged for European goods such as beads, cloth, and weapons. It was that great English adventurer Frederick Courtney Selous who apparently delineated much of the boundary between English and Portuguese ambitions when he explored the region in September 1889.

In the valley of the Umkaradzi River, Selous discovered old native gold diggings and a number of quartz reefs that appeared to hold promise. At the head of the valley, he took notice of a distinctive, lofty mountain called Fura by the natives. Selous, expressing his admiration for the eminent British scientist Charles Darwin, renamed it Mount Darwin. This was also an opportunity to label an important geographic feature with a distinctively English name—because he desired to clarify once and for all that these eastern lands were British, not Portuguese. Selous recorded that he had been unable to find any native who had ever seen a Portuguese subject in these lands and subsequently obtained chiefs' signatures to a document formalizing these observations. The country remained under British control, and Mount Darwin evolved into a small administrative center, both for a slowly expanding group of European pioneers and for a far greater number of native tribesmen in surrounding tribal trust lands.

One might have expected that a gold rush could have heralded the settlement of Mount Darwin. The discovery of what was to become Shamva Mine in 1909 brought a brief flurry of gold prospecting to the district, but this was short-lived. Although mines were developed and operated, it was agriculture that became the long-term mainstay of the northeastern economy. At about the same time Shamva Mine was being developed, a forty-thousand-hectare concession was granted for services (in connection with the construction of a railway line between Salisbury and the Mozambique seaport Beira) to the partnership of Pauling and Lawley. Minerals were discovered there and several small mines brought into service. But with time, the land was divided and farmed.

In the early 1920s, three large farms were developed for tobacco cultivation, but by the end of World War II, they were lying idle. An exception was the Cullinan family of Ruia Ranch, which successfully battled with disease and predatory leopards and lions to introduce cattle onto the land.

There was little development in the period of World War II, when many of Rhodesia's young men were serving overseas. Their return at the cessation of hostilities—coupled with a sudden glut of recently demobilized adventurous young men—heralded an era of pioneering in Africa. Rhodesia's Lands Department Board interviewed suitably qualified candidates and granted tenure to Crown Land for farming. In most instances, the land was virgin bush without even road access. Often with the aid of contract African laborers, boundaries were staked out, timber felled, and stumps removed to facilitate cultivation. Housing tended to be primitive in the early stages while farms got on their feet, the production of cash through sale of crops being all important. Tobacco remained a highly viable crop that could be raised in virgin soil; but that also meant that drying sheds were necessary and of a greater priority than personal accommodation. These large, high-walled sheds were constructed by skilled African masons and carpenters, invariably from locally manufactured bricks.

The profitability of tobacco allowed wise farmers to build fencing and develop dams in a country known for its unpredictable rainfall. It also provided the means for diversifying production to cattle, maize, and ground nuts. Farmers in the northeast played a critical role in producing agricultural products that fed Africa and provided cash crops to trading partners, both regional and international. They were a dynamic force, ever expanding in a commercial sense, but largely also careful conservators of the land.

The 1972 farm attacks by the Zimbabwe African National Liberation Army (ZANLA) were thus a symbolic attack against the pioneer Rhodesians of European decent as well as an attempt to cripple important agricultural production. Farm families rallied, pulling together to defend their land, livelihoods, and the vast array of Africans in their employ who were virtually dependent on the farms for food, shelter, salary, and medical attention.

The government rushed to supply farm radios and a purpose-built alarm system for use in the event of attack or emergency. Subsidized security fencing sprang up around farm houses, outbuildings, and labor compounds. Farmers themselves formed into highly effective Police Anti-terrorist Units (PATU), formally trained and outfitted with modern weaponry. Women volunteered for police auxiliary duties, operating radios, overseeing catering and a myriad other support tasks. A number of farmers owning small aircraft became important assets to the police reserve air wing, providing surveillance capabilities and critical air support.

The British South Africa Police (BSAP) provided farms with police auxiliary members serving their call-up stints to stand watch at night, giving farm families a much-needed opportunity to rest, sleep, and run their enterprises with at least some degree of normalcy. Affectionately called "Brightlights," the reservists became an integral part of Mount Darwin's social fabric. In later years, army sections were posted to farms under threat.

As frightening and unsettling as the war was for the farmers and families of Mount Darwin, it was poor indigenous Africans who bore the brunt of the war's brutality. In the surrounding tribal trust lands, terrorists invaded once-peaceful kraals to coerce and forcefully proselytize tribes people. Food and women were demanded and taken, while killings of suspected "sellouts" served to frighten people into submission. The methods for these killings were every bit as heinous and imaginative as I had experienced with the Viet Cong: driving a sharpened, still-burning stake into an anus or vagina was certain to make a strong impression on peasant farmers, as did ritual cannibalism and horrific mutilation.

Later in the war, insurgent gangs advanced their subversion aims by cutting into the fenced compounds that housed farm laborers. This was not recruitment by winning hearts and minds to the cause of black nationalism; it was terrorism and intimidation. Farms lost cattle and other livestock both to theft and intentional mutilations such as hamstringing.

In the worst-affected tribal trust lands, the Rhodesian government had by 1975 begun establishment of defended "keeps" to shelter tribespeople from enemy depredations. To me, there seemed an air of the forced relocation about a program not unlike that President Ngo Dinh Diem's government had attempted during the early 1960s in South Vietnam. Vietnamese peasants, profoundly attached to their ancestral lands, largely spurned relocation. The British had used something similar during the Malayan Emergency, whence Rhodesian decision makers adopted the concept. I, for one, had misgivings about protected keeps, thinking that they would eventually build resentment unless another solution could be found soon.

It was into this environment that G Troop deployed in two vehicles early one weekday morning. I drove the 1950 Bedford RL that had been assigned to Training Wing, a doughty old four-wheel-drive British army design five-ton truck. Of cab-over design, driver and passenger were seated over the front wheels—not an ideal circumstance when dealing with mined roadways. Conversely, visibility was excellent, and an observation port had been installed in the cabin roof through which an observer could stand. Tomlinson Depot's handyman/artisan, World War II Royal Air Force pilot "Tug" Wilson, had meticulously painted in black on each olive-drab door the image of a descending martial eagle, the official Support Unit insignia.

Behind the truck was a large two-axle trailer, into which nonessential gear was packed: sea bags, rations, and extra ammunition. Our troops were seated in full webbing and with rifles loaded along two back-to-back bench seats mounted in the center of the truck bed such that every man faced outward and could do his part in observing the country through which we would be passing. All had been trained in vehicle counterambush tactics and were ready to return fire and attack if so ordered.

The Bedford was in many ways a copy of a General Motors truck of the era. The metal engine cover between the two cabin seats enclosed an in-line, six-cylinder engine that was pure Chevrolet. The RL was never built for speed. To allow the relatively small motor to work efficiently, transmission and transfer case gear ratios were on the low side. With four large wheels, the truck had good ground clearance, and a winch was mounted centrally under the chassis, meaning the vehicle could be winched out from several different directions. Driving required careful concentration and no small amount of strength, because the large steering wheel was connected to the front wheels without benefit of any power assistance.

On that morning, the troop had organized itself quickly. Gear was carefully stowed, radios checked, rifles inspected and loaded. A row of sandbags had been placed over the steel truck bed bottom to offer some degree of protection from a land mine. As I pulled out of Tomlinson Depot loaded with troops and pulling a full trailer, I was conscious that my old vehicle was as laden as ever it should be. We labored up the first suburban street in second gear and once on the open highway northbound, I finally shifted into fourth gear and built speed up to about forty-five miles per hour.

Truck-mounted Support Unit troops in the operational area. (*Rhodesia Herald*)

While the road remained paved and with gentle gradients, our modest convoy managed similar speeds.

Our route took us due north to the rugged Mazoe Valley, Rhodesia's citrus-growing region. An undulating road with spectacular views of granite outcroppings and carefully manicured citrus orchards carried us slowly into the cluster of buildings that was Mazoe, which consisted of an old pub, shops, and a few farmhouses. We stopped near an African trade store, where the men bought freshly baked bread and large bottles of Fanta orange drink for the trip ahead. Nearby was a farmer's fruit stand, where bags of oranges and tangerines could be had cheaply. Half an hour later, the trucks were remounted and we resumed the journey, the Bedford's load now greater still. The next township would be Bindura, another farming community and also the beginning of what most of us considered the war zone. Mazoe's citizens had at that point been spared.

The war had not yet come to Bindura in any significant way, but it had taken on the feel of a township on the edge. There was a Joint Operations Center, the air force maintained a presence as did the army and BSAP. There was a bustle in Bindura, and no shortage of camouflaged vehicles and uniformed men in and around the town.

Passing through Bindura and finally on the final stretch to our destination, the road narrowed and began to feel more like a farmers' access road. The country was verdant, native grasses lush and damp and fresh growth in the green tree canopies. Everywhere, streams seemed to be full. With the cabin windows all open, the air was laden with the odors of fresh earth and recent rain. Often at the narrow stream crossings, called *spruits*, I would call back to the men behind. "*Chenjera*, men. Take extra care; this is a good ambush site we're going through." To safely negotiate the downward roadway, I had to gear down—and on the way out of the narrow valley carved by the waterway, I was double clutching the old truck down through its gears. There was little that could stop us when a road grade forced me to use first gear, but I found myself nervously staring into lush grass and scrub on our uphill side and rechecking to ensure that the rifle in the adjacent rack was ready.

No insurgents decided that day to try their luck with an ambush against our slow-moving convoy. I was personally pleased that the men seated behind me were veterans, many with a decade of service. They had heeded my warnings about potential dangers: we arrived safely in Mount Darwin.

In common with many small Rhodesian towns, the Darwin community had sprung up around the original police camp and administrative center. BSAP Mount Darwin was situated on a small, elevated bluff; it was to be our operating base. We ground up the hill to the compound and found a shade tree to park the truck under. A short distance away stood the old cell block, surrounded by security fencing and concertina wire. The police buildings had been there for many years. Neat, whitewashed, and all with broad verandas, the single-men's quarters and mess stood apart from the original charge office. I reflected that this must have been a pleasant district station in the prewar years, with its lawns, gardens, and shade trees. Now the added influx of various security forces elements had added an air of urgency and tension to the daily policing routines, which nevertheless went ahead as usual. Brown-booted district policemen in their gray shirts and leather leggings still investigated complaints of criminal conduct and as much as possible maintained a patrol schedule to surrounding farms and the African tribal trust lands.

After the requisite courtesy calls at the office of the member in charge to announce our presence and make arrangements for accommodation and messing, Ormonde and I left G Troop in charge of the young national service police officer (NSPO) we had brought along. As good soldiers do, the troop quickly set about finding comfortable places under the trees to check

Mount Darwin police post. (Courtesy Dave Parry)

weapons and organize their packs, rations, and webbing. Ormonde and I headed off to visit the offices of nearby JOC Mount Darwin, where we could expect to be given our operational instructions.

In charge of the operations desk that day was a blond, sunburned Rhodesian Light Infantry (RLI) lieutenant. He was in his late twenties, and I guessed he had been promoted through the ranks, a fact I regarded with more certainty as he spoke to us in the unique patois of the RLI troopie. He had, he said, been expecting us, and, in a ten-minute briefing using a wall map, he outlined the factors that led him to believe that a small but well-armed cell had arrived and was operating in nearby Kandeya Tribal Trust Land (TTL).

I studied the topographic map on the wall as the briefing continued. Kandeya TTL bordered the north area of the district in a broad pie shape, with the point being Mount Darwin community. The Ruya River coursed between the township and the hills and mountains of Kandeya. All of the information about the group was of an inconclusive nature, virtually raw information as opposed to intelligence. Nevertheless, there had been more than one report received and the JOC believed a response was warranted. G Troop would enter the general area in which the enemy group was thought to be operating. There we would observe, lay night ambushes, and hope for a chance encounter.

After the initial situation summary, the briefing became less formal. We took notes, particularly map grid references, and plotted important way points on our own topographic maps.

"How soon can you be ready to move?"

Ormonde and I glanced at each other. It was early afternoon. There was no reason to delay our deployment. A road drop and careful night march could well get the troop positioned covertly before first light.

"We'll be ready to drop at dusk," Ormonde said.

"Good."

"We'll aim to quietly get into this area," he continued, pointing to the concentric brown contours on the chart that indicated a dome, or *gomo*.

That agreed, we noted operational radio frequencies for the patrol and planned reporting times. The plan was to operate in the area for about a week, depending on operational exigencies.

Thirty minutes after we had begun the walk from the police camp, we had returned to G Troop's position under the trees. Most of these veterans had completed repacking and weapon readying and were napping—a smart move, I reflected, given that we were facing a sleepless night. I hoped for a few minutes time to rest also, but I suspected that this would not happen in the time remaining before our short truck ride to the drop point.

There were some important decisions to finalize if I was to be my best in the week ahead, with no resupply possible. Because G Troop had no indigenous Africans yet trained to use a machine gun, Ormonde, the NSPO, and I would serve as gunners as well as commanders. Ormonde, with his British army background, had comfort and familiarity with the Bren gun. That was his choice. I would be carrying the large, belt-fed FN MAG lent to me from the main armory by Eric Kennelly. In the gun would be a fifty-round belt, carefully draped over the weapon, and as backup a further one hundred rounds. As the gun had a high cyclic rate of fire, the gun ammunition supply would be further augmented by additional belts carried by my "number two," Constable Zivinai. He would also carry the radio.

I had chosen Zivinai to live next to my elbow for the next week mostly because I felt certain he would stay calm under fire. A Support Unit veteran of nearly a decade, he had a squat, solid body, with just the start of a belly. I was comfortable with my choice for the operation. There under the trees at Mount Darwin police station, I checked ammo belts with Zivinai, reminding him that they needed to be kept clean and dry—and that if we came under fire, he must be by my side to assist with the gun.

"Yes, *Mambo*," he grunted.

I adjusted the backpack radio straps for him, ensured that extra batteries were in his care, then moved away to carry out last-minute preparation of my own gear and rations. We would be traveling very light—without back packs—living only from what could be carried in our webbing pouches.

As usual, Ormonde and I would cook together and share rations as necessary. He carried a small gas stove; I would have the backup fuel canister. My rations, carefully prepackaged at home, were small packets of rice flavored with dehydrated soup—supplemented by several sticks of *biltong*, cans of Vienna sausages, sardines, and canned fruit. These were carefully compressed into an aluminum British army pattern mess kit (always referred to as a dixie) together with tea bags, fruit flavoring for water, water purification tablets, and the sulfa guanidine tablets that were necessary for overcoming the diarrhea that always became a problem after several days in the bush.

My entire food ration for the patrol, enclosed in the dixie, fit neatly into one of two kidney pouches that were suspended from a heavy web belt; the other contained neatly coiled belts of ammunition for the machine gun, and two Mills 36 grenades. I carried two plastic canteens, one enclosed in a metal drinking cup that could be used to heat food or water. My compass and first aid kit hung from the webbing belt. A tightly wrapped bundle composed of two groundsheets and my parachute sleeping bag was secured to the rear yoke of the web suspenders that bore the weight of the waist belt and all that was attached to it. I would carry no pack. Left behind was my toothbrush, toothpaste, soap, insect repellent, and razor. All exuded odors that our enemy could use to identify the presence of a patrol or an ambush.

Next, I quickly fieldstripped the MAG, first sliding the butt off, then removing the central bolt assembly. They were clean but received yet another wipedown and application of light oil. Then I pulled a swab through the barrel with a weighted cord known as a pull-through. Satisfied at last that I was nearly ready, I carried out a final check of pockets and pouches to assure myself that notebooks and maps were where they should be—all encased in waterproof membrane—and that I had my pocket knife on a lanyard and spoon stuck in an ammo pouch. Everything seemed to be in order.

I glanced around me. The men had been briefed, at least to the extent of where we were going and when. Most lay with heads cradled on their gear, dozing in anticipation of our deployment. I wished there had been time for me to nap for even a few minutes. The day had begun before dawn, and the drive in the old Bedford was hard work. Determined to at least try, I stretched out and had closed my eyes for what seemed like moments when I heard our truck arrive. I arose and with Ormonde walked over to speak to the driver, a seasoned African constable who had made the effort to arrive a few minutes early.

"You'll take us out the north road in a few minutes. I'll knock on the roof of the cab when we are ready to get off. Drop us and leave as silently as possible," Ormonde instructed.

"Sah."

The men were on their feet, hefting rifles and webbing in readiness for the drive. Soon, we were all loaded into the troop transport, seated with rifles pointing outward, every man uncomfortable because of the profusion of webbing and equipment that poked and prodded in the confined space of the bench seats.

The sun was getting low as G Troop drove through Mount Darwin, heading northward. Soon we were on single-lane dirt bush tracks, our driver driving as quietly as possible. There were no other people out—because a strict curfew came into effect at dusk: anybody out and about at night was assumed to be the enemy.

Twenty minutes later Ormonde tapped on the cab of the truck, and the driver glided to a silent, near stop. The men off-loaded as quickly as possible and faded into the bush. The weight of my MAG made my landing awkward. Zivinai was waiting for me, and we moved quickly to where Ormonde had the men assembled. Using hand signals and a few words uttered in a low voice, we divided into two enlarged sections. Ormonde and I did a quick visual reconnaissance and map plot, agreeing on our bearing, and we moved off carefully in an elongated single file.

Kandeya showed the effects of native African agriculture. Our drop point was in an area where goats and cattle had been allowed to graze on native shrubs and trees, so there was little ground cover. Tracks created by livestock seemed to be everywhere. It was rapidly becoming dark. We had seen no *spoor* to indicate that people had used any of the trails recently. Spreading out just enough to ensure that nobody became lost, the patrol began moving toward the Ruya River.

It was a warm night. With nearly twenty pounds of gun suspended on a strap over my shoulder and the weight of my gear, I began to sweat almost immediately. It was more than a half hour before my webbing had

A Support Unit patrol shakes out at a creek crossing in the northeast operational area. (Courtesy National Service Patrol Officer Sebastian Winch, *Outpost*, magazine of the B.S.A. Police)

finally been adjusted to reasonable comfort. Nightfall came quickly. Our pace slowed as the men concentrated on moving silently, keeping a close watch on others and always looking for suspicious signs that might indicate an enemy ambush. Ormonde, preceded by a point man scout, led the column.

The early night was particularly black. Stars came out, but there was no hint of a moon. There was more stumbling, more equipment clatter as we groped through the bush, finally reaching the banks of the Ruya. Here in the open, I began feeling vulnerable. This was a sizeable river, the banks cut almost vertically by flood waters that fortunately had abated. There was *spoor* that indicated that animals and perhaps humans crossed at this point. I quickly moved several men to a covering position as the scout and two others made a relatively silent crossing, the water reaching up near their armpits.

All was quiet except for the sound of the crickets. So far, so good, I mused. Ormonde and several more men crossed and spread out on the opposite side in a defensive semicircle, while the remainder began making the crossing one at a time. From my position it was difficult to see how the men were faring, though there were no sounds to indicate that the river was moving at any speed.

Finally, it was my time to cross. With the gun balanced over one shoulder and my webbing on the other, I started across—feeling my way forward as I went, pointing my toe to find the next step in the uncertain river bottom. I checked constantly around me for signs of danger, moving as quickly as my load and the steady pull of the current permitted. After perhaps fifty meters, the river bottom began sloping upward and I began making out the silhouettes of the advance party providing security. I joined them as the last of the party made their crossing.

Again, we started off slowly—now aided by the rise of a sliver of moon. The stars formed a glowing canopy in the clear African sky silhouetting mountains in the distance. It was nearly midnight.

There were more signs that we were entering an area of habitation, trails with the *spoor* of cattle and donkeys. The Shona people of Kandeya had managed to cultivate several fields of maize. These appeared without warning, each a vast open area enclosed by trees that could have sheltered any enemy group. Both to avoid leaving our tracks and to better conceal movement, the scout faded back into the bush and we began a slow, circuitous route toward the objective.

We were all tired. Webbing and gun straps cut and chafed through clothing damp with perspiration while wet socks and boots abraded feet. I quietly mused that even with my daily participation in rigorous physical training, I could have been fitter for this patrol. But nobody lagged.

We had been guiding on a compass bearing designed to lead us into the area where suspected insurgents were believed to be operating. There was some high ground in the area that we assumed would make good observation points, where we might lie up without attracting the attention of the local Africans. At about 3:00 AM, a sharp-sided conical *gomo* appeared as a silhouette on the horizon. We guided on it and about half an hour later made the bottom of its slope.

There was considerable evidence of local habitation: cattle tracks, tilled farm plots, and firewood collection. All remained quiet, but not for much longer. We had a little more than an hour before roosters would crow and kraals begin to stir. Confident that we could shelter on the *gomo* behind us—and that it would be foolish to attempt its ascent in complete darkness, we climbed the lower slope a short distance and called a halt. The men clustered silently into a rough defensive position, drank from canteens, and stretched out. They would be allowed a short rest and could nap alternatively so there would be no lapses in the patrol security readiness.

Ormonde nodded my way, and I gratefully lay my head on the ground, resting against the machine gun butt, and fell instantly asleep. Minutes later, Ormonde was shaking me awake, whispering that I had been snoring—always an unacceptable practice. I slid over to a nearby tree, propped myself upright, and drifted back into slumber for a further thirty minutes. By no means rested when awakened, I nevertheless felt far more inclined for the task ahead. As the first hint of dawn began to light distant hills, the patrol formed up for the climb.

The *gomo* was remarkably steep, and there was little or no evidence either that local Africans or their livestock ever climbed its slopes. Large boulders were strewn about—some interlocking—and hearty native trees grew in abundance among them. We ascended one step at a time through damp, treacherous undergrowth and over slick granite boulders until finally an opening in the tree canopy appeared. This was the top.

We had been lucky. The position was not ideal, but it would serve as a shelter from prying eyes until we could maneuver to a better location. Density of tree growth and the hill position were not ideal. It became lighter and we began hearing the sounds of herd boys moving cattle from a kraal but could not see them. We could not observe as well as we needed to, but undoubtedly could defend our position, if necessary.

Sentries were posted slightly downslope. Others began to search out places to cook, shelter, and sleep. Good soldiers have an instinctive eye for what can be translated into relative comfort in the bush, and it was not long before shelter halves were tied over saplings and boulders. Soon there was a faint hissing of portable gas stoves as men cooked *sadza* from ground cornmeal.

Ormonde and I did similarly while discussing options for moving to a better position after sunset. There was another *gomo* nearby that appeared to be far better suited to our purposes. While I brewed tea from the all-valuable clean drinking water that I had carried in, Ormonde rigged an antenna and got the radio operating in time for the morning scheduled check-in. With his shackle code book balanced on one knee and a notebook on the other, he prepared the encoded message that would advise JOC Mount Darwin where we were and that we were in a fully operational status. From our elevated position, radio reception was good, and the call-in was completed without difficulty.

The meal, cooked very quickly over the tiny gas stove, was little more than a gut filler. I was tired from the long day yesterday but felt an almost-immediate surge of energy as protein and hot rice hit my stomach, together with an infusion of strong Rhodesian tea. Watch standers had received their orders. We were both ready for some sleep. Zivinai was already asleep, wrapped up nearby in a blanket and poncho—trusting that he wouldn't be interrupted by a rain shower.

I was not so confident, rolling out my poncho/shelter halves, one to sleep on, the other tied taut with parachute cord to nearby saplings to provide at least some overhead cover from weather. Sharing with the gun, which stood loaded on its bipod, I rolled out my parachute sleeping bag, removed my soaked black canvas hockey boots and socks, and climbed gratefully into the cool silk. Before dozing off, I did a mental checklist of what had been accomplished and what remained to be done.

As always, there was the question of drinking water. I mused briefly about this critical question in the awareness that the events of bush wars always seem to hinge on the availability of drinkable water. In Vietnam, we learned with time to search out Viet Cong and North Vietnamese army jungle camps by their proximity to water. Water collection points were a favorite ambush site for both sides.

In Africa, there were areas where a man dare not venture during the dry season. While elephants and some other large game proved adept at finding and digging for water from the sand of seemingly dry riverbeds, few of the men who became insurgents had these bush skills. When the rains came to fill streams, small ponds, and even puddles, it was safer to transit into Rhodesia.

If the gang we were seeking was being supported by the people of a kraal, their replenishment worries were over. Our troop, however, would likely need water that night. Finally, I dozed off, soon awakening to a desultory state of semiconsciousness, my ear attuned for radio traffic that didn't come.

There was little activity nearby that we could discern. Sentries always listened carefully for sounds and conversations from nearby herd boys and female firewood gatherers, but none ventured close enough to pose a risk of compromise.

In the early afternoon, I walked quietly around—checking on men to ensure that all were fed and fit. There were no health issues, although there were a few small blisters from wet socks. Weapons had already been wiped and oiled, as rust—particularly in the bore—is a genuine risk in damp conditions.

Ormonde and I later sat together under the trees on two adjacent boulders with maps spread out between us, plotting our movements for the evening. The objectives would be our relocation to a more suitable observation point (OP) and the establishment of night ambushes on nearby trails. We expected the enemy would use the cover of darkness to move within the area.

A nearby *gomo* looked attractive for our layup area and OP. We decided to move out at early dusk—down the south slope, then into cover and, finally, ascending the hill. As darkness came, the men gathered and rechecked equipment to ensure that no items had loosened that might rattle. Most had managed a few hours of broken sleep. Zivinai stood next to me wearing the radio on his back. He had carefully wiped the garlands of machine gun ammunition that were draped over his shoulders. I nodded to him, then followed the single file as the troop began moving slowly down the steep slope—stopping often to look and listen. We were still enclosed in a low canopy of trees, unable to see more than perhaps twenty meters downslope and all was very quiet. Earlier in the afternoon, we had heard the sound of the *mujibas* herding cattle and the occasional call of women tending a small patch of maize. Either, I speculated, the local folk were particularly conscious of the risk of curfew breaking—or they had somehow deduced that we were somewhere in the area. Or perhaps it was both.

In some ways, the descent was harder work than the climb up. Footing was precarious. The MAG, carried on its sling pointing forward and slightly left, affected my balance, and I came close to falling more than once. Zivinai followed close behind, once grabbing my webbing suspenders as one foot slipped off a smooth stone. It was with some relief that we reached level ground at last light, turning to move into a tree line for cover. The intended destination loomed ahead, already becoming a darkened silhouette in the twilight. No need for a compass bearing. The column spread out and moved south.

We discovered a well-worn pedestrian track at the base of the *gomo* that was our intended OP. Even in the fading light, I could see that a particularly determined bicycle rider had managed to negotiate—with some difficulty—the soft sand of the trail.

The patrol moved on a short distance to the concealment of nearby trees. Men were deployed by hand signal into a long line facing the trail, while Ormonde and I huddled behind them for a whispered conference.

"Lots of traffic on this trail."

"Ja. We should set up ambushes here now and worry about the OP early tomorrow."

So it was agreed. Ormonde took a small group eastward about one hundred meters, positioning them back from the trail in dense cover. I did the same, walking slowly to the west, back in the trees—tailed all the way by Zivinai—to a location that offered views both ways of the trail. The two out groups would serve to warn the main killer group of an approaching enemy; they could also act as stop groups against those attempting to escape the ambush. After a radio check, I left our NSPO in charge and made my way back to the central position that overlooked the killing ground.

The men had a good eye both for concealment and cover. Most had already assumed positions in a gentle arc, facing the open area that was the intended killing zone. Each was assigned an arc of fire. The two machine guns were positioned, and we settled down to wait.

It had become a very dark night. Stars stretched across the heavens, and I waited for the appearance of the moon by stretching out prone in the grass and peering around a low boulder—doing my best to observe the trail. Zivinai, facing rearward to watch for an approach from that quarter, was close enough that I could reach out and touch his leg. The machine gun butt lay cool against my right cheek. I played imaginative games with myself to keep my eyes moving, not focusing in any one area for too long, always looking and listening for signs of the enemy. I wore a face net over which was a camouflage bush hat. White faces are more difficult to conceal than dark ones, and I was taking no chances.

After several hours, the stars were concealed by clouds and rain began to fall gently. No ponchos or rain gear was permitted in ambush because of the distinctive pattering water makes when striking it, another sure giveaway to an attentive enemy. I zipped up my battle smock and buttoned the sleeves at the wrist. It was a slow rain, but with time it soaked us all. Water coursed in rivulets under my body. I concentrated on staying perfectly still, in the knowledge that my body would warm the water closest to it and make wetness more tolerable.

In the very early morning hours, the rains stopped. A sliver of moon defined the horizon and all remained absolutely quiet. Slowly, warmth returned to my body. Zivinai quietly attempted to stretch the stiffness from his limbs, and I wished it were possible to push time forward to dawn.

It had been a very long night. Perhaps, I mused as the first slivers of daylight showed to the east, the gang sensed we were in for a damp night and elected to stay some place dry and warm. But where? We would have to be lucky to bump into an enemy group. There were not at that time many in the area, but the effort had to be made.

Finally, when I could make out Ormonde's position with the snout of his Bren gun pointing toward the trail, I raised my hand. He did the same, then held one hand over his hand in the signal for a rendezvous. This, I knew, meant the night ambush was over. The radio crackled, calling in the two stop groups, and I stood up, shaking off leaves and grass from my damp clothing. There was no time to scout out water, but the rains had left enough standing in puddles that I was able to half-fill a canteen. There would be a component of grit in it, and the water purification tablet would render it nearly undrinkable, but it was water nonetheless. Others did as I had done.

Soon, we pulled back well into the trees and began the climb to the top of our selected observation point. Once again, there was no evidence that the *gomo* had been visited by man. Vegetation and trees were dense but not so dense that a track had to be cut. This time I was behind the forward scout, who climbed a short distance, then paused and listened. Near the top, the boulders became larger and there were fewer trees and much more light. At last, I could see that the dome was open on top with expansive views of the countryside. Fortunately, the crowns of trees in the forest ringing the top served as a screen between our new position and the nearest kraal. By careful positioning and movement discipline, our muddy camouflage uniforms should not attract attention from below.

With the patrol gathered, defensive sectors were established. Sentries carefully checked their sectors, then pulled back to an established observation point. Others not then on duty began locating positions in the rocks for cooking and sleeping.

Ormonde and I chose a spot in the open—but well back from the edge—at the crest of the *gomo*. Radio reception was excellent from the elevated position, but the view to the south was even better. I set down the gun on its bipod, shed my webbing, and stood in the early morning sunlight, enjoying a gentle breeze while staring out over the vast panoply of

Africa. In the far distance was the community of Mount Darwin, backed by the massifs of Vuma and Mount Darwin. Slightly to the east of the town, I watched activity on the airstrip, where Rhodesian air force Alouette helicopters were being serviced. Nearby farms, their fields of maize glistening in the morning light, began the day's activities.

Closer still, the country transformed into what Africa must have looked like two centuries before. A low range stood to our southeast and stands of native trees flourishing in the draws where water accumulated from adjacent exposed granite. Closer to us still were several patches of cultivated land. Women from the kraal located to our east walked on narrow footpaths through the grass to these fields, each clothed in brightly colored cotton print wraparound skirts fashioned from the bolts of cloth sold at trade stores. They chattered back and forth, carrying hoes for their work over shoulders much as a soldier would his rifle. Far away, the distant muffled clang of a cowbell announced that the herd boys were moving kraal cattle out for a day of grazing. I was quietly relieved that we would not need to worry about the prying eyes of those boys while we established our new position.

Ormonde crouched on the bare granite to start the gas stove for the long-awaited morning brew up of tea.

"This feels a little more like home," I quipped. "A good OP, defendable and hopefully not far from where the terrs are plying their trade."

We both knew very well that there would have to be an element of good fortune in our getting close enough to kill a small band of elusive armed men in the vast area before us. The enemy would need a reason to move; we would need to somehow be in his path, within shooting distance, to neutralize him. We would now watch how people moved during the day to see which paths were most favored; we would try to think like the enemy to make educated guesses about where he might like to go. And we would do our best not to let people know that we were operating in the area.

I sat on a low boulder enjoying tea so hot that a piece of cigarette packet foil had to be folded over the edge of my metal drinking vessel to prevent me burning my lower lip. Breakfast that day had been capped with a small can of fruit cocktail. The morning sunlight was gentle and fresh as were the breezes that carried heady scents of damp grass and moist earth. We were all beginning to stink, as only soldiers who cannot wash smell. After several days, one becomes mostly inured to his own body odor and that of his fellows. Much has been said about the particular pungency of overheated Africans, but in my experience, an unwashed European meat-eater takes on a particular fetid, feral rankness. That was happening to me: Unshaven, face with a gentle crust of dirt with courses of perspiration through it. My camouflage shirt and trousers were permeated with red mud and stiff to the touch. Flies were finding me attractive and I didn't really care. We were a long way from the parade square at Tomlinson Depot.

On a shelf of water-worn granite, I located a shallow pocket of earth—doubtless the product of millennia of erosion—on which to sleep. Scraping out a gentle indentation for my hip, I lay out a groundsheet and rigged my poncho as a low overhead cover. With watches posted and our morning sitrep safely transmitted by radio in shackle code to JOC Mount Darwin, it was finally time for some sleep.

I fell into a deep slumber almost immediately. Clouds gathered and a light rain began to fall, a gentle patter just inches above my face on the poncho above. The rhythm and odor of fresh rain conveyed my dreaming back to Vietnam—intense images of the monsoons in a surreal setting of muted light, backlit by the urgency of war. Then rivulets of water began to accumulate under the small of my back, drawing me for a time back to consciousness, but I willed myself back to sleep. This time my dreams were about my childhood sweetheart, Judith, whom I had not seen since my departure back to Vietnam in 1971 on the final of my three years there. She was talking to me, asking what I was doing—and where was I going?

Dreams while on operations were a rare event for me. These had been lucid enough to awaken me and remain in my consciousness. I wondered whether I had reached some significant milestone in my life. I could not get back to sleep despite an almost overwhelming weariness. I consciously wrenched my thoughts back to the reality of my mission and the responsibilities inherent in it. Getting up after a scant few hours of rest, I walked a few feet to the high ground, where Ormonde was standing and staring intently into the valley.

"What do you make of that, Doug?" he said pointing in a southeasterly direction at a low bluff.

"Quarter left, see the lone tree on the skyline? Follow the ridge down; there is a kraal there. Lots of people running around and some smoke too."

I watched the spot carefully—and also saw smoke, much more smoke than a cooking fire would create.

"I see it, but can't make out what's happening."

We stood together just back from the cliff face watching, concentrating, before deciding that it was worth contacting JOC Mount Darwin about our observations. Our radio transmission made it clear that we could not ascertain what was happening with any certainty; neither could we dismiss the possibility that enemy had attacked, particularly as a group was believed to be operating in the area.

Several minutes passed. Then we watched two air force Alouette helicopters take off and head directly toward the area of the kraal we were watching. One landed at a nearby *mealie* field, while the other circled at distance. Perhaps because we were not operating on the same radio frequency, we could not determine what events were unfolding several kilometers away. It might have been a domestic house fire, but the Rhodesian security forces were taking no chances. After a time—and another quick check of the perimeter watch, we both returned to our respective shelters to rest.

The troop was drawing together, becoming more close-knit as only the sharing of danger and adversity can do. The constables and sergeants with whom we interacted daily in the relative civility of Salisbury did not lessen protocols of discipline and respect by attempting to create familiarity; it would have been considered poor form to do so. There was little that would change cultural considerations, diet, and habits between indigenous members and those Africans of European origins, me included. Nevertheless, there was a perceptive melding as proximity taught men more about each other—and themselves. Orders or requests—whether verbal or as hand signals—were required less often because men knew or sensed what was expected. This produced in me a pleasurable satisfaction. Our small group—despite enormous differences—was truly operating as one, and the ever-present Zivinai seemed always to be where I needed him without prompting.

As yet another dusk came to Mount Darwin, ambush parties prepared. Weapons were stripped and oiled, magazines cleared and reloaded, gear repacked. From our cliff-side perch, Ormonde and I stared quietly out over the valley, where all was apparently quiet now at the kraal that had previously excited our attention. In the township far away, lights began to come on up on the low hill where the police camp was situated. It was still quite warm. The muddy, chemical-laced drinking water sloshing around in our canteens was better than nothing, but I was already beginning to battle bouts of diarrhea, which always seemed to accompany the use of drinking water acquired under less-than-ideal conditions.

"Those brown boot bastards are already in the club sucking up a *chibuli*," Ormonde growled. My salivary glands reacted involuntarily as my imagination considered what the first mouthful of bitterly cold, bubbling ale might taste like at that very moment. I simply groaned, earning a malicious grin from my off-sider in return.

"The first round at the 234 Club is yours, china," I said as we both fell to silence and I wondered what might occur in the remaining days of the patrol.

That evening, Ormonde was to take his team down the eastward slope to ambush a trail not far from the nearest kraal. I had decided that another track running east and west, not far from the south side of our OP, would be a good secondary ambush area. My group left the *gomo* first, descending a slope so steep that I realized that we would need to find a different approach when it came time to return. At the foot of the dome, breathing hard from our exertions, we gathered quietly under cover to allow darkness to set in further. I took the moment to plot reference points with compass and map from silhouetted domes and features. Usually a better-than-average navigator, I had frightened myself on previous night movements by virtually loosing sense of direction in extreme darkness. I wished for a better night compass, noted the bearings, and committed back-bearing to memory—then motioned the men ahead.

Our destination was a grove of trees perhaps six hundred meters away; I believed it would lie in close proximity to the ambush trail. We moved at a slow but steady pace, watching around us constantly. The women had left their fields long before, and none of the calls or cow bells of the herd boys could be heard. I imagined that the people of the nearest kraal were sitting down around a fire to enjoy the evening meal. Perhaps they would have guests?

The patrol glided silently into the narrow tree line. As I had hoped, a well-worn dirt track was situated in the open just twenty yards or so away. The tree line position would not have concealed us in daylight, but the dark, dirty faces and camouflage rendered the men virtually invisible. I let them stand silently in the trees and began to look around us, considering the best way to position a small ambush team. As I was doing so, a distant metallic sound carried across the grassland toward us. I tensed, looked to men on both sides of me, and signaled them to listen and be ready. I took a deep breath, released the machine gun belt to hang freely from the feed ready to fire, pulled the gun tightly into my side, and with my right hand tightly grasping the pistol grip, gently touched the trigger in anticipation. It would be me who would initiate any attack with a burst from the gun.

We stood utterly motionless in the shadows. The noise came to us again, this time closer, and I thought I might have heard a voice too. I stared intently down the trail to the west, trying to make out the shape of what seemed likely to be insurgents advancing to the kraal. It was well after curfew, and thus no prudent person walked around after dark.

At last a shape began to emerge, apparently that of two men pushing a bicycle rather unsteadily and talking as they walked. I could see no weapons but that didn't mean they weren't present. I could feel Zivinai's presence immediately behind my right shoulder as I waited for the men to close on us, tensed and ready to fire. He had been listening to scraps of the conversation through the dark. Suddenly, he whispered in my ear urgently, "*Mambo*! Don't shoot! These are not terrorists; they are young men coming back from a beer drink." This piece of unexpected information caused me to withdraw my trigger finger and whisper back testily, "Watch them when they pass to see if they have weapons." If any were seen, I reasoned, I could step out into the trail and take them down from behind.

Every eye was on the two as they walked slowly past our position, giggling. Both were barefooted, dressed in simple dark-colored secondhand trousers and shirts. There was nothing martial in either their attire or demeanor, nor were they carrying packs or parcels. I slipped quietly out of the trees, alone, for a final look at them at close range—from behind. There were, I knew, many in my place who would have taken both men out, and perhaps I was being a little naïve, remiss in my duty, but I felt it better to err than to kill two innocents. Our enemies would make much of that type of incident at a time when we genuinely were trying to maintain the goodwill of the Kandeya Tribal Trust Land.

Those two young men, jolly with beer, had come very close to death without realizing it. Moments later, they had advanced into the gloom and could no longer be heard. I returned to the trees, signaling the men to follow on the forward scout and ordered him to guide on another point several hundred yards away, where it was my intention to set up an overnight ambush.

That ambush, set up in a slightly elevated position of a gentle bend in the trail, offered converging fields of fire into the killing zone. Here we set up—ever hopeful—and spent another uneventful night without seeing or hearing another human. But in the distant background during several periods in the night's darkness, I heard a high-pitched squeaking far away. From a whispered discussion an opinion was proffered that these noises were being created by a traditional donkey cart in need of axle grease.

I thought long and hard about this. Who would drive a cart around in the tribal trust land after curfew? Why would they do this? Could it be somebody trying to arrive at the market before dawn, or was the cart perhaps carrying heavy implements of war—such as mortars, ammunition, or land mines?

There had been a short-lived temptation to lead the patrol in the direction from which the sound seemed to be coming. Every time the noise carried through to me, I became frustrated again. But in the extreme darkness, aggravated by overhead cloud cover, even if I chose to illuminate my topographic map, there was an excellent chance that we would become lost. That would mean my patrol might not be able to reach a suitable hide and OP by first light, increasing many times the odds that our presence would be noted and the enemy alerted to leave the area. We stayed where we were, lying next to the trail with Zivinai's big boots a reminder that he was watching my back.

I pulled us out with more than an hour of darkness before first light, guiding on compass back-bearing. The first way point—the tree line where I had so nearly shot the two partygoers—was relatively easy to locate, although the position appearance seemed somehow altered since we had transited through the evening previous. I calculated a further back-bearing intended to carry us slightly south of our original path, hoping that this would place us farther east of the extremely steep path we had forged down the *gomo*. The men were tired, more so at the low-ebb predawn period, and I hoped for an easier climb to the heights of our OP *gomo*.

The march seemed to last forever. I could not see enough of surrounding features to estimate our position. In frustration, I finally halted the patrol as I became increasingly concerned that with every step I might be leading us away from the intended destination. We would wait for the first hint of dawn and hope that I could reorient myself in time to cover the final distance before light. I sat anxiously and waited, wondering whether G Troop would soon be sharing a joke at my expense about my navigation skills, or the lack of them. I recalled a number of cruel sayings from Vietnam, chiefly the dictum that held that there was little that was more dangerous than a new lieutenant with a map and compass.

It ultimately took me far longer both to determine our position and to move the patrol back to the *gomo*. I anxiously radioed Ormonde as dawn broke to explain our predicament and warn his group of our intended avenue of approach. It was dangerously close to first direct light when we stopped very briefly to fill canteens from a small rivulet within a few hundred meters of the eastern kraal. From there we would guide directly across the *vlei* and into the trees that covered the bottom fringe of the dome.

I was anxiously signaling the patrol to saddle up and had reshouldered the machine gun just as a young African woman in a bright blue cotton wrapped skirt appeared on a path perhaps two hundred meters away. She was carrying a water vessel with her. I froze, hoping she might be looking another direction—hoping that she might not notice us—but it was not to be. Suddenly stopping dead in her tracks, she turned and trotted back the way she had come.

Tired, frustrated, and not a little angry with my navigation performance, I turned the patrol back to give the appearance that we were heading away from the settlement. Then, where the ground was harder and less likely to record the imprint of military footwear, I turned suddenly and we made our way quickly into the shelter of the gomo's trees.

At last, the line of men ascended the crest of the *gomo* after passing Ormonde's sentries. I dismissed them to eat and rest and then set the gun down and shed my webbing. Ormonde had boiled water for tea and I gratefully squatted with my tin cup to enjoy a brew-up.

"Nothing on your side last night?" I queried.

"No. Very quiet. It really makes me wonder whether perhaps they have moved on."

I shared his sentiments, wishing it were possible to know what intelligence reports had come into the JOC since our departure. Surely the Ground Coverage source network should be providing pieces of information about the group? We would likely not be told over the radio, although it was possible that we might be withdrawn and reinserted to another, more active zone.

I then related my experience with the two young beer drinkers—and I asked whether Ormonde's group had heard the peculiar squeaking noise that we had tentatively identified as a donkey cart. They had not.

"I don't think we've got a Ho Chi Minh Trail in operation down there, but I have bad feelings about this. Who in his right mind would operate a cart after curfew?" I said.

"Perhaps you can get in closer to the sound tonight?"

I thought about Ormonde's suggestion. Moonlight would be minimal or nonexistent when my patrol would be moving into position, meaning that navigation could be difficult. Moreover, it was important that each of us had a pretty accurate idea where the other was operating. I pulled my now-battered map out of my long thigh pocket, extracted it from its waterproof pouch, and unfolded the relevant section, considering our options.

While I pored over contour lines, trail markings, and the small squares that indicated a native settlement, Ormonde took care of the afternoon radio schedule. From what I could overhear, JOC Mount Darwin was issuing instructions. This was soon confirmed.

"JOC says we can pull out tomorrow. Activity reports have gone cold; maybe our terr group has moved on?"

"I wonder," I reflected.

We hated to leave without some tangible result; we also knew, given the size of the area and the fact that we were up against a small, mobile band, that good fortune played a greater role than we cared to admit. Perhaps it made sense to return to Mount Darwin to resupply and assess the latest operational intelligence.

Sitting with maps spread out between us, we considered the options—ultimately deciding to put in two ambushes in reasonably close proximity to a kraal—the kraal I guessed might be near the source of the cart noises. If the ambushes were unsuccessful, we would rendezvous, rest several hours, and march back across the Ruya for pickup.

That evening, both patrols moved out together in the gathering gloom, moving carefully from the OP and out across the grassland below. Two hours later, Ormonde's group dropped off on the side of a well-worn trail within sight of the objective kraal. Continuing westward, I led my men well away from the conical thatched roofs of the village and after we were on the other side, turned sharply back and moved silently to the kraal's far side trail. With the outbuildings and *rondavels* perhaps fifty meters away, I signaled a halt at a point slightly above the main trail.

We were close enough to hear conversation. A couple in the nearest hut had a particularly long-winded argument. Zivinai reassured me that there had been no discussion about visits from insurgents. I eventually burrowed down further in the long grass and watched the kraal and its trail. Tired after a week in the bush, my mind wandered, and I found myself wondering who in the animal kingdom might at that moment be sharing this small patch of Africa with me? A variety of venomous snakes were native to the region, but most would quickly move away from an intruding man. I had learned that it was prudent to make just enough noise in the high grass to let other creatures know of my presence. Unless one was unlucky enough to encounter a black mamba on a warm day or the laconic but deadly Gaboon viper underfoot, the bush was reasonably safe. Man had lived in the area long enough that most of the dangerous large game had migrated toward the Zambezi Valley, although it was not unusual to encounter fresh leopard *spoor* near the *kopjes* where clans of baboons sheltered. That night, we coped with nocturnal ants and an occasional mosquito. They lunched on the unwary—unimpeded by insect repellant, forbidden because of its distinctive odor. Eventually, the last of the village people quieted and went to sleep. As the long hours ticked away, the ambush team struggled to remain awake. I eventually issued orders that men could pair up, with one man at a time catching a short nap.

In the early hours of the morning, I once again heard in the far distance the creaking squeak of the cart. I hoped it would come our way, but it did not. Frustrated, I pulled the ambush at the first hint of dawn and withdrew a short distance to a wooded area, where we were soon joined by Ormonde's patrol. They took the first watch, and I fell into a welcome sleep propped up against a tree with my hand resting on the machine gun.

Several hours later, somewhat refreshed, we began the walk out—now unconcerned about our presence being obvious to local inhabitants. We were leaving the area, but they didn't know that. We would show the flag, in much the same way the BSAP had in years previous, but in the garb of a modern warrior.

The Ruya River seemed less threatening when we reached its banks in full daylight. With good visibility to the far bank and area beyond, the potential of a river-crossing ambush had been eliminated. As the patrol neared the river, Ormonde called over his shoulder, "Keep an eye out for flat dogs; there have been people taken in the river here recently." I thought instantly of how vulnerable we might have been when we made the original river crossing in darkness, a time crocodiles can be particularly lethal. There were nervous grins from several of the troops, one or two of whom made hand signals signifying large biting animals to their peers.

But there were no crocs in the vicinity. We watched carefully as the men made a relatively easy crossing at a low point, then resumed our march, my discomfort increased by wet, chafing trousers aggravating an already-raw crotch. Though we never wore underwear—and sometimes left trouser fronts unbuttoned for ventilation—"crotch rot" was a condition that worried many of us. A combination of chafing and perspiration in the extreme temperature together with an inability to wash was almost certain to bring the condition on. Each step reminded me how tender my legs had become—and of how good a shower and clean shorts would feel that evening.

The remainder of the march was uneventful. We encountered nobody. When I estimated that we were within an hour of our rendezvous point for pickup, I radioed Mount Darwin to send transport.

We arrived at the road in the stillness of a hot afternoon and pulled back into shade and relative concealment to await the arrival of transport. Now unconcerned about where the next water would come from, the men drank deeply from canteens and relaxed. A short time later I heard the distinctive sound of the RL laboring up a distant hill, and in moments the big blunt nose of the Bedford swung into view on the slight incline, throwing up powdery dust under its wheels. The driver halted, grinning, and we were quickly aboard and returning to the land of hot showers, clean clothes, and cold beer.

Though there was a fairly constant train of transient personnel through the single men's mess at BSAP Mount Darwin, the quarters were always well cared for by domestic staff and individual batmen—menservants—in the employ of single-duty branch members. Ormonde and I had bunks to sleep on and access to a communal bathroom. The troops were billeted nearby. I reminded the senior sergeant that all weapons and ammunition were to be cleaned and securely stowed before the men were released to eat and rest, and then turned my attentions to my MAG, while Ormonde fieldstripped the Bren gun on a corner of the veranda. One of the mess domestics came to see if we needed anything washed. He must have smelled our musty unwashed state from yards away. He was an older man, graying, with whom Ormonde joked in native dialect about our filthiness. "Yes," he said, "We'll be showering just now. Then you may wash everything that we are wearing."

As the *madala*—old man—shuffled down the veranda, I handed Ormonde some money, my share of the laundry stipend, and reminded him that the first round at the nearby 234 Club was his. We wasted no time with our weapon maintenance and were soon showering.

One shower is never enough to remove the filth of a week or so without exposure to soap and water. Feet, toenails, and calluses are permeated with grime that remains for days. Even our short-shorn hair seemed to be a habitat for living things. My camouflage shirt and trousers, stiff with mud and sweat, were retrieved from the floor as I showered, working to scrub the worst of the dirt away.

Finally, feeling like a man reborn, I toweled off with a small olive-drab towel and donned shorts and a clean camo shirt. An old pair of *veldskoens* completed the transformation. Together Ormonde and I walked perhaps ten meters to the club.

The 234 had once been an underground water reservoir for the police station. Discovering that it leaked, resourceful policemen drained it, installed a large center support pole in the middle of the concrete floor, and built a roof structure over it that was ultimately covered. From outside, it was only the round, thatched roof that could be seen; all else was below ground. A set of narrow steps had been hacked out of one of the concrete walls and a bar and refrigerator installed. With whitewashed walls, the carefully varnished center pole decorated with trophies and memorabilia, it was a very pleasant refuge. We descended the narrow stairs and moved directly up to the bar, Ormonde ordering two pints of Lion lager from the barman. The old African deftly pried the bottle caps from dark brown bottles that had been refilled many times and placed them in front of us with glasses.

Neither of us spoke as we poured the cold amber, and with a quick pronouncement—"Cheers!"—savored the first mouthful. It tasted like nectar. With never enough water to drink, we remained dehydrated even after gulping pure water at Mount Darwin.

I turned to Ormonde: "Now it is we who are the rear echelon slackers. Here's to those poor pricks in the bush, especially the ones who can see the bright lights of civilization as we did."

Two beers went down quickly, and I noticed their effect almost as soon as the fluid reached my stomach. The bar was beginning to fill as the men finished afternoon shift. There was a good deal of friendly chatter and banter, none of it about things operational. Soon hunger overtook thirst as a motivator and we decided to seek out the mess trailer.

As Rhodesia became increasingly swept up in the bush war and more members of the regular police force were called to duty in the operational area, members of the BSAP Reserve filled vacancies at police stations across the country. Reservists, many of them fulfilling call-up obligations, carried out a vast array of tasks on the street as policemen, in the air as police pilots, and in the stations manning radios and typewriters. And some of them were cooks in the operational area, feeding men hungry from days of living on subsistence rations. One could always count on a substantial, hearty meal from one of the police messing trailers. Off we went, with stomachs rumbling, to see what was being offered down the hill from the police camp.

The smell of *boerewors* and onions preceded our arrival at the chow line, where a few other hungry souls held out plates and mess tins to the caterers in the open-sided trailer. The reservists were a cheery bunch, both male and female, and old enough to be my parents. There was plenty of lighthearted banter as plates were heaped with steaming food. I thanked my server, who noticed my American accent and smiled. "Plenty more if you want it!"

We found a place at a picnic table under an overhead canvas cover and savored the first real meal we'd had in a week. I had lost at least ten pounds while on patrol. My body seemed to gratefully soak up the nourishment it was being offered.

Afterward, sated and full, we walked back under towering eucalyptus trees to the mess. The JOC watch standers knew that G Troop was in camp if there was a flap. We hoped there wouldn't be a crisis that night. After hopefully getting a good sleep, Ormonde and I would check in the next morning to learn what we could about enemy activity; that would determine what G Troop would be doing in the days ahead.

Back at the mess, we again checked to ensure that arms and equipment were secure. The sergeant who was present did not tell us that all of the men were actually in camp. We all knew what that meant—and we knew that the noncommissioned officers (NCOs) had their own ways of ensuring that men were present and fit for duty when the time came. For my part, although sounds of laughter and the clinking of glasses wafted periodically up from the nearby 234 Club, I fell gratefully into my bed and fell into a deep sleep. The old military cot felt utterly luxurious.

We were not disturbed that night. Feeling much refreshed the next morning—and after ensuring that all men and equipment were present and accounted for—Ormonde and I drove to the operations center. Here we discussed with the duty officer our observations from the recent patrol and learned that the trail of our elusive band had gone cold. There had been no new sightings or agent reports. They had, it was surmised, moved elsewhere; if the Ground Coverage intelligence network was functioning as well as we all hoped, more current information would filter in and there would be another opportunity to pursue and eliminate the group.

We left JOC Mount Darwin an hour later and drove slowly back to the police camp in the doorless Land Rover. G Troop was to remain in standby mode. Neither of us was disappointed at this development. It seemed far preferable to have fresh intelligence as the basis for a new operational plan rather than relying on good fortune to locate and destroy the enemy. BSAP Special Branch was an efficient organization, with an extensive network of sources and informants. Hopefully, we would not have to wait long for them to deliver tangible information that could be acted on. In the meantime, the men would be readied to move on ten-minutes notice.

Moments later, back at the police camp, we had parked the vehicle. The senior sergeant approached us to receive instructions for the day just as an army Land Rover wheeled into the camp at some speed. Recognizing the driver from the morning briefing, Ormonde hurried over to speak with him while I reminded our senior NCO that the men needed to be placed in readiness to move on very short notice: weapons clean, ammunition checked, water bottles full—and basic rations packed away. I was confident this had already been done, but this was my way of following up. Bracing to attention, the sergeant uttered a simple "Sah!" and was turning to walk away when Ormonde trotted up: "We are moving now. There's been a sighting nearby. Get the men who are ready here now!"

We ran to gather up our webbing and weapons from the mess. There was an air of urgency in the sergeant's voice as he called together the men and headed them toward the vehicles. I learned that Special Branch had reason to believe that one or two armed insurgents were then harboring on a small *gomo* not far from the town. We would be provided with a guide; we would move out immediately.

I hurriedly donned webbing and picked up the gun, paused to ensure that the ammo belt was correctly loaded and ready, then trotted down to where two Land Rovers were loading up. I took a passenger seat in one of them, carrying the gun across my lap with barrel pointing outward. There were then a total of about ten men ready. We could wait for no more. Ormonde gave the signal and we pulled out on to the road, moving at a good pace. The information about the enemy was very fresh; it was thus important that we act as quickly as possible.

The dirt road out of town had recently been graded, so we made reasonable speed. Our operational plan was simple. Because the low hill on which the insurgents were thought to be hiding was quite near the road, we would approach as quickly and quietly as possible by vehicle, debus, form up on the trot, and attack. With any luck, our quarry would be surprised and/or would stand and fight. G Troop's men were well armed and had the advantage of better marksmanship skills than our opponents, so I was confident we would do well if contact was made.

Less than thirty minutes after receiving our orders, G Troop glided quietly to a halt at the side of the road in the two dark-green Land Rovers. Our guide indicated that the hill was a short distance inland through light forest. The men quickly unloaded and shook out into an extended line facing the hill, with Ormonde and me at either end. The young NSPO—armed with a Bren gun—was positioned between us, Zivinai at my side with radio and extra ammo belts for the MAG.

We stepped out moments later, walking quickly to the east, where I could see the bottom of the *gomo* through the trees. The men were keyed up. I glanced to both sides quickly to satisfy myself that everybody was focused on our objective, watching for signs of movement.

Moments later, Ormonde's Bren gun boomed out with a three-round burst that struck adjacent to a large boulder near the crest of the far end of the facing slope. I had not seen movement, but Ormonde was closer than I and it seemed quite possible that the large rocks might be concealing a possible hide. Pausing for just a few seconds, I unleashed two bursts into the same area in the hope that the fire would keep our quarry in cover long enough that we could close on him, then motioned for my men to move forward quickly.

As I did so, a Rhodesian air force Alouette helicopter flew over us, very low and at speed. Our radios crackled with a message from the army officer overhead who was taking control and hopefully directing us to our elusive enemy by using the advantage of overhead observation. The chopper flew over the low hill that was by now looming in front of us, banked, and circled. Zivinai handed me the radio handset and I acknowledged the call, asking whether a contact sighting had been achieved with the enemy.

"Negative. No contact," was the response.

It had been movement on the hill that caused Ormonde to fire. A heavy cover of brush made detailed observation of the hill difficult, but that was very typical of this type of war. The enemy could be adept at using nature to hide, but as we moved in close to the lower slope, it was quite apparent that nobody remained. We posted a small team to cover the front of the feature and moved quickly around the ends of it to sweep the reverse side. In the distance, the helicopter clattered in its sweeping pattern, looking for movement or possible *spoor* created by men being pursued.

The reverse of the *gomo* was hard and rocky. We were unable to find tracks. Neither did we find evidence that men had been hiding on its slopes. A detailed clearing sweep was carried out while the remainder of the patrol readied itself for a follow-up in the event the helicopter crew got lucky.

They did not. We had all been unlucky. Whether it was faulty intelligence or a particularly crafty quarry, on this occasion the joint security forces pulled a blank.

Even in these early days of the bush war, these joint air/ground team efforts had frequently been successful. The army's Fire Force—a helicopter-borne reaction team—was even then using vertical envelopment tactics against bands of insurgents. Young, fresh troopers were dropped at strategic points in the bush to act as attack-and-stop groups against the enemy, their tactics controlled by an officer in a gunship-configured Alouette called a K-Car. We had reason, after this frustrating episode, to envy Fire Force; they were seldom deployed without a confirmed sighting by other security force elements, either a ground patrol or a patrolling reconnaissance aircraft.

This operation was the culmination of that G Troop patrol in the Mount Darwin area. Our time was up. The demands of headquarters and an unrelenting Support Unit training regime required our presence back in Salisbury. For me, it had been a frustrating but valuable experience, one that would help me make training relevant and useful to the men who were spending most of their time sleeping under the stars in Rhodesia's northeast.

CHAPTER 8

Seeing Rhodesia

After a year of service, my exposure to the land known as Rhodesia had been largely limited to operational forays into the northeast and weekend trips to Lake Kariba. When it came time to use some of the generous leave due from the British South Africa Police (BSAP), the decision about where to take a holiday was simple: we would tour the country on a large circuit.

Jennifer and I had married the previous year in a small garden ceremony at our rented home in Marlborough that was attended by our growing circle of Rhodesian friends. Ormonde stood up as my best man; the prison chaplain, Douglas Waugh, conducted the ceremony.

In the interim months, while we both worked, Jennifer and I carefully studied the automobile club guide, trying to build an itinerary that would allow us to see as many of the very different regions as possible in a period of about thirty days. We decided to drive a large, clockwise circle that would originate in Salisbury, take us eastward to the beautiful mountains that formed the border with Mozambique, and then strike southward. We would turn west, drive across southern Rhodesia to the Matabeleland capital city of Bulawayo, then head northward toward Wankie National Park and Victoria Falls. This would be our opportunity to see a full range of African game in the environment of the nation's superbly maintained national park system. At Victoria Falls, on the northern border with Zambia, we would drive west along the course of the Zambezi River to the headwaters of Lake Kariba before making our way finally back home to Salisbury.

The itinerary decided, the next phase was decisions about where we would stay en route. Jennifer patiently wrote letters to country hotels and bed and breakfast establishments; their responses allowed us to make final decisions and make reservations.

As the date drew nearer, I went to our admin officer to draw the fuel ration coupons necessary to purchase gasoline along the way for our journey. I calculated mileage carefully and decided that, with a frugal 1600cc Volkswagen, we would not be stranded.

Finally the day came for our departure and arrangements had been made to ensure that our domestic helpers, Ephraim and wife, Edith, would be regularly supplied with rations—and that they had bus fares for their own holiday home to visit family. They waved us off, with Roscoe the eighty-pound Rhodesian Ridgeback occupying almost all of the rear seat, and our personal gear carefully packed in the front storage compartment.

It was quite wonderful to be taking a leisurely drive in our car, seeing new country, and, in particular, not having to worry about maintaining an operational schedule. Typically for the breed, Roscoe settled in immediately and was soon snoring peacefully from his bed behind the seats, yet ever alert for a changing noise or sound. The VW hummed along at a steady fifty miles per hour as we headed toward Rhodesia's highlands, passing first through the *kopje* country, past the Goromonzi turnoff, then into the pine plantations as Marandellas neared. At one of Rhodesia's many roadside rests, we stopped for a cool drink and to allow Roscoe a chance to run. It was peaceful on the road, with the exception of the occasional passage of large trucks. I found myself wondering if perhaps some of them were hauling goods originally landed at the port of Beira, in Mozambique.

I pointed out signs for The Three Monkeys Inn to Jennifer as we came into Marandellas and the local police station—but we continued on for another hour or so and stopped in Rusape for fuel. Three young Africans came out: one to pump fuel, one to wash the windshield, and the older one to collect cash and petrol rationing coupons.

We were soon on our way again, but this time off of the main Salisbury to Umtali Highway. The road sign directed us to Inyanga, a secondary road traveling northeasterly toward the mountains. This was an aspect of Rhodesia neither of us had experienced. Now familiar with the relatively flat high veld, we were traveling through larger *kopjes* and gently climbing to mountain country, something that I had never imagined I would see in Africa. Indeed, a number of European friends had encouraged us to spend time in the east of Rhodesia, where high mountain air, trout fishing, and mountain climbing were all possible. My focus had always been on experiencing the low veld national parks, where Africa's unique animals could still be seen in a natural habitat—but the more I saw of the mountains that arose ahead of us, the more I was glad we were planning to visit them.

Inyanga town, I had learned, was situated at an elevation of about fifty-five hundred feet; but there were nearby mountains almost two thousand feet higher. We had arranged to stay in a private bungalow on a rural property outside of Inyanga. The literature suggested that it was both comfortable and affordable, as well as remote and private.

A small hand-lettered sign at the roadside announced that we had reached the property of our hosts-to-be. A narrow gravel drive ascended a bluff. We followed it and climbed up through a small meadow to a final steep hill that skirted a deep chasm. I was delighted to see a small waterfall, its slender traces falling over granite and creating gardens of ferns and moss with attendant spray. To one side of the cliff I noted that a penstock had been constructed; this carried water to a modest turbine that created electricity for the farm. We were indeed in the country.

Our bungalow stood perhaps fifty meters from the farmhouse. Both were built on high ground, with mountain views that extended clear into Mozambique. Successive azure ranges rose into the distance, many forested, most of a uniquely appealing granite formation. The cottage itself was a painted brick rectangular structure, spacious, with the feel of somebody's private home. We settled in easily, savoring the relative cool and forest scents of the mountains, while our host explained the operation of hurricane lamps and the stove.

There was enough daylight remaining for a walk. It seemed as though every path and road on the property was steep; there simply were not many level spots. It was grazing country. We returned to enjoy the spectacle of the tiny waterfall and the wildflowers and ferns, Roscoe cavorting in doggy pleasure after a long day of travel confinement. That night we cooked supper on an open fireplace in the cottage courtyard and fell asleep early with the sounds of wind blowing through tall trees. It had been a suitable start to a good holiday.

We had decided during planning that the purpose of this first trip would be an overview, a chance to see and assess what we would later plan to return and see in more detail. It had seemed practical at the time, but neither of us was anxious to move on the next day. We eventually did so, thanking our hosts and driving onward to see some of the sights of Inyanga: its mountains, streams, and the hotels that had served British trout anglers since the early days of Rhodesia's settlement. Cecil Rhodes himself had reveled in the cool climes and clear mountain streams. We would look for the old stone hotel that bore his name in the vast national park he bequeathed to the nation.

Duncan Eddy, a Scot compatriot at Tomlinson Depot, had explained that Inyanga felt to him like a small parcel of the highlands of his native land. Duncan was a golfer and an angler; it was easy for me to see his attraction to the country. We spent most of a day wandering the narrow roads, stopping for tea and a chance to soak up the splendor of the Rhodes Hotel's colonial trappings. Yes, we decided on the road southward to the mountains called Vumba, Inyanga would be a most satisfactory spot for a restful holiday someday. I found myself quietly wondering for how much longer this idyllic area could avoid the war with Mozambique—so close and always seemingly more hostile.

Jennifer had identified the quaint, stone Leopard Rock Hotel in a travel brochure. With round turrets, steeply pitched roof, and imposing facade, its appearance was similar to that of a French chateau. We were both curious as to how such a structure came to be built in the Vumba Mountains a short distance south and decided to investigate and overnight there.

The drive to Vumba took us through Umtali, the provincial capital of Manicaland and an important entry point for trade from Mozambique. Only a few months earlier, Rhodesians had passed through Umtali on the short drive across to the port of Beira. I had heard the many stories of fabulous dinners of freshly caught prawns cooked in traditional *piri piri* seasoning and washed down with a bottle of cold Portuguese white wine. Jennifer and I were too late for Mozambique: the border was closed to all but the most necessary travel.

We were both naturally curious as to what life in Umtali might be like, since I thought that at some undeterminable point in the future, I might be asked to serve there—perhaps in more peaceful times. We found a pleasant small town, laid out with tree-lined streets and surrounded by hills and mountains. A mixture of colonial architecture—broad verandas and hip roofs—mixed with more contemporary business structures. Umtali had been an important city and railway town since before the turn of the century, built to access the seaport at Beira.

The twenty-five-kilometer drive to Vumba was on a winding, spectacular road that seemed to climb most of the way. The air was cool and heady with the scent of surrounding forests, ferns, and flowers. As we entered the grounds of the Leopard Rock Hotel, I sensed that this land had been very important to the builder of the unique building before us. Across the front of the brick two-story structure were three turrets, much as one might expect to see in a Norman castle. Massive doors had been painstakingly assembled from native hardwood. And everywhere were gardens, a riot of color, and scintillating aroma. Despite the rather imposing appearance of our accommodation, our hosts were very much in the pattern of typical Rhodesians: warm, friendly, and perhaps a little curious as to what had brought us to their part of the highlands. We felt very much at home—and soon heard the story of the hotel's origins.

The original owner of the hotel land was a prospector and miner from Bulawayo who found and purchased land in the 1930s. Mr. Leslie Seymour-Smith saw potential for viable orchards, and after planting thirty-seven acres of apple trees, set about building a farmhouse. World War II interrupted the owner's plans, and after his return to Rhodesia from overseas service, he decided to turn his energies to construction of a hotel on the exceptionally beautiful hill site. After more than two years, the building was complete, and visitors began to arrive, many from overseas. We learned that Queen Elizabeth and the Queen Mother had spent several days as guests in the years before Rhodesia's independence. We felt at home and were anxious to walk the trails and explore the native forest. I was pleasantly surprised at the proliferation of birdlife in the foliage of trees and shrubs. Vumba was a large, green perch overlooking Mozambique and the nearby quite-tropical Burma Valley.

Our days at the Leopard Rock were much as a dream—to be savored in the certain knowledge that one moment soon, all would evaporate. The structure was damaged by rocket-propelled grenade (RPG) fire in the years ahead, but it has survived to this day after a prolonged restoration in the 1990s.

Reluctantly departing our hilltop home, we struck out for the town of Melsetter and the Chimanimani Mountains. This was more eastern highlands country very close to the Mozambique border, an area favored by outdoor enthusiasts and the home of Rhodesia's Outward Bound School. Although we had no ambitions about scaling rugged mountain peaks with a group of young people in training, I had heard much about the mountains—the distinctive African nature of their shapes and covering vegetation.

We were not in a hurry, and in any event, the national speed limit of eighty kmh (fifty miles per hour) encouraged a leisurely pace for sightseeing. Our southerly path took us initially across relatively level country, with the mountains to the east a constant reminder of our relative position. Later in the day, we tracked parallel with the upper waters of the mighty Sabi River before once again swinging left and slowly climbing up a valley.

Near the border the road forked, and we took the south track paralleling the international boundary and through plantation forests, the higher ranges beckoning in the distance. Eventually, as we entered Chimanimani National Park, they rose to more than seventy-five hundred feet, and at our ultimate destination—the Chimanimani Hotel—mountain peaks towered over us much as they do in the European Alps. These mountains were indeed different from what I had grown up around in the Sierra Nevada of the western USA. As day's end neared, mists swirled over and around splintered granite peaks, and everywhere below were verdant natural displays of grasses, gorse, and trees. Rivulets of water and small streams coursed their way over rocks and tumbled hundreds of feet, their mists supporting ferns and mosses.

The hotel itself was certainly not of a luxury type: a friendly fireplace, bookshelves filled with dusty tomes, and a friendly, rather somnolent staff, who gave us a second-story room facing the ranges. Decorated in variously fading shades of red velvet that might once have been quite stylish, the room was large and comfortable. A massive old English bathtub nearly seven feet long graced the bathroom, where we discreetly put Roscoe's bed for the night. Unlike most hotels in Rhodesia, dogs were not especially welcome at Chimanimani. Typically, our big Ridgeback was more than happy to quietly bed down after a good run through a nearby pine forest. It became cold once the sun cast its last rays on the range. We walked down to the dining room, had drinks in front of the fire, and ate a filling if unremarkable supper before calling it a night. There was time for a morning walk before we again struck out the next day. I was certain that we could enjoy the flowers, birds, and scenery of Chimanimani for much longer at some future date.

We had decided to round out our visit to the eastern highlands by driving south to the hills of Chipinga before finally turning westward and crossing the country. We spent a long day on narrow mountain roads, ascending ridges and driving through valleys with carefully tended farms. There were many Afrikaans names on farm gates and obvious pride in the way their farms and grazing properties were managed.

Finally returning to the hot, open flatlands of low veld country late in the afternoon, we spotted the towering silver superstructure of Birchenough Bridge in the distance. Spanning multiple channels of the Sabi River, the imposing structure had been erected in the 1930s as an identical copy of Sydney's Harbor Bridge. Silver arch reflecting in the sunlight, it appeared wholly out of place in the open African veld resplendent with baobab trees and thorny shrubs.

Two bridge traffic lanes entered the span between large, white buttresses in the art deco fashion of the 1930s. I slowed, enjoying the spectacle of the mighty river meandering below us on the single span of more than a thousand feet. There was not another car in sight; neither was anybody on the river waters. It was a moment when I felt a melding with Africa, as though I was truly blessed to have experienced those moments above the shimmering waters and afternoon glow.

Though I had stopped in Fort Victoria on my initial drive into Rhodesia, there had not been time to see the nearby Zimbabwe Ruins. This time, we would not miss them. This was the land of the Karanga tribe, the people who for several generations had made up the bulk of the nation's proud black army regiment, the Rhodesian African Rifles. Many of the young men of rural Gutu and Buhera had come forward to volunteer for service in Support Unit, too.

We had identified a small family-operated hotel at nearby Lake Kyle as a suitable base camp. There we settled into a small *rondavel* with splashes of bougainvillea blossoms on its walls. Our hosts—being of the rural English mentality—were unconcerned about our large canine passenger. Roscoe, as usual, made himself immediately at home after his meal, while we walked along the path to the dining room, where the African staff served us.

Arising very early the next morning, we drove to the Great Zimbabwe Ruins, a carefully preserved archaeological site of towering dry masonry granite walls and once the source of much conjecture as to who its builders had been. Early morning sunlight reflected off the granite range and the boulders and outcroppings that were a backdrop to a series of mostly circular structures. These had the appearance of defensive walls: high, strong, and probably difficult to breach.

The site reminded me very much of an open-air medieval fortress. We learned that it had been constructed around AD 1000, had been inhabited by as many as twenty thousand souls, and had been abandoned after about five hundred years of habitation. The builders' construction skills were stunning: perfect courses of granite blocks, some in herringbone pattern, with not a trace of mortar and seldom more than a minute gap between stones. Although many lesser constructions remained from the kingdom of Monomatapa, Great Zimbabwe has been identified as the largest such site in Africa.

Late that afternoon, thirsty and tired from hiking up the *kopjes* and stone stairs of the vast ruins, we drove in to Fort Victoria for an early supper and a chance to see the old town together. Back at Lake Kyle the next morning, we enjoyed a drive through the national park, seeing rare white rhinos and native antelope. I found myself becoming more anxious to see some of Rhodesia's large national parks. Ahead was the historically significant Rhodes Matopos National Park and enormous Wankie National Park, whose boundary abutted the Botswana border.

Our drive to the southwestern corner of the country was a pleasant trip that took up most of the day. To avoid as much as possible the city atmosphere of Bulawayo, we decided to explore from nearby Rhodes Matopos National Park. Jennifer had located a small old hotel with guest *rondavel* accommodation. From the hotel we could explore the national park, an area steeped in contemporary history. It was here that Rhodes had concluded his treaty with the Matabele king—and it was here too that the great entrepreneur was buried on the top of a *kopje* aptly named World's View.

The Matopos Hotel was a relic from a bygone era, a fine old watering hole with souvenirs, foreign currency, inscriptions, and memorabilia displayed wherever room could be found on walls, shelves, and even the ceiling. I felt certain there must have been names from the original pioneer column etched somewhere. The structure itself was constructed of plastered brick with a metal roof. A veranda spanned the front, where several chairs were pushed up against the wall. A beer seemed like a fine idea after a long but pleasant day on the road.

Our host was a classic publican—friendly and a gold mine of information about the locale and its people. Clearly, the locals made a point of stopping for a drink and a chance to exchange information. We savored cold drinks and acquired ideas for the best way to explore the national park and historical sites in the region.

Matopos is a place of fantastic granite outcroppings, small hidden valleys, and *kopjes*. The hotel itself was in a spectacular location, a harbinger of what might be expected a few miles farther along. Our accommodation was a very pleasant *rondavel*, well elevated above the road and overlooking the old pub. There was not an abundance of water in this part of Matabeleland, but hardy plants like bougainvillea grew in profusion. An old African gardener, his beard white against black skin, patiently worked the soil with a hoe, pausing to grin and raise his hat to Jennifer.

The next morning, we were out on the road with our guide map in hand. We had learned that Cecil Rhodes had met with King Lobengula, son of Mzilikazi, in 1886 in these very hills to negotiate a concession with the Ndebele leader. Of equal interest was evidence that man had hunted and occupied the myriad caves for millennia. Matopos caves bore the unique, ancient artwork of the San people (Bushmen), chronicles of hunts and important events that stretched back forty thousand years. From the turn of the century, small white farms had been established, and somewhat later, the national park had been formed. There was much to see in a quite small area.

The national park had a modest system of narrow, carefully maintained dirt roads. We encountered few visitors as we set off into the hills, enjoying the ever-changing spectacle of ochre boulders balanced in gravity-defying postures, one upon the other. It looked to me the ideal habitat both for leopards and baboons—but I could also imagine that early man would have found comfort in the high shelter of the caves in the outcrops.

We stopped to walk to one such early cave to view the wall art of its early inhabitants. As we walked up a steep, narrow track to the hidden cave mouth, I instinctively looked above at the trees and huge boulders under which our path followed. Though the San were not a warlike race, I could not fault their eye for defensive position. The murals were faded red depictions of great events, in particular hunts: animals and men with bows splashed across the shaded granite panels of the cave walls, a vast and complex tale of antiquity. The characters were drawn beautifully to scale, and every animal was recognizable as to its species. It was easy to imagine the valleys of Matopos thriving with game. The national park service had managed to preserve herds of kudu and other antelope, although the environment could make them difficult to spot. We later came upon two rare white rhinos grazing peacefully in an open area.

That afternoon, we parked the car and walked up the *kopje* known as World's View, the final resting place of Cecil John Rhodes and his trusted lieutenant, Leander Starr Jameson. Although Rhodes had died in his seaside cottage in the Cape Province of South Africa, his wish had been that the top of this granite dome would be his burial place. There was no doubt that Rhodes had an eye for beauty; World's View took in a vast panorama of the rocky hills of Africa, all of which became increasingly apparent as we ascended the hill. All was quiet, except for the faint sound of the wind. There were no other visitors present.

The grave had been cut out of solid granite, facing on the forward slope and capped by a large bronze tablet that bore the simple inscription, "Here lie the remains of Cecil John Rhodes." Nearby was the grave of Jameson and, far more noticeable, a large, cut-granite rectangular monument bearing bas-relief tablets depicting early mounted and infantry soldiers. This was the tomb of Major Allan Wilson and thirty-three others of the ill-fated Shangani Patrol, overrun and killed by an Ndebele *impi* (war party) near the Shangani River in 1893. These early member of the BSA Company Police had been memorialized as heroes by their employer.

We continued the history lesson with a visit to nearby Bulawayo, a city established in the 1870s for the kings of the Ndebele empire. This proud warrior nation—an offshoot of the Zulu kingdom—expanded its sphere of influence first under King Mzilikazi and then Lobengula. In particular, the Mashona people of the north and east were frequently subjected to raids by Ndebele impis, a factor that was to play out in future relations when Rhodesia became Zimbabwe.

Bulawayo's broad avenues—purportedly laid out in a manner such that a full team of oxen could be turned around—belied the origin of its name, "place of slaughter." Not only was the city the nucleus of Ndebele culture, but it also had played an important role in the early colonial development of Rhodesia. The railway northward passed through; there were fascinating examples of colonial architecture and one of the finest museums of natural history on the African continent. Government institutions, including the BSAP, administered the country via a system of provincial divisions; Bulawayo was the seat of Matabeleland Province. Salisbury and Bulawayo, the nation's two largest cities, were quite different in both a historical and cultural sense. Provincial rugby teams competed fiercely for honors, always in a spirit of friendly rivalry.

It was time, finally, to explore the vast Wankie National Park, midway northward from Bulawayo toward the northern border. This preserve of more than five thousand square miles had been laid in the late 1920s adjacent to the Botswana border, thus facilitating the natural migratory habits of large native mammals, in particular the vast herds of elephants and species of large antelope. The national park service managed its mission of preserving the habitat and animals while also assisting visitors to enjoy this piece of unspoiled Africa. A modest, circular road system connected several fenced camps where park visitors could stay overnight. We had reserved accommodation at several of them, on sequential nights.

Roscoe, however, was not welcome in the national park. Fortunately, the government vet had kennels available in the town of Wankie, the nucleus of a huge underground coal mining operation that had been developed soon after the turn of the century. The town itself had an industrial air about it as we drove in from the main highway. Steam locomotives were busy shunting cars in the rail yard—and the massive mine works were humming with activity. How strange, I mused, that this example of industrial activity was poised on the edge of one of the world's great national parks and game preserves.

Although we missed our canine friend and protector, we were glad that afternoon to be leaving Wankie, finally to be traveling to the park. The atmosphere of Africa returned as we drove down the long, flat road, where stands of flat-topped native trees grew up to the verges. The fine dust that we breathed carried with it the unique scents of vegetation and the animals of the forest.

Once inside the park, those animals became more visible. At a water-hole, we stopped to watch a troop of baboons gathering to slake their thirsts in the hot, dry afternoon. The antics of both the group leaders and juveniles were a source of amusement to me—not at all unlike human behavior at gatherings such as business meetings.

The baboons were displaced by a family of elephants led by a large matriarch with every sense focused on the security of her babies, of which there were several. Elephants also have interesting patterns of group behavior, with the mostly female herd rallying to defend, feed, and care for the young. All other species deferred to the huge mammals as they frolicked, sprayed water, and rolled in the soothing balm of African mud. When finally they had tired of this particular water hole, the group silently transformed into a long column and moved away, over the brow of the water hole and into the distance. Several impalas ventured in, skittish and vulnerable in the certain knowledge that four-legged predators favored the moment when animals lower their heads to drink as the moment for an attack. I watched the brush around the lip of the hole for signs, perhaps, of the twitching tail of a hunting lioness. There was none—this time.

We drove the remainder of the distance into Main Camp, arriving hot and thirsty but happy and quietly excited about these first brushes with Africa's animals. We checked in at the office and were shown to a large thatched *rondavel*, basic but open and comfortable, with a screened porch. In the time before sundowners and the evening meal, we were entertained by a large yellow-billed hornbill. Curious to a fault, he turned his massive beak from side to side to peer at us from a low tree bough.

In typical Rhodesian fashion, park employees and rangers had gathered for sundowners—cold pint bottles of local beer—before the evening meal was served. We introduced ourselves and were treated to a rendition of the day's events in the unique atmosphere of a national park that is home to more than a hundred species of mammals. Some of the solitary bull elephants had been given names and were known to all because of habits and preferences. The traveling patterns of animals were always a topic for discussion: where had a pride of lions made their last kill? Had anybody sighted a particular cheetah with cubs? It was all interesting and certainly served to whet our appetites for the days ahead.

Although there was a fence around the camp, night and early mornings had the distinct atmosphere of the Africa bush. Roaming lions roared and grunted over a nearby kill, and there were nocturnal bird calls from owls. But for me, the rich odor of the bush in the dawn hours was always a particular delight—a rich compendium of fragrant soil, vegetation, and the animals unlike anything I'd ever encountered. I sat on the porch silently soaking in a sensual reverie.

In the days that followed, we followed the roads to Sinamatella, where the camp had been built on a low hill overlooking the vast plain, then to Robins Camp. Each camp was different, and every day we encountered new species and fresh experiences. As this chapter of our Rhodesian reconnaissance drew to a close, I was grateful for the opportunity to sample a little of what Africa must have been just fifty years earlier. With this amount of change in five decades, I found myself wondering how long the continent could remain unspoiled—despite the best efforts of dedicated preservationists like the Rhodesian national park service.

Our next stop was to be Victoria Falls, also home to another important national park as well as the famous bridge and Zambezi River. We had reserved a modest national park cabin for a couple of days. It was also the home base of a colorful gentleman named Michael Marion Grant; we planned to enjoy Mike's company and that of his Australian wife, Jan.

Grant, a relative of Ormonde Power, was a large, sunburned Celt who had pursued adventure in various corners of the world. Initially, it had been Africa. Until recently, he'd been in New Guinea earning a living as a bush pilot in one of the world's most dangerous flying environments. Africa had drawn him back. Mike had a job flying visitors over the Victoria Falls cataracts, certainly a less hazardous lifestyle than he was used to—but I soon learned that he had discovered ways to break the tedium.

We were completing our drive on the long, straight road northward as we passed Victoria Falls airstrip and cleared the last rise to see the town and

Victoria Falls. (Author collection)

river basin ahead. We decided to first check into our cottage. By this time, Roscoe had learned to lie perfectly still behind us, below the luggage that shielded him from view. At the entrance boom gate, two smiling African game rangers waved us through, and we were soon settled into a small cabin in the camping area.

The Grants met us after work for drinks and supper. There were several fine hotels deserving of our attentions, Mike advised, so we began with sundowners at the Elephant Hills, entertained by a family of warthogs frolicking around the lawns. Then we dropped in to the original Victoria Falls Hotel, with its magnificent view up the Zambezi River to the famous bridge that spans the cataract. I was again enchanted by the richness of the old furnishings and wonderful art that decorated the entire structure. Finally, we got around to eating—and making a plan about what we might do for the remainder of our stay.

The next morning, Jennifer and I walked into the national park preserve that encompasses the south side of the Zambezi and its waterfall. Not only was there the attraction of seeing an enormous volume of water spilling into a split in the earth's surface—but the spray attendant with so much water also created a lush rain forest quite unique to a normally dry area of Africa. We walked along the footpath, dodging puddles, shielding under raincoats at times, anxious to enjoy the palms, vines, ferns, and mahogany trees that had sprung up in the river's verdant jungle oasis.

The paths wandered along the edges of the successive chasms that the Zambezi had spilled into over the millennia, huge clouds of mist roiling up from the incredible turbulence of water falling on rocks and forcing its way out of the gorge, eventually to find its way under the bridge and onward toward Lake Kariba and Mozambique, where it feeds into the Indian Ocean. No wonder the local people had christened it Mosi-O-Tunya, The Smoke that Thunders.

On our return from the falls, pleasantly soaked, we stopped to ponder the statue of David Livingstone, erected to commemorate the Scottish missionary's 1855 sighting of the great waterfall, the first white man to do so. The famous explorer returned in 1860, when he christened the falls in memory of his queen, Victoria. There Livingstone stood, caught midstride, looking intently out from under his cap—as though he was walking briskly to the edge of the precipice.

Our adventures continued later in the day when Mike Grant came to collect us in his small Fiat sedan. We would drive through the nearby portion of the national park that was home to most of the large African mammals. Late afternoon is a good time to view animals that have been sheltering from midday heat and are moving about to eat and find water. But an element of prudence is required to ensure that the viewing experience hasn't extended into hours of darkness, when viewers may find themselves the food source for a large, hungry animal. I sensed that the African game ranger was apprehensive when he waved us through the boom gate after noting the details of the car and asking for the correct time. But Mike Grant was nothing if not an adventurer—and he launched us down a narrow, single-lane dirt track, the brush and trees forming a virtual barrier in some parts.

This made for some surprising, close-up game viewing. I nearly missed a beautiful female kudu standing just a few feet back in heavy brush. The afternoon sunlight played on her large, upright pink-lined ears and doe-like eyes. We jerked to a stop and sat staring until she suddenly turned and was gone. Next, a group of hyenas loped across the road on a cross trail, watching us furtively and making haste to get away, possibly to a nearby kill sight. We were getting into the spirit of this small adventure, wondering how we had lucked into this unexpected display. The sun was sinking, but visibility was still good. We drove on.

As we rounded a gentle corner in the trail, I unexpectedly found myself looking up at the bulk of a nearby bull elephant. With full set of tusks and enormous ears gently fanning back and forth, I suspected that the old boy had been surprised by the meeting nearly as much as had we. Mike halted our forward progress by stabbing the brakes just as jumbo wheeled into the road and faced off. Grinding the gearbox into reverse, our driver wasted no time beating a hasty retreat in reverse. Sensing victory, the elephant staged a noisy mock charge to within a few feet of the withdrawing car—close enough to get me thinking about the perennial stories that circulate in game parks about subcompact cars being flattened by angry pachyderms. We veered suddenly off the track, over a couple of large rocks, and sped away back to the gate.

It was all grist for stories over supper at the Grant's apartment that evening. Mike rounded out the evening by announcing that he had a spare seat available on the morning flight over Victoria Falls. As I had previously seen the wonders of the river from the air, I suggested that Jennifer might like to ride along in the right seat—an invitation she graciously accepted.

Not unexpectedly, another adventure ensued. After circling the rising mists at the falls gorge, Mike took his passengers up the river then dropped down to treetop height in a fast flit over the border area of the national park, where large herds of Cape buffalo, elephants, and wildebeests obliged by running away from the obnoxious noise in the treetops. Given the time the flight lasted, I was quite certain the flight path had extended well across the Botswana border—but as they say, all's well that ends well.

After the relative civilization of Victoria Falls, we wanted very much to see some of the wilder country downstream. Amid waves from our friendly hosts, we drove back down the road toward Bulawayo, then turned eastward on the gravel road to Msuna. It was hot and dusty. We traversed country that looked every bit as wild and undeveloped as the lands I had patrolled in the northeast, except that here there was not as much water. Now and then, we would pass a small, thatched kraal, where near-naked kids waved, while their mothers tended wilting *mealie* patches or ground cornmeal in a wooden mortar.

Msuna is situated on the banks of the Zambezi not far downstream from the point where the river stops flowing and becomes the upper reaches of Lake Kariba. The walls of the mighty Zambezi gorge rise on both sides, but here the river is very deep and seemingly motionless.

Our hosts were two young men with several spacious *rondavels* for guest accommodation situated a short distance back from the edge of the Zambezi. Of perhaps more significance to most of the local inhabitants, it was also the only watering hole and restaurant for many miles. Msuna was an important, if quiet outpost for elements of the Rhodesian security forces. That was because the cliffs on the opposite side of the narrow gorge were Zambian territory—and there had been a history of incursions launched by guerrillas from those shores.

Hot and thirsty, we didn't take long to settle into our accommodation and head over to the shade of the pub veranda for cool drinks. Though far more of a bush setting, it had the feel of an English public house; the hosts knew all the regulars and vice versa. It was the end of the working day. District policemen arrived, as did several off-duty soldiers of the territorial army, assigned to the camp on rotating call-up assignments. Historically, patrolling the waters of the Zambezi had been the responsibility of the BSAP, with its flotilla of patrol boats. Extra army personnel were intended to supplement the force—to act as a deterrent to guerillas and to pursue those tempted to make the crossing.

As was typical in Rhodesia, introductions were quickly made and friendships established. We listened to stories of the days' events, learning something of this remote life. I very soon found myself thinking about how life might have been had I been assigned to a remote police post in northern Matabeleland, responsible for patrolling a pristine river and looking after a very occasional transgression of the law. I was anxious to see this country—and the opportunity did not take long to eventuate. The army troops said they had a patrol downriver planned in the morning. Would we like to accompany them? I accepted on behalf of Jennifer, Roscoe, and me.

Roscoe was very much at home, normally managing to sandwich himself into a cool corner under our table. Untroubled by the comings and goings of soldiers and policemen, he was somewhat less accommodating of a tamed male duiker that was the darling of the publican and his partner.

The small antelope was unaccustomed to the presence of females—females of any species—and had the temerity to butt Jennifer's shin, thus launching a full-on chase around the pub. Roscoe came very close to catching this recalcitrant antelope, but never did.

The resident policeman quietly begged me to stop the chase: "We'll all fucking starve around here if anything happens to that little bastard—they love him, you know." Taking pity, I eventually distracted Roscoe long enough for the duiker to escape, though he continued to hang around after dark, hoping for another opportunity to ambush.

The river was very close, but that night there were none of the noises of moving water—just the occasional splash of a crocodile. The Zambezi was full of crocs. They had not been hunted in years, and the rather tense nature of the Rhodesia/Zambia border meant that few men were in the area.

Next morning, we all climbed into a dark-green aluminum dingy of about fourteen feet, equipped with outboard motors and an MAG machine gun. It was pleasantly cool, the river was like a millpond, and the morning sun reflected in multiple colors off the water. A large white-headed fish eagle soared past looking for his breakfast. These waters are the habitat of tiger fish, but we were looking for game of a larger variety.

Rounding the first bend, I was watching the far (Zambian) shore intently for indications that man might have crossed the narrow sandy verges of the river. All that moved were a half dozen very large crocodiles that slid quickly down the bank and into the green waters. The corporal driving the boat grinned at me.

"They might sleep on the Zambian side, but they work for us," he said.

Indeed, I couldn't think of a way to launch a boat silently through such a congestion of hungry reptilian predators.

The wildlife on the Zambian side was prolific and in splendid condition; there were no human predators in the area to bother the magnificent kudu or the hippo families. Perhaps there had been some positive spin off from the war. No self-respecting poacher would dare venture to the banks of the Zambezi.

We were not in a hurry. The outboard hummed along at a gentle pace as I stared up at the towering cliffs on either side of the broad expanse that was the dammed river. It was not unlike the experience of sitting in a cathedral, staring up at stained-glass windows, soaking up all that was moving gently past. Nobody spoke. Roscoe dozed on a coil of line in the bottom of the boat.

Ahead was a small island, close in to the Zambian side.

"Let's take a look," the coxswain said. I nodded my agreement. Jennifer was game. We were well armed. I would enjoy an opportunity to experience a small patch of pristine forest. Because large mammals often swam to islands, we might see game resting there.

We swung into a tiny patch of sand, grounded the bow, and hopped ashore. With the boat firmly tied to a nearby tree, we walked very quietly on a game path toward the center of the tiny islet. Only the sound of a gentle breeze blowing through the treetops could be heard. The brush was very dense, and though we all scanned the sides of the track, I hoped any large game might hear us and move away in good time.

While that thought was passing through my mind, a patch of dense scrub perhaps twelve feet away suddenly erupted as a male bushbuck broke cover and bolted away, his head held high displaying a needle-sharp rack atop and legs a blur of white and dark tan. We all reacted by quickly pointing weapons but nobody fired. After a moment, we walked on.

Half an hour on the island was enough to verify that no humans had been using it as a staging point. It was actually Zambian territory, but the army considered that this was a small technicality. I had to agree. When finally the patrol pattern was complete, we turned around and cruised comfortably back to the landing—in time for a late lunch and a *braai* that evening.

"I guess you can tell your work mates that you made a quick trip across the border to Zambia, but I wouldn't recommend it," I mused with Jennifer that night.

"The same applies to the flight into Botswana, I guess?" she said.

We were once again back on the road tracking eastward to yet another patrol post—the last on the western edge of Lake Kariba. Binga was our destination. Msuna had been a very pleasant stay. We were now even more curious about Binga, sensing that we were moving even farther away from civilization. Once again, we were on a graded gravel road that gently traversed the gentle hills of dry, dusty Africa. There was almost no other traffic on the road, nor were there many signs of habitation. We admired baobab trees, looked out over shimmering bluffs of exposed rock, and were glad that a waterside cottage awaited us at the end of the drive.

We discovered that Binga was home to a large commercial crocodile farm; thus, the community, though tiny, had a little more of the feeling perhaps of a typical Rhodesian community. Binga perched on the shore of Lake Kariba, at that point much wider than the Zambezi had been farther

Roscoe the Ridgeback joins us for a Zambezi River patrol with the Rhodesian army. (Author collection)

upstream. Our cottage was a comfortable rectangular structure painted a faint green color and featuring a screened porch from which the lake was our view.

Our hosts were also hosts to the community after dusk, when locals gathered for sundowners. On the evening of our arrival, an open-air movie had been scheduled for showing immediately after dusk, and preparations were being made to erect a 16-mm projector on a low table in front of our cottage. John Wayne, starring in *The Green Berets*, was to be shown. The publican reckoned this fare would draw a good crowd, at least by Binga standards.

Always a John Wayne fan, I was ill-prepared for just how awful *Green Berets* was. North Carolina pine forests just did not feel like the highlands of South Vietnam, where the epic was supposed to have occurred. An old Lister single-cylinder diesel generator thumped away in the background, providing flickering power for the projector. Patrons used the opportunity provided by reel changes to recharge pints of beer and chat about the movie. A young district policeman I'd met that evening asked me in rather guarded terms whether *Green Berets* represented how the United States special forces were fighting the war in Vietnam.

"Not the way I remember it," was my response.

He later that night invited me to accompany him on a fast boat patrol on Lake Kariba. I accepted. Jennifer and Roscoe would have a relaxing morning and early afternoon at the cottage.

I left them both sleeping just after dawn, hopped into the dark-green police Land Rover with my newfound friend, and drove to Binga police station, where I was introduced to the member in charge, Inspector Tom Naude. Tom presided over the people of a large section of northern Rhodesia from his office on a dry bluff overlooking the lake. I'm sure he wondered what I was doing on his patch, but he readily gave me permission to accompany his subordinate on the boat patrol.

The BSAP maintained a fleet of fast, inboard fiberglass patrol boats for deployment on Lake Kariba. Roads in this region were primitive and often not maintained, meaning that water could be a better means of reaching the isolated, largely uninhabited lands between Binga and the dam wall at Kariba. It was in one of these boats that we would be carrying out the day patrol.

We were to look out for anything unusual. Because of tensions between Rhodesia and Zambia over support the latter provided insurgents, few recreational users ventured very far from the facilities of Kariba. This region of the preflooded Zambezi Valley had originally been the native home of the Batonga people. They had been forced back to the shoreline of the lake that inundated their lands, where they conducted desultory agriculture and animal husbandry. I had learned that the Batongas smoke cannabis in pipes fashioned from gourds. Cannabis, or *dagga*, grows readily in southern Africa, where its hemp is used in some forms of native construction. Batongas were not known as warlike folk, and their business with district policemen tended to be low key.

A black African constable accompanied us. He pushed us off from the dock and leaped aboard easily as we idled away into the lake. Soon, we were up to full power, planing across the calm, smooth water in the shadow cast by abruptly rising mountains on the shore.

We were armed with FN rifles and binoculars. There was no sign of other craft on the waters, either on the northern, Zambian side or ours. The Rhodesian shoreline had the appearance of hard, dry country—unlike what I had observed farther upriver. There was little flat country to attract game, and I did not see signs of antelope or small game.

But the crocodiles were there, though not nearly so obvious away from their upstream sandy riverside basking places. At a now-closed research station, my patrol partner told me that a scientist had been taken not long before. A novice boatman, he had restarted the outboard with tiller pushed to one side, lost his balance, and fell overboard, where curious crocs quickly made a meal of him. The very deep, green waters thereafter took on an even more sinister quality, and I was ever vigilant for floating logs or other objects that might force us to swim.

That did not occur. It was a pleasant if uneventful patrol that had me back in the relative civilization of Binga late that afternoon, pleased to have seen a stretch of the lake that few in those days ever saw.

Jennifer and I enjoyed an early supper, then went for a walk—eventually stopping to sit and watch as the last of the sun slipped over the western horizon. Our holiday was drawing to an end. We spoke about our trip and how much we had enjoyed finally seeing Rhodesia together. I felt relaxed and happy, but Jennifer had other things on her mind, things she had probably spent the afternoon considering.

"Doug," she said, "I'm really starting to wonder about our future here."

I was taken aback. I had never thought of Rhodesia as my long-term home, but I also had never been happier at any job. It seemed a perfect fit for me, training young, motivated Africans here. I knew it would likely not be something I would want to do forever; but neither was I ready to think about changing vocations soon.

Jennifer had observed Rhodesian life for nearly two years. Although we had not spoken about it in such direct terms, she now said that she thought things were going to get a good deal worse in this tiny country before they improved. And she was astute enough to know that my aspirations of a quiet district police posting were unrealistic now that I had made my place at Support Unit. In any event, I had another year to serve of my hitch in the BSAP—unless I requested an early release.

I sat and quietly pondered as the sun finally set. The old Lister generator fired up and lights were switched on. There was logic in her argument; it was probably only a matter of time before we moved on. This was no longer my sole decision to make. I had the future of my twenty-four-year-old wife to think about. Finally, I acknowledged that perhaps she was correct in saying that we should be thinking about moving on. I didn't like to admit it, but she was likely right—no matter how much I loved being Section Officer Hubbard, BSAP Support Unit.

The next day, we began the long drive home to Salisbury. At the mandated fifty-miles-an-hour speed limit, it was just as well that we were relaxed and could use the time to consider important decisions about our life ahead. Jennifer felt confident that we could make a good life together in her native Queensland, Australia; I was much less certain. The strange vocational hybrid that I was at age thirty seemed unlikely to be understood in rural Australia. Though I was not enthusiastic about returning to the United States, it seemed more likely that I could resume a career from there. We did not resolve these questions, but we did explore many options as the kilometers ticked away and we neared our home in Marlborough, Salisbury.

Two days later, we were both back at work, Jennifer at the Italian civil engineering firm where she was a bookkeeper. After weeks away, my first PT session was tough going, but it felt good to be back.

CHAPTER 9

Unexpected Events

IN ADDITION to the usual quotient of recruit squads and returning trainees, there was a particularly notable group of national service patrol officers in training to be section commanders. Known to us simply as Training Troop 4/74, these men were, in the main, volunteers. Many had been educated at Gwebe Agriculture College, country boys with good bush skills.

Ormonde and Mike Davis worked to refine their parade square drill, while my focus was on field craft. I liked what I was seeing in the leadership qualities of these young men, who worked well with their new constables and gained their respect. With men like these coming through the system, it seemed to me that the leadership plan espoused by headquarters had a good chance of success. Small teams, well led, were what a low-level bush war seemed to need.

After weeks of depot and field work, Training Troop 4/74 was nearing the final phase of the cycle when it came time to evaluate what they had learned in a final field exercise. On 16 September 1975, Section Officer Mike Davis and I loaded up the squad and drove to Goromonzi.

Our objective was to put this small group of junior leaders into a realistic operational environment, to provide them with a series of problems to be solved individually and as a group, and to push them to create the stress of actual field operational conditions. There would be a good deal of strenuous physical activity and not a lot of time for rest.

I knew the squad well enough to feel quite confident that all would manage the impending challenges, but I was less certain as to who the best of the group were.

On a bright, beautiful spring day, I drove a canopied Land Rover loaded with targets, ammunition, first aid kit, and our personal gear past the Goromonzi police station and onto the gravel road that descended through *mealie* fields to the valley below. Behind me came the truck, carrying the squad. Our destination was Lonely Park Farm, the owner of which had welcomed Support Unit, making a small valley available to us for field training.

That morning at depot, Mike Davis—the quintessential drill instructor—had a glint in his eye as he turned to me and said, "This feels a bit too much like a picnic outing to me. What say we run the *ounes* around a little when we get there?"

Mike's experience had equipped him well to read the moods of young troops. Training Troop 4/74 was in good spirits that day, largely, I suspected, because they were out of the cloistered environment of depot and headed for the bush, where most felt much more at home. But Mike was right; the men needed to be put under stress as soon as possible for the exercise to be effective. A few minutes later, I wheeled the Land Rover off the road up a steep track into the bush and parked beyond an old water tank. Mike followed in the truck, grinding up the slope in first gear. As he braked, I heard his shrill command, "Debus!" This prompted an instant response, the men spilling over the sides and falling into formation.

"I'm watching you," he growled. "I want to see the last man back from the top of that hill over there." The men tensed, clutching rifles, and Mike yelled "Go!

The squad of perhaps a dozen men ran hard across ground broken with rocks, shrubs, and small trees and headed up the far slope, flowing around the trees and struggling to keep up the pace. There was always a good chance that Davis would send the last man back again for another involuntary ascent of the hill.

We lost sight of them; then the first men burst from the trees, rifles held at high port, running toward the starting point. There were no stragglers. The better runners had helped those who needed it, a good sign. Moments later they were formed up under the canopy of a large shade tree, all breathing heavily, with patches of perspiration showing through camouflage shirts. Every man was focused as I explained their first exercise.

"There will be times when you and your men should dig in. The enemy has not been using mortars against us much, but the Mozambique Liberation Front (FRELIMO) has them, and you can bet the day will come

Battle training at Lonely Park, Goromonzi. (Author collection)

when you'll need protection from them, or even from RPG fire. This is when smart soldiers dig shell scrapes. You all know the principle: body length and deep enough that you won't get your arses shot off by grazing fire. For purposes of this exercise, that piece of ground over there is where your group is to stop. Get together. Make a plan. Read the ground and think about what it might be like to take fire, where it might come from. You've got twenty minutes to prepare and get dug in."

They moved away quickly, talking quietly but in an animated way, as we moved back to some high ground to observe how they read the ground, sited their positions, and worked together. One or two of the men were taking charge.

With the sound of tools scraping and chopping at the earth, I opened our demolition box and prepared a charge made up of a 250-gram block of Soviet TNT. This would produce a large, unpleasant explosion for the men, hopefully one that would remind them in future times of the value of terra firma as a defensive medium.

"Time's nearly up!" Mike warned, prompting a last desperate spurt of digging. Moments later, he fired a burst of blanks over the heads of the group, which took the hint by leaping into the new positions, which resembled shallow graves. I moved up from the opposite quarter, placed the charge and lit it—prompting a sharp-eyed recruit to shout "Incoming!"

Mike and I moved away quickly, sheltering behind a tree as the blast—loud and potent—reverberated through the valley, casting a few clods of dirt around the squad position. Nobody, we noted, had attempted the easy way out by digging a shellscrape that was not deep enough. Their heads were down—ears undoubtedly ringing—but rifles were aimed outward and they were ready to defend.

Next, there were tests of basic skirmishing tactics and leadership. The men were well tested in the skills of fire-with-movement tactics. But what we wanted to see was how well they had learned to command a section and make good decisions under stress. We changed scenarios and plans often to assess how each man coped and performed. Each candidate took charge of a small group of his fellows, assessing, giving orders, and leading them forward against an entrenched "enemy" position, firing round after round of live 7.62 rounds at Figure Twelve targets. We kept tally of target hits.

It was a long day, even for fit young men of the land. Davis and I consciously pushed them in many different ways, even to small but critical issues such as how much drinking water remained available to each section.

"You must know!" he barked at one aspirant who dithered for a suitable answer.

"Right. For purposes of this exercise, assume that you are likely to be on follow-up at any moment and there is no water resupply nearby." Water discipline, however ill advised (as we know today) was necessary and practiced in the harsh conditions of Africa.

The men were tired, but most were thinking, anticipating what might be asked of them next, planning how they would respond to the next challenge thrown their way by their instructors. Finally, as it became dark in the small, wooded valley, the group was told to select a harboring-up position for the night. Their choice would be the base area. They would eat, rest, and be prepared to move on a few minutes notice. Their choice was a small area of "dead ground"—good defense against small-arms fire, with observation over a track that could be used by transiting insurgents. The trees were dense, affording good concealment and cover. They had, I surmised, decided that these advantages were more important than the risk posed by high ground to one side.

"Very well," I murmured to Davis as they moved away to take up the position. "We'll pay them a little visit in the wee hours to see how they perform." I could envisage a crafty enemy rolling grenades toward the position.

It was a quiet, very beautiful African evening. The sunlight vanished quickly behind the western horizon and was replaced by a dazzling canopy of stars. The only sound to be heard was a distant cow calling.

Support Unit did not have the thunderflash explosives that are typically used to simulate grenades in training, just one more item on the list of war supplies our commander was trying to obtain for us. That did not mean, however, that our trainees could be shortchanged in this critical training phase. I would make up charges, improvised from what was available in the red demolition box. Here we had fuse, detonators carried separately, and captured Soviet TNT demolition charges. I selected a 250-gram block from the box, noting the Russian Cyrillic black letters on the waxy brown cover over the hard, yellow explosive material. Next, I measured and cut a length of fuse for suitable delay, lit it, and timed the burn rate. Then I broke the TNT block into two equal pieces and hollowed out an indentation in which to insert the detonator and fuse. Finally, two fuses were cut, detonators carefully crimped on to one end and then slotted into the TNT and taped in place. Not ideal, I mused as I stowed the box and the improvised charges away from the ground where we would sleep next to our vehicles. After a meal cooked quickly over a gas stove, it was time to sleep. Not a sound came from the nearby reentrant where the squad was harboring.

Goromonzi was not at that stage of the war in an area considered at risk from enemy incursions. Nevertheless, although we could not safely issue ball ammunition to our trainees in these circumstances, Davis and I both had full magazines of live ammo ready. For the most part, we would be sleeping with our ears open, ready for the unanticipated. I knew with certainty that we would both awaken soon after midnight, in time to mount our imaginary attack.

I stretched out on my assembled Hounsfield stretcher in a light sleeping bag and relaxed, staring skyward at the panoply of heavenly attractions, noting the Southern Cross and other stellar formations. I found myself wishing that it might somehow be possible to transmit the sights I was observing to those whom I loved far away. Finally, with Mike Davis snoring gently in the background, I slipped off into a light slumber.

When I awoke at about 1:00 AM, the moon had risen—a clear half-circle suspended in a clear sky, casting faint shadows through the canopy of the huge tree overhead. I stretched and murmured quietly in the direction of Mike Davis, who was already awake. After carefully checking my boots for any unwelcome visitors, I sat and laced up. As I finished and arose, Mike was at my side.

Visibility in the faint moonlight was good enough for a silent approach across the open ground. I retrieved the two made-up charges, handing one to Mike, and we began to move slowly to the nearby slope that would give us downward access to the trainee position. In less than ten minutes, we had climbed to a point just below the brow of the slope. Here we were in dead ground, invisible to the men lying in ambush just twenty meters away.

I halted, and we both crouched. The plan was to light fuses on the charges, move quickly to the brow, and throw them a short distance over. This would indicate immediately how alert the group was; either they would react when they saw or heard our "simulated grenades" being thrown, or the explosions would rouse them to action. In either event, we hoped they would mount an immediate and spirited attack on us.

With fuses lit, and holding the charge by dangling fuses, we stood and quickly made the last few steps to the throwing point. Midstep, there came an enormous cracking explosion that hurled me to the ground. In a millisecond, my life changed forever. The charge had detonated prematurely, taking with it my right hand and wrist.

I called out to Mike, who had already jettisoned his charge and rushed to my aid. From the bush position below the hill brow, the trainee section burst into action; men had surrounded me seconds after my call for help.

I was fully conscious and determined to remain so. I was the only individual present who had ever dealt with major trauma. My injuries were serious and potentially life threatening, depending on how well blood loss could be controlled and what the delay for medical treatment would be. I knew it was important to remain conscious to ensure that I arrived alive at the hospital in Salisbury.

With a flashlight held by a helper, I could see that my right arm now terminated in exposed bone and burnt flesh. There was no evidence of arterial bleeding, a consequence of the extreme cauterizing temperatures that burned my body. Though I could not see with my right eye, it was intact, and a quick check confirmed that my genitals were intact despite painful injuries nearby.

One large young trainee, characterized by a shock of red hair and huge hands, stood ready to help. I told him to hold my shattered arm tightly below the elbow to curtail blood loss. He understood perfectly, grasped it firmly while another man helped me to my feet and supported me on the walk down the hill to the vehicles.

I was very aware that I might be in serious trouble. Our first aid kit was rudimentary. Plasma kits had not yet been issued to Support Unit, nor was morphine available. Shock was setting in quickly. Although it was only moderately cool, I had begun shaking uncontrollably by the time we reached the vehicles, and I was placed on the stretcher in the back of the Land Rover.

"Drive for Goromonzi police station," I instructed. "Get on the radio, describe my injuries, tell them we need help. Maybe the air force has a helicopter available."

We lurched out on to the gravel road and raced for Goromonzi, perhaps twenty minutes away.

Pain was starting to course through me, ratcheting up in stages like loud static on a radio. Nerves in my nonexistent hand signaled my brain. My pain in my burned right hip, lacerated by shrapnel and open blast wounds, made it difficult to lie still, and I knew my face was a mess, my lips and nostrils torn by blast overpressure. My erstwhile nurse hung on to my arm bravely as we bounced and banged over the road—and after what seemed like a very long time, we pulled up in front of the station.

"Get every blanket you can find, even if you must clean out the cells," I ordered as the driver and another trainee jumped out and trotted toward the radio room. They were back moments later, laden with blankets—but they did little to control advancing shock.

"Sir, they say that the air force can't come in a helicopter. But there is a B Car coming now from Salisbury Central. He should be here in less than half an hour."

I did some quick mental calculation and reasoned that this was likely true. B Cars—town patrol cars—were capable of 100-mph speeds, and each driver had been exhaustively trained in pursuit driving. Somewhere out on the road at that moment, a Peugeot sedan was hurtling toward us at whatever speed the driver could coax out of it.

We heard the B Car well before it arrived. Motor revving to a coarse whine, it burst over the rise with blue light flashing and wheeled into the gravel where the Land Rover was parked. After a quick consultation, it was decided that I would lie on the back seat, my helper reversed in the front passenger seat to hold my injured arm. Moments later, the Peugeot was screaming down the two-lane road, the driver working the four-speed transmission skillfully, and once out on the Salisbury-Marandellas Road we reached 100 mph.

By this time, I could only focus on getting pain relief soon and not bleeding to death. The sedan had a heater that helped reduce my shaking, and my assistant hung on throughout the blue-light and siren ride to

Andrew Fleming Hospital—but I was ragged when we pulled up to the door at Casualty at about 3:00 AM.

A large, strong black hospital orderly wheeled a gurney out and skillfully lifted me onto it unassisted either by a tiny young nurse or my colleagues. I thanked them and was quickly wheeled into the hospital.

It was very quiet in the cool, sterile halls of Casualty. I was met by the duty doctor, a kindly British lady of my mother's vintage, who installed an intravenous drip and gave me an injection that I assumed was morphine. Coming so late after my injury, it helped very little. Doctors had been summoned to perform emergency surgery; now it was a matter of waiting, cutting off my bloody, crusty uniform, and listening to the doctor's comforting stories.

She had received medical training in England, coming after qualification to what was then Nyasaland (now Malawi) as a missionary doctor. She and her husband now lived on a small farm near Goromonzi, where both delighted in bush walking and observing Rhodesia's animals.

"I've had some interesting experiences with snakes over the years, but never any bad ones," she related—doubtless trying to distract me from waves of pain that seemed only to get worse. "Unless one encounters an unruly Mamba, snakes will move away from man in the bush. My husband and I seldom see them, also probably because we walk with canes to tap the ground and give the animals warning."

"Of course," she continued, "there is one large, lazy, very venomous snake that an unwary walker can step on. It's called a Gaboon Viper; I learned about these animals when I began my missionary duties." The minutes ticked slowly by, but I listened with interest as she spoke of her early life as a young lady doctor, rowed from village to village in a canoe around the shores of Lake Nyasa by boatmen from the mission, stopping at each place to treat poor African fishermen and their families. She had not felt danger from the local populous, but when it became known that a sack of coins used to procure food and services along the way was stowed in the boat, there was concern that the schillings might be a source of potential danger.

"My supervisor at the mission solved the problem by putting a big Gaboon Viper in one of the bags. Nobody would go near it!"

I managed a small, sardonic smile that could not have looked very attractive and imagined the Africans staring intently at a heavy, ever-moving fabric bag containing the unhappy snake.

The first of the awakened doctors arrived, the orthopedic surgeon. There was a cursory examination of my arm, a few words of encouragement, some questions about blood typing tests, then he walked away to prepare. Another twenty minutes passed before the anesthesiologist bustled in, wiping sleep from his eyes.

"I'm glad to see you, doctor," I mumbled.

"You'll feel better very shortly," he told me, shoving a hypodermic needle into my left arm. Seconds later a warm comfortable sensation overtook the pain and I was unconscious.

I awoke the next morning in spotlessly clean hospital linen on a bed next to a plate glass window, beyond which was a hallway and a nursing station. A nursing sister in her late twenties stood up and walked into the ward, moving aside a portable screen that shielded me from the rest of the room. Sister Mathews brought with her a tall drinking glass with a straw, greeted me quietly, and helped me insert the straw past my sutured, swollen lips. I was terribly dehydrated and grateful for the drink. I thanked her, and she moved off, promising to return shortly.

I took stock, at least of what I could see; my right eye was bandaged, my right arm was now a stump that terminated perhaps ten inches from the elbow, now tightly wrapped in bandages. My right thigh still burned and was also apparently bandaged. My left arm, thankfully intact, was immobilized with an intravenous drip installed. I was filthy, but that would soon change.

I dozed, pain never far away, until Jennifer arrived. She was remarkably composed, cheerful, and encouraging, wanting to know what she could bring to make me more comfortable. All I could think of was carbonated lemonade, something to cut through whatever it was that made my mouth so very dry. We talked a few minutes about how best to tell my parents about the accident, and then she left for work.

Though I later learned that my position next to the observation window had been arranged because there were concerns that I might expire from loss of blood that first night, I began gaining strength almost from the first. Sister Mathews, sensing my determination, soon had me moved to a new bed at the far end of the eight-bed ward, adjacent the window.

In Ward B1 with me were several Rhodesian army men, also recovering from serious injuries. It was a cheerful group, despite amputations, multiple fractures, and other injuries. A buzz of gentle banter soon began, at least at meal times when men felt better. The low point of the day was when wounds were cleansed and redressed, each man privately enduring behind portable screens the pain of the removal of dressings stuck to wounds by coagulated blood and serum.

My twice-daily injections of morphine were soon replaced with codeine. Baths in bed slowly cleansed me. It appeared that there was little needing to be done about my amputation but allow it to heal.

Then I met a very interesting man, Mr. Owen-Smith. I soon learned that it was he who had come in to reconstruct my facial injuries that first night. Rhodesia's finest plastic surgeon was small in stature but exuded command presence. He was in his fifties, and I immediately noticed that he had been badly burned at some point earlier in his life. This, I was to learn, was the consequence of having been shot down in flames while piloting a Royal Air Force Hurricane fighter during World War II. His hands, fortunately, had been spared in the fire, and after the war he had attended medical school in England, where he honed his skills to become a surgeon of rare skill. When eventually I was able to see the scores of small, tight sutures that repaired my lips and nostrils, that skill was apparent. I felt an enormous obligation to this man who had responded in the dark of the night to repair me rather than leave the work to one less skilled.

On the day of our meeting, he looked intently at my face for a few moments, then asked a nurse to remove the dressings on my thigh. This exposed the still-open blast wounds and burns. He nodded, and said he would call in to see me the next day.

That afternoon, the ragged band in B1 did their best to raise spirits in the tiny group. Opposite and one away was an engineer warrant officer, formerly of the British army, whose left leg had been amputated below the knee. He had lost his balance while laying mines; the terrible injury had been inflicted by one of his own mines. I could imagine the grave self-doubt and criticism the man was then enduring and watched tearful meetings with his wife and children. With his family out of sight, however, the sapper managed to regain a modicum of cheerfulness.

In the bed directly opposite mine was a young Rhodesian Light Infantry (RLI) trooper not long past his eighteenth birthday. His limbs appeared to be a mass of casts and traction apparatus. He was Afrikaans, quiet and not inclined to chat much—but we tried to cheer him up. His young mother came to visit regularly, sitting by his bedside, often touching his bare shoulder and speaking softly as if to comfort him. On one occasion, she asked him how he had come to be injured; her son told her that he had fallen out of a helicopter—some distance off the ground. He had been a machine gunner, so carried the gun on a strap over his shoulder, cradled in his lap with the muzzle pointing out the open door. During takeoff, he had lost his balance, tumbling out of his seat to the earth below. The gun had landed on top of him, and thus was undamaged.

"But why didn't you throw the gun away, my boy?"

"Aagh. I was afraid of what the Sergeant Major would do to me if I did," came the utterly serious response.

With others in the ward, I struggled to stifle an outburst of laughter, even though it hurt to do so. The young man's explanation was such a candid illustration of army life—that he would prefer certain physical pain to having to deal with his sergeant major was utterly quixotic, but it was also understandable to anyone familiar with the culture.

By the end of my first week in the bright, modern environment of Ward B1, Mr. Owen-Smith had visited me every day and was taking an interest also in the healing of my amputation. Following one such examination, he announced that he would like to have me moved to his ward for more surgery. I would soon be saying good-bye to my army cohorts.

The burn ward, more commonly called Ward 9, was a section of Salisbury's original hospital. Some distance from the main multistoried Andrew Fleming, the old building nestled in among large, old jacaranda trees. With a full-length screened veranda, ten-foot ceilings, and individual rooms, it was a vast change from the modern environment of the main hospital. As I was wheeled on a gurney down the impeccable, polished hallway of the old ward past wheelchairs that must have been modern in World War I, I could imagine mustachioed soldiers of the Empire making their home comfortably in its confines.

My room directly across from the nursing station had tall French doors that led out to the veranda. Clearly, I mused, the ward's constructors believed in the therapeutic value of fresh air—and I was looking forward to enjoying the smell of fresh flowers and the trees that I could see through windowpanes in the doors.

I was soon settled in, enjoying my new view and the relative quiet of the old ward. There was a knock on my door and, like a whirlwind, the ward matron entered. With the firm authority of a sergeant major, Matron Alice Mutch introduced herself, asked me about my progress, and was immediately critical of the manner in which my arm dressing had been applied earlier in the day. With a distinct Scottish brogue, tiny matron explained, "You'll have no end of trouble with that stump unless we shape it; the dressings must be firm."

Noting that my long legs were nearly touching the foot of my bed, she made a note on her clipboard and bustled out the door. An hour later, I was enjoying the new view from my veranda while two wardsmen assembled an enormous bed of at least seven feet in length under matron's direction. I would be more comfortable while recovering from the next round of surgery.

In some ways, I began to dread the nights. Never a good sleeper, a combination of pain, discomfort, and the soldier's phenomena of sleeping as if on ambush all mitigated against even a short night of uninterrupted slumber. In the previous ward, there were morphine injections to challenge the pain signals being sent to my brain by a myriad of now-destroyed nerve endings in the hand that no longer existed. I had quickly weaned myself off the highly addictive drug, taking instead a potent codeine tablet called Propon.

In my private room, where the door was left open by my preference, I awoke many times during the night, staring into the hallway and the dimly lit nursing station and pondering whether pain-killing drugs would help me sleep and whether it even made sense to ask for them. Sometimes a cup of tea and chat with the duty nurse was a better idea.

As luck would have it, my trusted friend Jo Cullingworth often worked the night shift in Ward 9, while Brian was also on shift at Salisbury Central Police Station. Jo brought her three young children in to work and bedded them down while she did her rounds. Always attentive and with a good nurse's intuition about what might make things easier, Jo was a boon during those long nights. Being in charge of a burn ward at night was not an easy task, with many patients coming to grips with pain management and simply trying to get through another day.

Mornings began very early, at dawn, before the nurse's shift change. I was learning to eat left-handed, a particularly ungainly process. Matron Mutch, observing my efforts to shovel breakfast into my mouth, asked me to wait a few moments, then returned with a large bib, complete with a catch pocket at the bottom hem.

"Mustn't spill gravy on the sheets now," she counseled.

The food was basic, but good, and Matron always encouraged me to eat well.

Without a doubt, Ward 9 was the cleanest, most sterile environment I had ever been in. Owing to its age, the building was certainly a challenge, but one that Matron Mutch was more than up to. There would be *no* secondary infection on her ward.

Every few days, patients were wheeled in their beds on to the veranda. Then a team of wardsmen came in and—starting on tall ladders with the overhead light fixture—disassembled and scrubbed it and every square inch of the ceilings and walls with disinfectant. Then the floor was scrubbed and polished to a high sheen, and we were wheeled back in.

Separate rooms meant that camaraderie was absent. Most patients had been seriously injured, including Mr. Owen-Smith's own son, who had been serving as a district commissioner's assistant in the operational area. I never knew who was in the adjoining rooms.

My surgeon wasted little time getting me in for another session of repair work. I awoke from the anesthetic in my special bed feeling hungry and in good spirits. My right arm was slightly shorter and of a different shape. Earlier hints of infection were now absent. Skin grafts had been taken off my right leg and carefully affixed to the open wounds on my thigh. A good many sutures had been removed from my face. I was told that I must not move for the next several days while the grafts took hold.

Throughout, Jennifer had faithfully visited me twice each day—on the way to and from work. Roscoe the Ridgeback accompanied her, spending long days under her desk as she balanced the books of her engineer employers. In the afternoon, our VW would be parked for her visit under several large, old jacaranda trees opposite the ward veranda. Ever patient, Roscoe might fidget at first, but he usually bedded down on the back seat to await Jennifer's return for the drive home. However, one warm afternoon, the car window having been left down for ventilation, Roscoe wormed his way out, and, having heard our voices, was determined to track down his master and mistress wherever they might be. He made an immediate beeline for Matron Mutch's highly polished, sterile burn ward and, with nose to the floor, made a grand entrance into my room with much tail wagging. There was time for a quick pat, then Jennifer made a hasty retreat and actually got him back outside without staff seeing the hairy intruder. On her return, she managed to scuff out the most evident of the large dusty canine paw prints in the hallway.

We had begun to plan what we would do after my hospitalization and rehabilitation, though still uncertain whether we would try to make a new life in Australia or the United States. I found myself increasingly anxious to get well and get out. I tentatively set myself a goal: I would achieve my release within a month of my admission. Mr. Owen-Smith, I think, appreciated my ambition, but there were no promises.

I was dropping less food on myself at meal times. Never very skilled with my left hand in other than weapons handling, I knew that I needed to face the challenge of learning to write. Jennifer had written to my parents in Texas on my behalf, but she reminded me that there was no substitute for a message in my own hand. So, I began the tedious process of writing a letter on a tablet that would have taken minutes before. But, it was a start. And in something akin to a miracle, after several weeks, my brain had accepted that the left hand now was for writing—and suddenly all became much easier. My handwriting even began to look as it had before the accident.

Mail delivery from Rhodesia to the United States took about ten days, via airmail. Long-distance telephone service was difficult, if not impossible. When I finally got a letter from my parents acknowledging that they knew about my injury and asking if there was a number they could call to reach me, we had to tell them to wait a while longer. To add to the other unsettling events of the month, Jennifer received word from our landlord that he was selling our home in Marlborough. She began to sell our household goods and near-new furniture, a wedding gift from my grandfather purchased from a local manufacturer. Our Mukwa tables and chairs would be far too expensive to ship—and we would need the cash. Part of our daily visits always seemed to center on what might be sold and how much we could reasonably expect to take with us. While I lay in hospital, Colin Shaw and a truck load of recruits removed what goods remained from the sales and transported all to a small nearby flat. Support Unit's quartermaster issued us with a gas stove from the operational store.

I had officially informed my superiors of my intention to take a discharge upon my final physical assessment. There was support across the board for our decision, although some, I think, hoped that I might reconsider and stay on in a different capacity. I was offered a position as a questioned document examiner at the criminalistics lab at nearby Morris Depot. Though very appreciative of the motive for the offer, I had already convinced myself that I remained capable of driving something besides a desk in a musty laboratory.

One warm afternoon as I lay under a simple bedcover and enjoyed a breeze through the French doors, Matron Mutch called in to see me.

"Doug, do you enjoy a beer at sundowners?" she asked me.

"Yes, ma'am."

"You could have a daily pint here in the ward, you know. We have a small fridge across the hall where your beer could be chilled. Would you like that?"

"Yes, I would. Very much."

"Well, you can have your one-pint ration starting tomorrow. But there's a condition; you can't have beer and Propon both. Which will it be? Are you ready to give up the tablets?"

"I will give up Propon."

And I did, though it was not easy initially. I took my last pain killers three weeks after injury.

Friends and colleagues were very good about visiting me. The lads from Training Troop 4/74 had successfully passed out of the final training course, but they came in small groups to my room and finished their visit by presenting me with an inscribed silver tankard.

On a more formal note, explosives expert Chief Inspector Dave Perkins called in one afternoon and chatted about my recollections of the accident. He had completed a formal investigation of the incident and requested that I provide him with a written statement. Support Unit secretary Brigit Walsh followed, carrying her massive Underwood manual typewriter—and I dictated a two-page narrative that served to close the report.

I had been concerned that an outsider—unaware of the difficulties training staff faced on a daily basis—might be critical of my decision to improvise explosive charges for battlefield simulation. Thankfully, that did not occur. I was already struggling under a burden of guilt and self-doubt. However right my choices, the sad fact was that I had permanently disabled a body hitherto without serious defect. The long-term consequences of that were as yet unknown, but I now had a wife to consider and a very uncertain future. I was unable to bring myself to discuss these gnawing doubts and self-criticism with anybody. I resolved to begin writing letters to friends and former colleagues in the United States, asking them to keep an eye out for a position for a slightly used former special agent and Support Unit instructor.

One afternoon, Colin Shaw dropped in to see me. Colin knew we intended to leave Rhodesia once I was fit to do so. Knowing it might be the last such parade I might attend, he asked if I'd like to attend a passing out parade at Morris Depot, complete with mounted honor guard and band. I was enthusiastic but reminded Colin that my present regimental sergeant major was Matron Mutch. We would require her approval to remove me from the hospital, and I suggested that Colin see her and remind her of his qualification as a company medic.

Matron agreed to my short trip away, I suspect with a certain degree of trepidation. Colin must have been very convincing, because the next afternoon he arrived at the ward, commandeered one of the ancient wicker-backed wheelchairs, and rolled me out into the sunlight for the first time since my injury, with a blue fatigue cap on my head to protect angry red facial scars from the African sun. Colin and helper laid the chair back flat,

The BSAP Mounted Troop wheels onto the Morris Depot square, my last parade. (Author collection)

picked me up, and rolled me into the back of a covered Land Rover and set the brake. I had perhaps four inches clearance between my face and the ceiling, but Morris Depot was a drive of no more than ten minutes down the Avenues, and a short time later I was being lifted out and wheeled into a shady position under trees at the side of the grassy parade square, surrounded by friends and well-wishers. Moments later, the mounted column wheeled onto the grassy plain and formed up. It was a splendid march past and also my final passing-out parade.

My final days in Ward 9 were as pleasant as any hospital stay can be, but I was both anxious and impatient to leave. There were visits to the specialist surgeon, who confirmed that some tiny particles of material had penetrated my eye as a consequence of the explosion. Fortunately, he thought it would heal and return to near normal. The state of my hearing was more uncertain, but there was little or nothing to be done about it. The last of my sutures were removed, Mr. Owen-Smith counseled me on the importance of protecting my skin grafts from sunlight, and I was allowed to go home to our very temporary flat. I had been hospitalized exactly thirty days.

I was never to put on a uniform again. My stump was still bandaged daily in anticipation of the day when I could wear a prosthesis. I dressed in

Last day at Support Unit: my send-off photo. Front row, from left: Inspector Ormonde Power, Chief Inspector Pat Deasy, Chief Superintendent "Taffy" Pugh, Assistant Commissioner Guy Houghton, Superintendent "Willie" Watson, Superintendent Tom Naude, author. Rear rank, from left: unidentified sergeant major, NSPO Kaye-Eddie, Section Officer Mike Davis, Section Officer Barrington Goudge, Section Officer Colin Shaw, unidentified NSPO, Sergeant Major Isaac. (*Outpost*, magazine of the BSA police)

safari suits to make the regular outpatient calls to the hospital or nearby surgeon's offices in the Avenues. I was gradually gaining strength back, frequently walking on the broad earthen road verge under the canopy of blossoming trees. More than once, a farmer in town for the day halted his truck or car at roadside to ask whether he could give me a lift somewhere. It was so typical of Rhodesians, as was the example of the young African domestic who stopped to tie a loose shoelace for me.

Jennifer and I eventually settled on our travel plan; we would go first to Australia and look to see if there were opportunities there, perhaps to start or buy a small business. If that plan didn't seem right for us, we would continue onward to the United States, where I still held hopes that I might reenter the professional world.

I visited Support Unit from time to time as the process for finalizing my treatment and discharge went forward. I was fitted with a prosthesis at Andrew Fleming Hospital, attended a medical board, where it was determined that I was 65 percent disabled, and I finally turned in piles of personal uniforms and kit at the force quartermaster store. Jennifer managed to book our passage from Durban, South Africa, to Melbourne, Australia, via the Lloyd Triestino Line, with an onward air ticket to Texas.

We moved into Colin and Margaret Shaw's home in Hatfield, our personal effects now reduced to two or three trunks. Because we were traveling by sea, these would accompany us at least as far as Australia.

As the time to go grew nearer, my Support Unit colleagues and friends scheduled a send-off event for me, to be held in the unit's improvised canteen adjacent Tomlinson Depot parade square. The old corrugated metal building was packed with thirsty well-wishers at the end of a warm Friday, and there was a good deal of bonhomie. My system would not tolerate much alcohol, but I very much enjoyed the gathering, which had its poignant moments. Officer Commanding Guy Houghton said a few kind words about my service, as did a representative for the men I had trained. Finally, Ormonde stood, recalling our friendship and service together; then he presented me with a large sterling silver inscribed tankard "in left-hand pattern" (as he explained it).

We turned to leave soon after, and as Jennifer and I walked outside the old building, I heard somebody say, "Go well, *shamwari*." As tender a farewell as could be, I reflected quietly, as we walked away under the canopy of stars. There would be many things I would miss about Africa, but its people were foremost.

Brian and Jo Cullingworth took us to Salisbury airport. These good people who had guided and sheltered us throughout our Rhodesian odyssey were now bidding us farewell. They would airfreight Roscoe the Ridgeback to us after we had arrived in South Africa and had a place to stay while awaiting the arrival of our ship. As we walked together out to our awaiting South African Airways flight, they waved to us from the observation deck. Minutes later, we were in the air—and Rhodesia was gone forever. Little did we know that in a few short years, Rhodesia would cease to exist altogether.

We chose Capetown in which to spend some time before our voyage to Australia. Roscoe had a berth on a Danish cargo vessel, *Diana Skou*, due to sail from Capetown to Houston. Because of quarantine regulations, he was not welcome in Australia.

Jo and Brian had recommended to us modest cottages at Seaforth, in the old former Royal Navy port of Simonstown. We mastered the train and bus schedules, met many kind people, and enjoyed nearby sparkling waters—and found time to read and dream about our future, whatever it might be.

South Africa, for all of its friendly atmosphere, felt very much like a foreign country after our Rhodesian experience. The seaside neighborhoods of Capetown were much more English than my recollections of Johannesburg.

Capetown South Africans were curious about Rhodesia. I was invited by a friendly bank manager from Fish Hoek to speak to a gathering of old veterans at the local Shell Hole. As I had expected, they were genuinely interested and concerned about the plight of their besieged northern neighbor; but there was no indication that anybody had much idea about how to improve things—or even learn from others' bitter experience.

Roscoe arrived on time at Capetown airport, in a very large kennel. He was very glad to see us and was on his best behavior on the trains and bus routes back to our tiny, single-windowed cottage in Simonstown. Days later, we took him aboard his ship to America, where a large friendly Danish mate bedded him down on the couch in his cabin. Roscoe seemed assured of a pleasant voyage to America.

Soon after, Jennifer and I caught an overnight train from Capetown to Durban to meet our ship. Behind coal-burning locomotives, the old train carriages rattled across the Karoo desert and over the range to Natal's seaport. Not well rested, we found our hotel within sight of Durban's ocean passenger terminal and settled in for our last night in Africa.

I was still very unsettled, not sleeping and prone to spend long periods in reflective worry and self-doubt about what I had done with my life. Rhodesia was very much in my heart and my mind. I had been intensely happy; indeed, it had felt at times as though my destiny had been to train young Africans. Now I was telling myself that I had been delusional, that things like this can never last. I worried about tiny Rhodesia in its high-stakes game of international brinksmanship—but mostly I worried about the everyday people I'd left behind from all walks of life. What would happen to them all? This was the second time I'd abruptly left good people behind to an uncertain fate. This time I was leaving as a disabled man on a tiny pension, hardly able to shape the turn of international events, but feeling nonetheless responsible in some way, at least in my heart.

We walked around Durban's festive waterfront, enjoyed an Indian dinner at a restaurant, and readied to board ship on the following day. Late the next afternoon, we were crowded into Durmarine Terminal, a vast building now filled with a queue of passengers that seemed to stretch forever. It was both hot and humid. After a wait of more than two hours, Jennifer fainted just as entry doors were opened to the gangway. A gracious Italian crew helped us aboard, stowed our luggage, and escorted us to our stateroom. Exhausted, we rested for a while and then made our way to the upper deck for the vessel departure.

It was dusk. A soft, rosy glow shone behind Durban's palm trees, and the warm, damp air was full of the scent of the sea. Below us, stevedores and the ship's crew were in final preparation for the ship's departure. On our deck, groups of happy people, mainly couples, crowded the railing, waving to friendly faces ashore and throwing colorful streamers across. I sensed that the moments ahead would spell the end of a momentous chapter in my life. Whatever the legend was about Mother Africa's Embrace and the fact that she never truly lets go, I feared that this might be the last time I would see Africa's shores. I was sad and apprehensive.

Finally, the vessel moved slightly and the last lines cast off. The ship's horn blasted, and tugs began to push and pull us away from the dock. With the deep green expanse of water opening between the ship side and the wharf, a loud, drunken voice with a distinctly Australian accent arose from the after deck below where we stood.

"You're all going to fuckin' die!" a young man screamed, seemingly at every person ashore. "South Africa is gonna burn, and you're gonna fuckin' die!"

The tirade continued and with it my gorge rose until I was ready to fight the man. To my mind, here was yet another living example of the sort of ignorant intolerance that I had witnessed fueling African conflict. No matter that it may have been simply an outburst by a silly young man offended by the same boorish South African racial law that had first alienated me four years previously. What I knew with certainty after my relatively short experience in Africa was that malicious, emotive behavior and utterances can serve to further polarize people, forcing them even farther apart. I was convinced that Africans of all colors needed to learn to talk among themselves; they also needed to learn to disregard those whose proselytizing is done for personal aggrandizement. The incident had struck a distinctly dissonant chord on the occasion of my farewell.

Two large Italian seamen appeared suddenly on the deck below, taking hold of the man's arms and leading him off. Sad before the farewell, I was sadder after the offensive outburst ended. Jennifer and I stood at the rail together surrounded by other silent couples as the ship's engines took up their low rumble and watched quietly as Durban's bright lights became as distant as the stars—and then were gone.

EPILOGUE

RHODESIA'S BITTER CIVIL WAR dragged on for a further six years, increasing in savagery. The Zimbabwean African People's Union's (ZAPU's) and Zimbabwean African National Union's (ZANU's) allies, particularly the USSR and Communist China, poured aid into Zambia, Mozambique, and Tanzania to support the assault on Rhodesia.

Incursions were no longer confined to just the northeastern corner, but from all sides except the southern boundary with South Africa. In response, the Rhodesian army attacked the logistics and rear areas of their enemy. The Selous Scouts staged several large motorized cross-border raids into Mozambique and lesser ones in Botswana, killing hundreds of guerrillas.

The Special Air Service (C Squadron SAS) attacked targets deep in Zambia and Mozambique, dropping major bridge spans and disrupting operations. Casualty estimates vary, but indications are that at least 35,000 on all sides died in the conflict, an equal number suffered permanent injuries, and 1.5 million were displaced.

Support Unit continued to expand after my departure. Twelve operational units of forty men in 1974 soon swelled to twenty-five. Guy Houghton's efforts to acquire machine guns bore fruit the next year. Ultimately, Support Unit was equipped with mortars and was considered one of the most effective internal counterinsurgency forces in the war.

Despite ongoing initiatives to reach a settlement, none came to fruition. There are many reasons why key international players would not step forward to endorse the internal solution. Accusations suggesting that many black Rhodesians found the compromise unacceptable—whether true or not—weakened the cause, as did pressure on Britain from former African colonies in the Commonwealth that clearly found anything other than a black nationalist government unacceptable. And the two rival nationalist organizations that fielded insurgents determined that it was not in their best interests to negotiate while the possibility of a winner-takes-all scenario existed.

ZAPU, led by Ndebele Joshua Nkomo, and advised and equipped by the USSR, continued to build up a substantial conventional army in Zambia—planning the day when a lightening armor strike across the border would carry them through to Salisbury. Maoist ZANU, ultimately led by Robert Mugabe and supported by Communist China, favored a campaign of insurgency and intimidation, confident that it and the Shona majority would prevail. The war continued, and the innocents died while politicians skirmished for advantage.

The multiple demands of war were catalytic within the Rhodesian security forces. Black African numeric participation increased, as did the effects of their bravery and assumption of increasingly responsible leadership roles. The army and air force promoted blacks from enlisted status to commissioned rank, the effect of which was to further induce racial homogenization. The intent was much more about efficiencies than it was about appearance. The process—based on principles of merit—went ahead with little disruption.

Ultimately, after intense negotiations and pressure from both South Africa and U.S. secretary of state Henry Kissinger, Prime Minister Ian Smith agreed to return Rhodesia to British control and accept the results of internationally sanctioned elections. Bishop Abel Muzorewa became prime minister of a nation renamed Zimbabwe-Rhodesia, and, for a short time, many hoped for international recognition and reforms that would not discriminate against either whites or blacks. Despite the departure of Ian Smith from the prime ministership, that recognition was not forthcoming.

Britain in 1979 convened talks at Lancaster House, London, designed to iron out terms of transition. These included provisions for a cease-fire and a new constitution; there were also undertakings from the participants that there would be no intimidation in elections, that they would renounce the use of force for political purposes, and that they would accept election outcomes. Twenty seats were guaranteed for the white minority under terms of the new constitution. Land reform remained a thorny issue until the United States and United Kingdom established a fund to buy out farmers who did not wish to remain.

When the cease-fire was called, C Squadron, SAS, disbanded and slipped across the border to South Africa, where it was instated in the South African army as a new recce commando.

The election results when they came caught Britain by surprise. Robert Mugabe's ZANU PF won a majority in the newly elected parliament of Zimbabwe, successfully hoodwinking international observers in a massive preelection intimidation campaign that ensured their candidate's success. With the reins firmly in his hands, Mugabe—in a conciliatory move—named Ndebele Joshua Nkomo of the opposition ZAPU party to his cabinet.

Mugabe had not won a military victory and thus was required, at least initially, to operate within the legal framework he had inherited. There were guarantees of minority representation, at least in the short term, and to quiet the national defense establishment, the new prime minister appointed Lieutenant General Peter Walls to assume leadership as former guerrillas were integrated into Zimbabwe's defense establishment.

The British South Africa Police (BSAP) ceased to exist almost immediately, transformed into a new organization called the Zimbabwe Republic Police. White faces soon vanished from the ranks of leadership, replaced by appointees with suitable political credentials. Advisers from Eastern Bloc nations arrived to assume training responsibilities within the police establishment. Many members of the BSAP chose to leave the force, migrating overseas.

Mugabe, never comfortable with a democratically elected opposition, soon began a covert campaign against the minority Ndebele people, led by Nkomo and his ZAPU party.

After a series of events that were conveniently interpreted as an imminent insurrection, the newly created Zimbabwe army's 5th Brigade was ordered into Matabeleland, where, under the tutelage of North Korean instructors, as many as four thousand Ndebele were systematically slaughtered, many of them in public executions.

Though diplomats accredited to Zimbabwe were aware of Mugabe's ethnic cleansing program, it was ignored by the international community. With the main opposition removed, Zimbabwe quickly became a virtual one-party state.

Despite the government's political excesses, Zimbabwe's economy—underpinned by several thousand white commercial farmers—managed to struggle on while international tourism brought badly needed foreign currency.

In 1997, responding to internal pressures brought to bear by people purporting to be veterans of the struggle, Mugabe caved in and agreed to pay substantial amounts to the claimants from the national treasury. Clearly a move to buy and ensure personal power, the resulting strain on Zimbabwe's budget was unsustainable despite introduction of a range of new taxes.

Cash-strapped citizens rioted for several days after new taxes raised prices on essential commodities like maize. Mugabe blamed the disorder on the opposition Movement for Democratic Change (MDC)—and alluded to the role of white support for the party. The treasury began printing currency to pay its debts, and the value of the Zimbabwe dollar collapsed.

Just before Christmas 1997, the government announced that more than fourteen hundred white-owned farms had been identified for compulsory acquisition. Mugabe, again rallying the poor to sustain his rule, dragged out the land rights argument—claiming that white pioneers had taken the best land—despite the fact that 80 percent of these farms had changed hands since Rhodesia became Zimbabwe. What was not stated was that the Zimbabwe government in each instance had an opportunity under existing law to declare its desire that farms be used to resettle poor blacks. They had not done so.

A substantial international fund had been established during the Lancaster House talks to purchase farms for this purpose, and Britain established its own fund in 1980.

In early 2000, after Mugabe announced that Zimbabwe was sending troops to the Democratic Republic of Congo, and facing strong indications of increasing gains by the opposition MDC party, white farm invasions began. A sum of $500,000 had been covertly appropriated by the government to fund a rag-tag group of former guerillas, youth militia, and thugs to invade, beat, and sometimes murder the very people who fed the nation and provided its all-important agriculture income. The police were directed not to interfere in these "political" matters. Mugabe blamed the British government for reneging on funding land acquisition.

There had, in fact, been no such withdrawal of funds, but the British were becoming increasingly concerned that their money was buying land for wealthy, influential ZANU apparatchiks. Britain responded by promising additional funds, providing the farm invasions and illegal reparceling of land stopped and an orderly, transparent repurchase program was put in place. But Mugabe was determined that there should be a program of seizure without compensation.

Apparently, the opportunity to rid the nation of whites was too good an opportunity for the xenophobic president to pass up. In Washington, the administration ignored the land invasions and attendant human rights violations; Britain's Tony Blair canceled selected aid programs to Zimbabwe, while South African president Thabo Mbeki was characteristically silent. Only former president Nelson Mandela spoke out against Mugabe, suggesting that Zimbabweans should take up arms against the government.

Mugabe's efforts to intimidate the opposition—which was at the core of the farm seizure initiatives—left the opposition largely in disarray. Zimbabwe's agricultural sector has been destroyed, its starving people dependent on foreign aid. The national inflation rate has soared to record percentage levels, but ministers are still buying new cars with vital foreign exchange, and the president and his wife continue to commandeer the national airline for overseas shopping junkets. His cronies have taken possession of seized farms but cannot operate them. Hundreds of agriculture workers have been displaced or have fled the country. Where Zimbabwe once fed Africa, its citizens are now starving and rely to a large extent on food imports.

Libya, long a supplier of Zimbabwe's fuel, has taken payment in kind for petroleum the government couldn't pay for—and now has rich landholdings. Zimbabwean generals and politicians have enriched themselves via a series of scams involving blood diamonds from the Congo and exports of African hardwoods. The Chinese—ever mindful of the vital strategic mineral resources of Zimbabwe—spread largesse in Harare.

* * *

Friends and colleagues from Rhodesia days have had mixed fortunes. On the American side, SAS major Bob McKenzie miraculously cheated the odds and left Rhodesia after the elections, only to be killed some years later during an ambush gone wrong in Sierra Leone. His Selous Scout colleague, Marine Vietnam veteran Major John Murphy, was killed in a military parachuting accident in South Africa soon after the war.

Other Americans, particularly veterans of the Vietnam War, volunteered for service in Rhodesia. There were varying reasons for their service; many had been disillusioned both by America's domestic attitudes to Vietnam and by the national government's seeming indifference to Africa, where Russia and China were again fanning the flames of war. None was hired as a so-called mercenary. Each had been assimilated and trained, serving under conditions identical to other force members, earning modest monthly salaries.

And, in the course of the past three decades, I have met many exiles who, for political or economic reasons—sometimes both—have been forced to flee their homeland. There are thousands of Rhodesians (and other Africans) in Australia and almost as many in the United States, and their global networks offer support and friendship to all who have lived in the little country they once called home.

Events in Rhodesia eventually focused American attention on the Cold War in Africa. After Portugal's departure in the mid-1970s, Moscow cemented its position by providing direct support to the Samora Machel government in Mozambique.

In Angola, where United States companies had already made substantial investments in offshore oil, the Soviets, Cubans, and Eastern Bloc nations propped up the Popular Movement for the Liberation of Angola (MPLA) government in its fight against opposition National Union for the Total Independence of Angola (UNITA) forces under Jonas Savimbi. The United States covertly supported UNITA's war with cargo flights out of the Democratic Republic of Congo. Additionally, the South African army mounted a series of armored attacks into Angola, one of which reached the outskirts of Luanda. South African soldiers killed Cuban soldiers and Eastern Bloc advisers alike in these forays. The war was to last for more than twenty years.

Eric Kennelly retired several years ago as a colonel in South African special forces and moved to Europe. Ormonde Power, after five decades in uniform, recently did the same. Winston Hart, Brian and Jo Cullingworth, and Peter Cooper all survived the war.

The disabled and pensioners of Rhodesia, both black and white, have continued to bear the burdens of war. Zimbabwe stopped paying overseas disability and service pensions in 2002, and Britain has so far managed to avoid supporting Rhodesian pensioners, many of whom are destitute. Pensioners believe that an undertaking for support from the United Kingdom was given during the Lancaster House deliberations.

The citizens of Zimbabwe—ever hopeful that their lives can someday be returned to a state of the normalcy—continue to hang on, if they can. However, thousands of poor, hungry blacks have crossed the Limpopo River illegally into South Africa, where the Zimbabwean workers today form a sought-after cadre of motivated workers in local commerce. There are communities of the exiled in the United Kingdom and elsewhere as well.

What was once Rhodesia has today become a sad example of misgovernment at its worst. Zimbabwe has not only suffered enormous harm with the departure of so many talented citizens—both black and white—but it has also lost the last vestiges of democratic government through ethnic cleansing, arbitrary seizures, and state-sanctioned brutality.

* * *

Despite premonitions that I was leaving Africa forever when our ship sailed from Durban on that night in 1975, I have been back—and continue to live and work in the Francophone nations of West Africa and Angola. South Africa—the land so blighted by apartheid—emerged without a civil war, to be led by Nelson Mandela into a new era of democracy. South Africa today feels more like African countries in the north, but it is now a much happier place than in earlier times and a new generation of South African is coming to the fore.

Through it all, more than three decades after my introduction to Mother Africa, the land and her people continue to delight and inspire me.

GLOSSARY

Afrikaans: The language that evolved in South Africa from its seventeenth-century Dutch colonization; predominantly Dutch in origin, it has also been influenced by French, German, African, Malay, and other settlers to the region; though spoken at home by South African settlers in Rhodesia, it was not commonly heard in public

ANC: African National Congress

APL: Non–self-propelled barracks ship

batman: A manservant

biltong: (Afrikaans) dried meat, similar to jerky

boerewors: Traditional South African fresh sausage; translated literally "farmer's sausage"

braaivleis (braai): (Afrikaans) a barbecue

BSAP: British South Africa Police; Rhodesia's national police force; derived from British South Africa Company Police, the unit raised by Cecil John Rhodes to provide security for the original pioneer column that in 1890 opened up the land that was to become Rhodesia

Chenjera: A warning or caution

chibuli: A beer

china: (Cockney rhyming slang) "china plate" rhymes with "mate"; an endearment between male comrades

chopper: A helicopter or a machine gun

CID: Criminal Investigation Division

CNO: Chief of Naval Operations

COIN: Counterinsurgency
CPU: Crime Prevention Unit
dagga: *Cannabis sativa* (marijuana)
DMZ: Demilitarized zone
drill pig: A drill instructor, well versed in parade ground drill and procedure
EOD: Explosive ordnance disposal
Figure Eleven target: A full-size paper silhouette target depicting an armed enemy soldier
Figure Twelve target: Similar to the Figure Eleven target, except it depicts only a shoulders-up view of the enemy
flat dog: A crocodile
FN rifle: The issue small arm of the Rhodesian security forces, a 7.62-mm NATO-caliber semiautomatic, magazine-fed rifle designed by Fabrique Nationale, Belgium
FRELIMO: Mozambique Liberation Front (Frente de Libertação de Moçambique)
gap it: To move out rapidly; to run away
GC: Ground Coverage (protocol)
gomo: A hill or dome
Hounsfield stretcher: A sectionalized cot consisting of a metal frame and canvas
howzit?: How are you?
IED: Improvised explosive device
impi: A Zulu (or in Rhodesia, Ndebele) war party
ishe: (Shona) a title of respect for a superior; "Sir"
JOC: Joint Operations Center
jumbo: Elephant
KAR: Kings African Rifles
kopje: A small hill or dome
kraal: An African village; often just a collection of several round, thatched huts
lap lap: (New Guinea) a sarong-like garment worn by both genders
LCH: Heavy landing craft
LST: Tank landing ship
MAG: FN general-purpose machine gun
mambo: (Shona) chief
MDC: Movement for Democratic Change
mealie: Corn

mobile handbag: a crocodile
mopani tree: *Colophospermum mopane*; a native tree found in hot, arid regions of Southern Africa
MPLA: Popular Movement for the Liberation of Angola
msasa tree: *Brachystegia spiciformis*; a flat-topped tree native to African savanna forests
mujiba: An African herd boy and lookout, often a terrorist collaborator
NCO: Noncommissioned officer
NIS: Naval Investigative Service
NISOV: Naval Investigative Service Office, Vietnam
NISRA: Naval Investigative Service Resident Agency
nkosi: (Zulu, Ndebele) king; also sometimes used to address a superior
NS: National service
NSPO: National service patrol office; a Rhodesian of European extraction serving as a national serviceman in the BSA
NVA: North Vietnamese Army
OC: Officer commanding
OP: Observation point
OSS: Office of Strategic Services
ouens: (Afrikaans) people; in slang, refers often to a group of people
patrol officer: The starting position in the nonindigenous rank structure of the BSAP; indigenous Africans were first assimilated into this rank structure in the late 1970s
PATU: Police Anti-Terrorist Unit
PBR: river patrol boats
PGHQ: Police General Headquarters
pho: Vietnamese noodles
Pilgrim: Call sign for BSAP Special Branch
PT: Physical training
RAR: Rhodesian African Rifles
rev stick: A rifle
RLI: Rhodesian Light Infantry
rondavel: Traditional round African dwelling
RPG: Rocket-propelled grenade
RSM: Regimental sergeant major
RTU: Returned to unit
sadza: (Shona) thickened porridge, normally made from ground white maize called *mealie*-meal
SAP: South African Police

SAS: Special Air Service
shamwari: A friend
shebeen: An unlicensed drinking establishment
sitrep: A situation report
S/O: Section officer
SOE: Special Operations Executive
spoor: (Afrikaans) a track left by man or animal
spruit: (Afrikaans) a stream
stick boots: Boots adapted for drill and ceremonial use, typically with hobnails
stoep: A front porch
tackies: Canvas shoes
TT: Turned terrorist
TTL: Tribal trust land
UDI: Unilateral Declaration of Independence
veld: (Afrikaans) country, land—the bush
veldskoens: An ankle-high soft leather shoe commonly worn by Rhodesian men; sometimes referred to as "fellies"
vlei: (Afrikaans) an open area, often with a seasonal pond present
wanker: Literally, one who masturbates; used in slang as a term for an idiot or sometimes as an endearment

INDEX

ABOUT THE AUTHOR

DOUGLASS HUBBARD is an author and consultant to the international mining community who has spent more than three decades working throughout Asia and Africa. He served as a special agent with the Naval Investigative Service (NIS) in Vietnam from 1969 to 1972. In his book *Special Agent, Vietnam: A Naval Intelligence Memoir* (Potomac Books, 2006) he chronicles the work of NIS agents in Vietnam from 1962 until the fall of Saigon in 1975. After serving three years in Vietnam, Hubbard traveled to Australia in 1972 and then—with intentions of becoming a district policeman in rural Africa—to Rhodesia in 1974. Soon embroiled in the blossoming bush war against communist-backed nationalist insurgents, he was assigned to train young African recruits of the expanding security forces. His story is a personal account of a fascinating yet little-known period in African history. Hubbard currently serves as director of a Washington, D.C., nonprofit organization working with the disadvantaged and poor of Africa, and as a consultant to mining companies.

The Naval Institute Press is the book-publishing arm of the U.S. Naval Institute, a private, nonprofit, membership society for sea service professionals and others who share an interest in naval and maritime affairs. Established in 1873 at the U.S. Naval Academy in Annapolis, Maryland, where its offices remain today, the Naval Institute has members worldwide.

Members of the Naval Institute support the education programs of the society and receive the influential monthly magazine *Proceedings* or the colorful bimonthly magazine *Naval History* and discounts on fine nautical prints and on ship and aircraft photos. They also have access to the transcripts of the Institute's Oral History Program and get discounted admission to any of the Institute-sponsored seminars offered around the country.

The Naval Institute's book-publishing program, begun in 1898 with basic guides to naval practices, has broadened its scope to include books of more general interest. Now the Naval Institute Press publishes about seventy titles each year, ranging from how-to books on boating and navigation to battle histories, biographies, ship and aircraft guides, and novels. Institute members receive significant discounts on the Press's more than eight hundred books in print.

Full-time students are eligible for special half-price membership rates. Life memberships are also available.

For a free catalog describing Naval Institute Press books currently available, and for further information about joining the U.S. Naval Institute, please write to:

Member Services
U.S. Naval Institute
291 Wood Road
Annapolis, MD 21402-5034
Telephone: (800) 233-8764
Fax: (410) 571-1703
Web address: www.usni.org